A Different Path to Coming of Age

Michael Connolly
Richard Olive
John Tuohey

Published by
Vandamere Press
P.O. Box 149
St. Petersburg, FL 33731
USA

ISBN 978-0-918339-83-6

Cover Photo: The front entrance to St. John's Atonement Seminary on a snowy day around 1960. By permission of Gerry Whitfield.

To Rick,
my friend & teacher.
John Tuohey

Dedication

Dedicated to the priests at St. John's Atonement Seminary, who steered us over the shoals of adolescence with guidelines that have lasted our lifetimes.

Acknowledgments

This book would not exist without the inspiration of Brie Goolbis, Mike's wife. She, along with Ana and Pam, Ollie's and John's wives, provided continuing support over five years of writing and traveling in its production. There also has been significant support and encouragement from Father Emil Tomaskovic of the Franciscan Friars of the Atonement, former minister general and current director of special gifts of the religious order, who helped us with access to the friars' archives. We are grateful to Deacon Gerry Whitfield, who provided photographs of the seminary in the 1950s. (Both Emil and Gerry were our contemporaries at St. John's.) Others contributing significantly to our effort include Barbara Martire and Cathy Merritt of the Graymoor Archives and Records Center, who helped us focus on available photos from our years at the seminary (1956–1960), then transmitted selections to us over time, and Teresa Letteer, retired head housekeeper of the New York State Academy of Fire Science and Fire Science Library, Montour Falls, and others at the academy who so graciously allowed us free access to the building and grounds that once were our home away from home.

We also appreciate the contributions of our writing groups—the North Carolina Sea Quills, New Hampshire's Write Free or Die, and San Rafael, California's Tiptonites I and II—who offered painstaking reviews and edits. Additionally we would like to thank author and English professor James Tipton; writing teacher Margo Williams and members of her class; and Christopher Martin, rector of St. Paul's Episcopal Church, San Rafael, California, for their encouragement and support.

Thanks also to Carole Ganim, author of Being Out of Order, who introduced us to our publisher, Art Brown of Vandamere Press, who saw something of merit in three geriatric authors' work. Special thanks also to author Tim Pkelkovich, who traveled from the Midwest to meet with us to share his experience as a published author, and Kevin Sobalvarro, for his help on cleaning the photos.

Throughout this adventure we have met only interest and kindness as we had come to expect from those associated with St. John's Seminary.

Table of Contents

For many are called, but few are chosen

Mathew 22:14

Photo credit: By permission of the New York State Academy of Fire Science

We were barely teens in 1956 when we entered St. John's Atonement Seminary in Upstate New York, the first step in thirteen years of training for the Catholic priesthood. When we returned for a visit in 2012, it had become the New York State Academy of Fire Science.

Chapter One

Back to Another Time

Montour Falls, July 10, 2012 Together for the first time in fifty-two years, the three of us stood before the seven-story red brick building that was once home. It was as if gravity itself had pulled us back for a reunion to a place and time that had a profound effect in shaping us. We were barely teens in 1956 when we entered St. John's Atonement Seminary in Upstate New York, the first step in thirteen years of training for the Catholic priesthood. America was different then.

We were born during World War II. Each of our fathers, hard drinkers roughed up and toughened by the Depression, was in uniform. After the war, an optimistic but exhausted nation strove for normalcy even as Winston Churchill delivered his ominous Iron Curtain speech, referencing the Soviet Union's occupation of much of Eastern Europe liberated from the Nazis. American troops were still coming home when our stay-at-home moms delivered us for the first time to our neighborhood Catholic schools. Later that school year, we heard the buzz among adults about a startling development in Brooklyn: the Dodgers had a Negro baseball player.

In the '50s, drugs were Bayer aspirin or Alka Seltzer. Carhops, drive-in movies, and fairs occupied leisure time in small towns and rapidly expanding suburbs, where, just as in the cities, retail businesses shut down on Sundays when families streamed to church. Catholics heard unintelligible Latin from a priest whose back was to the congregation. Rock and roll was the rage. We were locked into Bill Haley and the Comets and a scandalous hip-gyrating guitar player from Tupelo, Mississippi, who busted out four No. 1 hits in one year. We thought the music from *My Fair Lady*, *Carousel*, and *South Pacific* was classical. Television was ascendant. Millions tuned in faithfully to an antiseptic, fanciful white world featuring the Andersons in *Father Knows Best* and the Nelsons in

The Adventures of Ozzie and Harriet, two ridiculously happy families in beautiful suburban homes with homebound moms in high heels, two well-adjusted kids between them, and jolly, helpful next-door neighbors who were always dropping by to chat and borrow a little cream or sugar for their morning coffee.

Much of the country, and certainly the three of us, could not even imagine such an existence. Our neighborhoods were hard-scrabble and working class in the Northeast. We were not poor, but going out to a restaurant was not in the family budget. Catholicism was drummed into our fibers by nuns from kindergarten through the eighth grade and touched every part of our lives. Baptism, First Holy Communion, Confirmation, and Matrimony were major events that ordered family gatherings, as did funerals. As mystical as were the many rituals, the religious life seemed a viable option when presented before we were out of grade school—especially for many Irish mothers and grandmothers with dreams their offspring might aspire to such heights as priests or nuns. We joined scores of other Catholic boys and girls who marched off to religious life at thirteen and fourteen years of age.

Now a state fire academy, the old seminary looked the same, but virtually all traces of religiosity, like statues, were gone. The three of us and Pam, Brie, and Ana, our wives, walked the halls and strolled to the footbridge over Catherine's Creek that had carried us to football and softball games in fields beyond. How many times had we anxiously watched storm clouds gather in the hills to the west? And how often had we squeezed in one more inning or series of downs before racing approaching squalls across the bridge, giddy as we entered the building just as the rain began pelting down?

We recalled the priests who inspired us, including Father Owen Murphy. He was instrumental in bringing us together again. He had been the disciplinarian back then, but he had been evenhanded and caring. In later years, he remembered each of us fondly, and we had come to feel great affection for him.

Knowing well what St. John's meant to each of us, our wives patiently endured our reliving the distant past and commented on how uncharacteristically animated and talkative we were. For our part, we were discovering things about each other—and ourselves—we could not have identified, much less acknowledge, in our teenaged pretense.

Each of us had come to Montour Falls deeply wounded. Perhaps we thought we were "called" to be priests at that tender age, but there was another motivation common among us.

We wanted to get away from home.

"You guys should write a book," said Brie, a published author herself with her husband. The idea had immediate appeal, and we went home to plumb our respective tales.

The deeper we went, the more we appreciated the defining influence St. John's had on our lives—long after we had left it.

Chapter Two

Mike—Beginning the Journey

The two most important days in your life are the day you are born and the day you find out why.

—Mark Twain

Waiting in the hallway outside my parents' bedroom, listening to the shuffling feet and whispering voices, I could feel the anxiety behind that closed door. The doctor had been in there a long time. I began to pace up and down the hallway. My brother, Paul, sat on the top step of the stairway leading down to the first floor, his chin resting between his hands. We had nothing to say to one another. My sister, Carol, two years old, lay asleep in her room. The door opened and Aunt Sarah came out, her arms open, reaching to encircle us. She was crying. As she knelt to embrace us, I looked over her shoulder into the room and could see the gray face of the doctor and my father, holding my mother's hand to his lips.

I don't remember how my father told us my mother was dead. I do remember the place—the parlor in our house in Pinehurst, Massachusetts. This room, once so comfortable and warm, a place where stories were told and read, ever after would be, for me, a frightening and forbidding part of the house. My brother sat in my father's lap whimpering softly into my father's shoulder. I sat on the couch, my seven-year-old body wrapped in the protective warmth of Aunt Sarah's arms, staring up at the stairs leading up to the bedroom where I had last seen my mother. Upstairs Carol was still sleeping.

That night, as I lay in bed, knots in my chest and pain in my stomach from crying, the vision of my mother coughing haunted me. I could almost feel the terrible spasms of whoops that shook her until she'd collapse on a chair or the couch or a bed, gasping for breath.

"Are you all right, Mama?" I'd ask.

"Yes, Michael, I'm fine," she'd say in a voice little more than a whisper. She would struggle to regain her breath and when she did she would look up and see me watching. "I'm all right, Michael," she would say. "Why don't you go on out and play with your friends?" And I would do as she asked. But before I went off to find my friends, I'd sneak around to the side of the house and watch through a window and see her slumped in a chair, holding her chest tightly as if she were trying to keep her lungs from bursting through. I'd see her body fold in upon itself like a rice paper fan and I'd be afraid.

One-year-old Michael with his mother, Ruth (left) and Aunt Helen in the driveway of 37 West Fifth Street.

All I can recall after my father told us our mother was dead is the crying—my own crying, my brother and sister crying, everyone who came to the house crying.

We weren't allowed into my parents' bedroom that night. The next time I'd see my mother was a few days later as she lay in a polished mahogany casket in O'Malley's Funeral Home. I hated the sight of her body surrounded by an artificial garden. The flowers couldn't disguise the fact that life, hers and ours, was no longer bright or beautiful. I hated the three-day ritual of the wake and funeral. Standing in the receiving line, I tried to be brave, tried to imitate the unemotional expression on my father's face. "Be a man," he had told my brother and me. "Connolly men don't cry." But I didn't feel manly; I felt lonely, abandoned.

"Doesn't Ruth look lovely?" I whirled around. My fists tightened, my chest began to pound. I wanted to scream: "No she doesn't; she looks far away—lost to me who loves her, who needs her." But I'd been told, "Connolly men don't cry." I excused myself and went to the bathroom, sat in a stall, and cried.

For years after 1949, I did not attend wakes or funerals. Even after the years had somewhat dulled the pain, I went reluctantly. My sense of loss and feelings of pain weren't exorcised by the rituals of wake and funeral; they were made more intense. I was only seven years old, but I knew my life had changed, and I hated that change.

None of us wanted to stay in a house where the memory of death festered. Eventually my father moved us from Pinehurst to Lowell so his sister, Aunt Helen, could care for us while he went to work. He left the house each morning for work at 6:00 A.M., before we were up and getting ready for school. After work he went to bars and seldom got home before we were in bed for the night. My brother, sister, and I were in the care of Aunt Helen, who was thirty-something, unmarried, and caring for her elderly mother, a stroke victim.

The house in which we lived, 37 West Fifth Street, was a household of women, but the world of males and of violence was only a few steps away, outside the door in a rough Irish neighborhood. Or inside when my father came home drunk and angry, slamming doors, shouting obscenities, and pushing me out of his way if I, at Aunt Helen's request, tried to help him to his room. We lived with death: my mother was dead, my grandfather too, my grandmother was dying, and for all the time he spent with us, my father was as good as dead to us as well.

Most of the time Grandmother Connolly lay in a dimly lit bedroom moving her lips but making only incoherent guttural sounds. Sometimes Aunt Helen moved her to a couch in the "parlor" so she could playact taking part in our ritual of daily living. But all she did was sit there making strange, throaty sounds and staring with uncomprehending eyes at what was going on around her.

Helen could be brusque and demanding with my brother and me, but she was an angel of mercy when it came to tending to her mother. She seemed to sense her mother's every need. If the old woman had to go to the bathroom, Helen knew. If she felt tired and needed sleep, Helen shepherded her back to her bedroom, holding her up as the old woman's fragile legs shuffled slowly along. Helen was there to anticipate her mama's every need, and, if she resented this constant preoccupation with the sick, she never showed it. Perhaps because she was so absorbed with the needs of her mother and my sister, Helen had little time for my brother and me. She was, no doubt, overwhelmed by the weight of the responsibility for her alcoholic brother's three young children, an invalid mother, and a house to take care of. She prepared our meals on time; we had clean clothes to wear; and the house was decently kept. But if there was love I was too oblivious to notice it—or to accept it.

I was determined. Nobody would take the place of my mother.

With my father seldom around and Helen too preoccupied, there was no one to oversee how we spent our time when we were out of the house. When we first moved to the city, I was alone—with my thoughts, my fears, and alone with my bitterness. There was no tight circle of friends here to comfort and support me. I'd sit on the front porch and feel sorry for myself.

"Hey, look at the little wimp in his cage." Three boys, a little older than I, stood on the sidewalk, looking at me through the screens on our porch. "Yeah, looks like they got a new animal in their zoo."

I jumped up and ran to the screen, the fury in me building like a fire out of control. I wanted to scream back at them, but nothing came out. Instead, I felt the tears demanding to have *their* way. I shook my fist at them, turned and ran into the house, slamming the door and leaving the sound of their laughter behind. But you can't cry forever—at least outwardly. So when the tear ducts dried up, the pain of loneliness and loss sent me to the streets in search of someone or something to soften it.

◆ ◆ ◆

In Pinehurst, where we lived when my mother was alive, I roamed through pasturelands of shoulder-high grass. One day some friends and I found an abandoned house. The cellar was flooded. Mattresses and a box spring floated around it in waist-deep water. We sailed around the dim cellar on those mattresses, imagining battles with pirates and savages from exotic places. At the end of the voyages around the basement of the haunted house,

I'd go home to a plate of Toll House cookies, a cup of hot cocoa, and the warmth and protection of my mother's love.

Lowell was different. It was a survival city. Men and single women struggled in grubby, pitiless factories, housewives absorbed the abuse of drunken husbands, and male children banded together in street gangs for protection from other street gangs. I was a stranger here, lost and alone, no friends, no feeling that I was part of a family, no promising future ahead for me.

One Saturday afternoon, several weeks after we moved to Lowell, my father sent me to Dempsey's Market, about two blocks from our house, for cigarettes and ice cream. He gave me a ten-dollar bill and told me not to lose it. In Pinehurst I'd grown used to warm and neighborly streets. You'd walk to the corner store accompanied by a melody of sounds: birds, bees and crickets, occasionally interrupted by a "Hi, Michael, where yah goin'? How's your Mom?"

In Lowell . . .

"Hey you, mama's boy." The shout came from a group of three boys about my age. "He looks like a mama's boy. He walks like a queer."

I felt the flame beginning to burn inside of me; rage I seldom felt except for when my father was drunk. I thought about shouting something back to them, but instead I kept on walking. The trouble began when I was on my way back home. A bad decision on my part made it easy for them. I could have approached Helen's house from the other direction and avoided them. I could have at least passed by them on the opposite side of the street instead of walking right through them. But I didn't. Something in me whispered:

The hell with them. Don't let those assholes scare you.

They surrounded me and started punching me and shouting at me. "Hey mama's boy; where's your mama?"

"What've you got in that bag, you skinny little shit?" one of the thugs shouted, grabbing it out of my hands.

"Give it back," I yelled, grabbing at it.

"Get lost, you little runt, you mama's boy." They surrounded me shouting and laughing. "You skinny little shit. Fight back, you little pussy."

I tried to but the punches came from every direction. When I dodged one, two or three more hit me. Even when I fell to the ground, they didn't stop. They kicked and punched. I tried to hunch up, an embryo refusing to unfold. But even that didn't help. The pain felt like someone was stabbing me with a red-hot knife. Lights blazed and darkened behind my eyes, as if a flashlight was being turned on and off.

Finally, tired of the game, they grabbed the bag with the cigarettes and the ice cream, took the eight dollars and seventy-five cents in change from my pocket, and ran off laughing, leaving me crying on the sidewalk. My nose was bleeding, my lip was split and my ribs ached, and my knees and elbows were skinned. I entered the house crying and shaking. Helen wasn't there, but my father was. He looked at me, uncomprehending.

"What the hell happened to you?"

"They beat me up," I said, choking back tears.

"Who beat you up?" He took a deep draw on his cigarette.

"Some kids from the neighborhood."

"What kids? How old where they?" he shouted, coughing out cigarette smoke onto me.

"I don't know. Just some kids. A little older than me, I think."

"Did you fight back? Did you make them pay?"

"I tried to," I said, the tears beginning to run down my face, "but there were three of them and they were bigger than me. They took the cigarettes and ice cream. And the money."

"What? What the hell!"

He jumped to his feet and headed for the front door. "Don't expect sympathy from me," he yelled back at me. "No son of mine who can't protect my money on the streets should come home whimpering and expecting sympathy from me. You'd better learn how to be a man; you'd better learn how to take care of *yourself.*" He slammed the door and was gone.

There it was. The declaration of what I could expect from him now and in the future: "You'd better learn how to take care of *yourself.*"

I did learn how to take care of myself. I learned to throw my sixty-five-pound body into an adversary with a fury few of them expected. There were more fights, street tests of endurance, most of them on the front lawn of the Presbyterian Church a few doors up from our house. When I fought, I always refused to give up and I was determined never to cry. Even when I was pinned to the ground by a stronger, heavier boy, when he let me up, I'd charge right back at him, an enraged tiger. In one fight I locked my teeth on an adversary's ear, prepared to bite it off, but he gave up. In another I had to be pulled off a boy whose head I was slamming into the ground, determined to split it open. My father had told me: "You don't have to win a fight; you only have to convince the other guy he never wants to take you on again." He was, I learned, right. Eventually I was admitted into the West Fifth Street gang.

But when a fight was over, I recognized anger had taken possession of me, made me someone I didn't want to be. Made me realize that in a fight I was willing to do anything, absolutely anything, to make sure the other guy didn't want to fight with me again.

I was terrified. What if I killed somebody? I'd be ashamed at what I had done, but remorse lasted only until the next fight. Something was driving me to be savage and cruel and it wasn't just the boys who challenged me. I roamed the streets, an explorer, looking, always looking. I was determined to know every street and alley and every hiding place in the neighborhood. Before long I'd found every warehouse door I could jimmy open, every alley I could disappear down, and every empty oil drum or discarded furniture crate I could use as a hiding place. I learned to navigate rooftops and fire escapes almost as well as I navigated the streets.

Neighborhood gangs in Lowell were protective of their turf. They didn't welcome strangers in their neighborhoods. The code was unwritten but powerful. Protect your own, defend your turf. Fight hard. Don't surrender. Don't let adults know what is going on in the streets. As a member of the West Fifth Street Gang, I followed the code. Most often the fighting on the streets in Lowell was to demonstrate our courage and establish our position in the pecking order or to maintain it.

Once I learned to master it, fighting provided me with an outlet for my bitterness and anger about my mother's death and my father's absence. As one of the scrawnier kids in the West Fifth Street neighborhood, I made up for my lack of physical size with determination. My father's reminder was a constant prod: you don't have to win a fight to get respect; all you have to do is convince the other guy he doesn't want to get into it with you again. At times, when he got up on a Saturday morning after a night on the town, I could tell from the dark patch under one of his eyes or the dried traces of blood under his nose and on his chin my father probably hadn't won. But he seemed content, nevertheless, assuming, I supposed, the other guy wouldn't want to mix it up with him again.

I developed another compulsion that would later get me into trouble and would contribute to my desperation to get away from the streets, from Lowell and from my family. I discovered, as I got more familiar with my West Fifth Street neighborhood, I could get something I wanted without working for it, paying for it, or asking God for it as we were taught to do at school, St. Michael's. I became an accomplished shoplifter. I "needed" things and so did other kids I hung around with and we had little money to pay for them. It was a sign of courage if you could walk into a market with a nickel and walk out with enough candy to satisfy the appetites of five other boys and your own. Patience and sleight of hand, I learned, could make a nickel purchase six times what it should.

Much as I cherished the booty, the challenge of pulling off a theft and the approval I got from the guys I was hanging out with meant even more to me. Supermarkets were a relatively easy mark because I could walk into them with a fake shopping list, grab a shopping cart, walk up and down the aisles putting milk and butter and other supplies I had no intention of buying into it until I came to the candy aisle. There I'd throw a few bags of goodies into the cart and then head for a quiet corner in the back of the store. When I was certain nobody was looking, I'd stuff the candy into my jacket and leave the cart with the rest of the groceries behind. Before I left, I'd grab a couple of empty boxes from the front of the store to make it look like that's what I'd been looking for in the first place.

I was a thief, but not a comfortable one. I went to Confession on Saturdays and Mass on Sundays to ask for forgiveness and do penance for my shoplifting. I was a frequent transgressor and an equally frequent confessor. Every two weeks I'd enter the darkness of the confessional and free myself of the weight of my guilt about stealing and fighting.

"Bless me father for I have sinned . . ." When I pulled back the curtain of the confessional and reentered the daylight of the church and walked to the altar to whisper the Our Fathers and Hail Marys

I'd received as penance, I felt relieved and determined to steal no more. My resolve seldom lasted more than a few days.

Life was full of contradictions for me now, and this was one of the many; I enjoyed the turbulent life of temptation on the streets, but I could never escape the guilt I felt about what I was doing or the feeling my mother was looking down from heaven, terribly disappointed in me: "Michael, look at you. Look at what you are becoming." I had mastered the art of pretending to be tough, but to do it I had to hide other feelings—feelings that what I was doing was wrong, very wrong. And that what I was doing would lead to more trouble in the future—if not in this life, certainly in the next one. I was, I felt, destined for hell unless I changed my ways and I couldn't see any hope of changing them. I needed to escape this life I was leading, the violence, the stealing, the loneliness. But there was no escape—not here, not in Lowell.

◆ ◆ ◆

In the old neighborhood of Pinehurst, the family who lived behind us, the Browns, had two boys and a mother with whom we played marbles. Mrs. Brown loved to take on the neighborhood boys. She was a tall wiry woman. None of us could look her straight in the eye until she knelt to line up a shot. She wore a red kerchief she hoped would keep her black curls under control, but didn't. She always smelled of Clorox or Ajax or furniture polish. And she had a collection of marbles, especially cat's eyes, we all envied.

After school I would gather with other neighborhood boys in the Browns' yard waiting for her to finish her work and come out to play. Sometimes, while we waited, we'd compete with one another. But the real competition didn't begin until Mrs. Brown joined us. She carried two socks filled with marbles we were determined to win from her. You could buy a mesh bag containing five or six marbles at the local market, but to get a sockful the size of Mrs. Brown's, you had to be a dedicated collector or a great competitor.

The door swung open, banging the kitchen wall. My mother turned from what she was mixing at the counter as I burst into the kitchen. "What's the matter, Michael?" she said as I rushed to her sobbing.

"Mrs. Brown took my marbles," I choked out between sobs. "It's not fair. It's not fair."

"What do you mean she took them?" my mother asked looking at me through soft brown eyes that never failed to calm the squalls of a five-year-old's spirit. "Do you mean she beat you again at marbles?"

"Yes," I screamed, "but it's not fair. I'm just a little kid and she took them all."

"Come over here and sit down," my mother said wiping her delicate hands on her apron, "I'm making some cookies; they'll be ready in a few minutes. Come over here and wait," she said, putting her arm around me and leading me toward the table. My eyes stung with the bitterness of the tears I was still choking back, but the tenderness in her voice and the smell of Toll House cookies were having their effect. My mind was turning away from the anger I felt about the lost marbles. "Wipe your face and blow your nose," my mother said, handing me a paper napkin. "Sit down while I get some milk for your cookies."

I sat at the table drinking milk and eating cookies, recovering from the heartache of my lost marbles as she talked to me in her sweet voice. "There's a difference between someone taking something from you, and you losing it to someone in a game, Michael. You keep going over to Mrs. Brown every time you get a new bag of marbles and challenging her to come out and play with you. And when she does and wins, you get angry."

"Yeah but she's got so many marbles and most of them belong to little kids like me."

"That's because other kids in the neighborhood want to play with her just like you, and for the same reason—because she's good and it's a challenge to beat her."

"Yeah, but she shouldn't keep our marbles even if she wins. We're just kids, and she's way older."

"Maybe you don't appreciate it, Michael, but Mrs. Brown is trying to teach you and your friends a lesson."

"What lesson?"

"I believe she's trying to show you that you have to learn how to lose." She put her arm around me and kissed me on the cheek. "You have to learn how to accept losses; we all do."

"Well, I don't want to learn that; I don't like losing. It's not fair."

"I know," she said brushing the hair back from my brow with fingers as tender as a baby's breath and pulling me tightly to her. I smelled the sweet scent of lilac and felt the reassuring warmth of her body.

◆ ◆ ◆

One night during supper at Aunt Helen's, two years after my mother's death, my father announced he was getting married again. I stared at him in disbelief. *How could he do this to us?*

I looked at my brother Paul, who appeared as puzzled as I felt. I looked at my Aunt Helen; she looked pleased. I asked to be excused to go to the bathroom. Instead, I went to my bedroom, locked the door, lay down on my bed and buried my head in a pillow and cried. No one, I believed, could replace my mother. And I'd thought my father believed that, too.

It can't be true. It just can't!

Young as I was, I knew my father had a special charm that attracted women. I'd seen it a few times when he had taken me to the Veterans Administration in Lowell where he worked part-time as a janitor on Saturdays or to Murphy Army Hospital in Waltham where he worked as a fireman on weekdays. He'd smile and say hello to all the women we passed, and most of them seemed to brighten, sit up straighter, or walk a little taller when he did. When he made idle conversation with one of them I could see he was turning on the charm and they were responding to it.

Later, Paul asked me what I thought of my father's announcement.

"I don't want to talk about it," I shouted.

"What do you mean? We're going to have a mother again. Aren't you happy?"

"What? You think she will be our mother? Our mother's gone. She's never coming back. We're never going to have a mother again. Never." I flung the words at him like they were rocks. They had the effect I'd hoped for. He began to cry. So did I.

When Aunt Helen asked how I felt about having a new mother, I replied without enthusiasm: "Good."

Marie B. Coyne was introduced to us at supper a week later. She sat straight up at the table like someone had starched her backbone. A pair of glasses hung by a string from her neck. She had a voice that you could polish fine glassware with. She was a telephone operator at the Army hospital. But not the gum-chewing type I'd seen in movies. My father introduced Marie as "our new mother." I stared at him across the table, my eyes burning with hatred, my lips trembling. The conversation around the table was mostly Marie talking about herself and establishing her past history as a mother. When she was seventeen, she told us, her parents died, leaving her in change of raising six brothers and sisters. She had, she said, raised them to be "fine men and women; not a bum among them. I had to sacrifice a lot for them. But I did it, and I've never regretted it, even though it meant giving up a lot of what I wanted."

Paul, my sister Carol, and I had had little preparation for the introduction of a stepmother into our lives. There was only the announcement from my father and word that we would be moving into a new home with "a new mother." Helen made a few unsuccessful attempts to explain what all of this meant, but then gave up. Paul seemed pleased that Marie would be coming into our lives, even though he tried to pretend to me that he wasn't. Carol seemed mostly confused; she liked living with Helen and couldn't remember a time when we were not living with her. What I knew about a stepmother was what I'd learned from watching movies like *Snow White* and *Cinderella*: they were nasty and mean.

The introductory supper with Marie included lima beans, a vegetable I hated. Helen knew my feelings about lima beans and we had had them only once. They reminded me of bird shit. I suspected Marie was responsible for this addition to the meal. "Just leave them if you don't want them," Helen said as she noticed me glaring at the beans on my plate.

"He hasn't even tried them," Marie replied. "He shouldn't be allowed to refuse food without even trying it."

"Looking at them makes me gag," I said.

"They are good for you; they have lots of nutrients." She turned to my father: "He shouldn't be allowed to leave the table until he at least tries them." My father usually paid little attention to his children's food preferences. But he nodded. The line of battle was drawn. I refused to try the beans. Marie was determined that I would. When the rest of the family started to get up and bring their dirty dishes to the kitchen sink, I was ready to join them. I pushed back my chair and picked up my plate.

"Put that plate back on the table and sit down," Marie demanded. "You're not going to leave this table until you at least try those lima beans like everybody else has."

I looked at my father, hoping he would rescue me.

"Listen to your mother," he said. "You need to start obeying her."

"My mother? She's not my mother, and she never will be," I wanted to shout. But I knew that would infuriate my father—and who knows—maybe Marie. I didn't need them ganging up on me; so I struggled to keep quiet, but I couldn't control the look of hatred I gave my father as he turned and walked away.

Long after the table had been cleared and with the family retired to the living room, Marie and I remained sitting across from one another, staring at each other, my plate with the untouched lima beans lying between us.

"Just try one forkful; then you can leave the table and join the rest of the family."

"I hate them."

"How do you know you hate them, you haven't even tried them?"

"I hate the way they look. I hate the way they smell."

"I want you to just try them. Then you can leave the table."

"You can't make me. You're not my mother!"

"We'll see about that," she replied through clenched teeth.

After what seemed like an hour, my father returned and sent me to bed. Alone in my room, I tried to savor the triumph of my resistance. But I recognized I had challenged Marie in a way that could only lead to problems between us. I would never have acted with my mother the way I did with Marie. But Marie was not my mother.

I listened at the door waiting for my father to take Marie home. When I heard the car drive off, I climbed out my bedroom window with a blanket and a pillow. I headed up to the Dempseys', two boys I hung around with. They lived in an apartment complex, and I could find a place under one of the stairways to sleep for the night. I was sure my father would stop off for a few beers after he dropped Marie off. Tanked up and angry with me for embarrassing him, he'd storm around the house when he got home looking for me. But I wouldn't be there. He probably wouldn't bother to leave the house looking for me. And even if he did, I was sure he wouldn't find my hiding place. I could spend the weekend there if I had to and return home on Monday when he was working and it was safe to go home.

Safe to go home?

It was soon clear Marie viewed marrying my father and adopting his children as a call to duty. I can't remember any signs of affection between my father and Marie. Her commitment in the marriage was the obligation to raise and discipline his children. He seemed okay with that. Marie had never been married before, but she believed raising her brothers and sisters had made her a mother. She was fifty years old by the time she married my father, a fine-looking fifty. And smart, but reserved. She was a strong-willed woman and I was a strong-willed twelve-year-old. No doubt my father had told her my rebellious nature needed a strong hand to curb it. She was determined to be my mother. I was determined not to allow it.

Michael, his father, Red; his brother, Paul, and sister, Carol, at 100 Myrtle Street in Lowell, which reminded Michael of Edgar Allen Poe's House of Usher.

My father and Marie had purchased a three-story Victorian house on Christian Hill. The big gray dwelling had a two-car garage, originally a carriage house when the house was first built in the late

1800s. Both the house and garage needed major repair. The paint was peeling on both. Clapboards on the house were missing and a few of its shutters looked like drunks, struggling to stay upright. Pigeon shit splotched the stairs leading up to the front porch. High above in one of the eaves of the house, a chorus of pigeons was constantly complaining, "What the hell are you doing here? This is our nesting place."

"You can have it," I wanted to scream.

For two months before we moved into that house at 100 Myrtle Street, I prayed our stepmother would disappear like a bad dream and our Edgar Allen Poe house would dissolve into the mist of that dream. As the weeks went by before the move, I became both more miserable and more of an outcast, looking back on a life I could never recover and ahead to one I could never accept. In the West Fifth Street neighborhood we were leaving, I had finally established myself as a tough, mean kid other boys didn't want to mess with. Moving to a new neighborhood would require I'd have to do it all over again.

The first battle took place on the front lawn of our house a week after we moved in. The lawn was big and bordered by several huge maple trees. Their branches spread wide over the driveway and above the front lawn. It was a sunny afternoon in late September and my father had sent Paul and me out to rake up the leaves and put them in piles for burning. We were about three quarters of the way through the task and I'd been keeping an eye on four boys across the street. They were about our age, twelve maybe or thirteen. They were laughing and pointing at us.

"Paul, those guys are planning something. We'd better be ready."

"Just ignore them," he said. I wasn't expecting much help from Paul, anyway. He was sensitive, *a real mama's boy*.

The four boys disappeared but soon appeared again, two of them carrying ropes with broken tree branches tied to them. They started toward our yard. "Welcome to the neighborhood." Two boys dashed toward the piles of leaves we'd raked up and began kicking them back over the yard. "You forgot to rake this spot," another yelled as he launched his rope over a low-hanging branch of the maple at the top of our driveway and started shaking leaves down from it.

"Son of a bitch!" I turned to see my brother, his rake held like a lance chasing after the kid at the top of the driveway. He caught him around the feet with the cast iron teeth of the rake as the kid ran across the road. "You bastard," Paul shouted, and the kid came crashing down in the middle of the road. His friends turned and started running to rescue him. I ran after them. One of them, the biggest, tackled Paul as he was about to bring the teeth of the rake down on the fallen boy's knee. I charged into the big guy, pounding him with my fists. He turned and started punching me. We tore into each other like enraged inmates of an insane asylum, punching and kicking. We struggled from the street back into our front yard. My brother and the other boys watched as we fought on, pushing and punching and hurling "fuck yous" and "you little shit" at one another. He got me in a headlock. I twisted out of it. He came at me again and I barreled into him with my shoulder. We were on the ground again punching and swearing. Finally, exhausted, we stopped. It was over. The four of them walked off shouting "fuck yous" at us. We shouted back at them.

Our new neighborhood had shown us one of its faces, one I was familiar with. But the neighborhood had another face, a competitive but less belligerent one. Once we were accepted by the gang on Myrtle Street, I would enjoy that other face. On West Fifth Street we seldom played street sports, but on Myrtle Street sports were a daily afternoon event during school days and a full-day activity on non–school days. We played wall ball and curb ball if there were only two of us. The sports we loved best and played the most were scrub (street baseball where you hit a rubber ball with your fist rather than a bat) and touch football. The street was narrow and there was a lot more foul than fair territory for scrub. The strategy for a batter was simple. Try to hit the ball hard and deep enough to get it over an outfielder's head or, much more difficult, try to strategically place it between infielders. Occasionally a ball would get away from a fielder and roll down the sewer. We would pry up the sewer cover with a branch and lower a tomato can with a number of holes in its side by a rope and attempt to scoop up the floating ball. If we failed and the ball floated deeper into the drain, the game was over until someone could come up with enough change to buy a new ball, or I could get downtown to shoplift a new one from Kresge's Five and Dime store.

Myrtle Street had some exceptional athletes, boys who could run like cheetahs, darting left and right to avoid a tag in touch football, boys who could spring skyward to snag a pass and then twist while still in the air to avoid a tag. Being good in sports was a way, other than fighting, you could gain respect in this neighborhood.

The most accomplished athlete was Ray Coleman. Sandy-haired, slim, and short, Ray was quick as a cobra and elusive as a mink. A natural athlete, he seemed to do with ease what the rest of us did with effort. The street from curb to curb was his stage and he dominated it with one dazzling performance after another. It was a problem for me to decide if I wanted to be on the same team with Ray or on the other team trying to beat him. Watching him fake and dodge and scoot by someone trying to tag him, I envied his skills. I never saw Ray in a fight. He didn't have to fight; he had respect.

Life on Myrtle Street offered new interests, but they didn't erase the old ones or flush away the resentment I was feeling. My mother's death taught me that nothing was permanent; that it is best to keep from getting too close to anyone because sooner or later you're bound to lose them. It was an attitude I would find difficult to let go.

Marie had decided that even as she assumed her new role of mother, she would continue to work as a telephone operator at Murphy Army Hospital, which meant that during the week she was away from home from early in the morning until late afternoon. As a consequence, my brother and I were each assigned chores to keep the house clean. My sister was too young for chores, so Helen babysat her at the West Fifth Street house until Marie or my father picked her up.

Paul developed a good relationship with Marie and he solidified it by being responsible, performing his household chores. Street games distracted me from my duties of vacuuming the living room, washing dishes, sweeping the kitchen floor, and cleaning my room. Something was always going on in the streets, and I wanted to be part of it. Paul joined in, but he would break away and begin his chores about fifteen minutes before Marie was scheduled to return home. When Marie got home at five thirty, she would find me still out on the street and Paul in the house, dusting in the living room or dry mopping his room. Paul was, she decided, "dependable." Michael was "irresponsible." When Marie found something broken in the house, she assumed I was guilty. I decided one day to put a door handle my brother and I had broken in a tug of war back into the door. *Good. The next person to open the door will think that she or he had broken it.*

The next person was Marie. The knob came off in her hand.

"Michael," she shouted. "Come here this minute."

I came with a dust mop in my hand and what I hoped was the look of a fatigued laborer.

"Yes."

She held the doorknob in front of my face "How did you break this doorknob?"

"Me? I . . ."

"Never mind, I'll have your father deal with you when he gets home."

What infuriated Marie more than anything else about me was my refusal to call her Mom. I called her Marie when I spoke to her or about her. When my father insisted I call her Mom, I refused and was sent to my room. Eventually Marie refused to respond when I called her Marie; that was disrespectful, she said. So I learned to converse with her without using her name.

"Can I go out?"

"Thanks."

"My teacher wants you to call."

One day an incident took place that would solidify the breach between Marie and me. She had been told I had a habit of taking small change from Helen's coat pockets and change purse. She often questioned me about the disappearance of loose change my father occasionally left around the house. She didn't leave any money, or her pocketbook, where I might find it. But she did leave two souvenir silver dollars in a bathroom drawer, perhaps believing I would not know it was real money, or, if I did, they would raise suspicion if I tried to spend them at the local market. But one Saturday she discovered the coins were missing. I could hear her and my father in heated debate as I sat in my room reading.

"He took them; I know he took them. Find out what he did with them," she said.

Suddenly the door to my room burst open and my father was standing there, his hands on his hips, a scowl on his face that would have made the devil himself want to get up and run. "What did you do with those coins that were in the bathroom drawer?"

"What coins? I didn't take any coins."

"Yes, you did; we both know you did," he said slamming the door behind him and storming toward my bed.

"I didn't . . . didn't take anything."

"You're a damn liar. Get the hell out of that bed and get downstairs; your mother and I want to talk to you."

The interrogation that followed felt like it lasted for hours. I denied any knowledge of the theft.

"We'll sit here until hell freezes over if we have to," my father warned.

As the minutes slipped into hours, I began to wonder if I should take the blame and end this misery.

"Did you take that money?" my father asked for what seemed like the hundredth time.

"No," I replied weakly, exhausted.

"Did you?"

"No."

Occasionally, they would leave the room. When they did, I was left wondering who the real guilty party might be. Was it my brother, who'd never admit it? Or was it my father, who took them when he was angry and drunk and didn't remember he took them? My father and Marie returned and my father's tone shifted from angry to the compassionate tenor you'd expect from a priest in the confessional.

"Look, your mother and I don't care about the money; we just want you to be honest with us. The money isn't the important thing; the truth is. So we are going to leave you alone for a few minutes to think it over and when we return we hope if you took the money, you'll admit it. That's all; then this will be over and done with this. So think it over. We just want you to be honest with us."

Bullshit. Who does he think he's kidding? Marie wants that money back, and she'll do anything to get it. I'm going to tell them I took them; they already think I'm guilty; I'm the only one being questioned.

But you didn't take them.

Yeah, I know, but they want me to say I did, so I'm going to. Then it will be over and done with.

You don't really believe that do you? They're looking to punish you for this. Don't you know that?

Yeah, but I don't want to sit here all day. And that's what'll happen if I don't take the blame.

What if they ask you what you did with the money; what are you going to tell them?

I don't know, but I'll think of something.

Don't do it. You'll only get in more trouble.

The battle of the voices inside my head kept up until I heard the sound of footsteps approaching. I confessed to the theft. Dark storm clouds began to sweep over my father's face. I thought Marie would be happy, but, as she rose to leave the room, she looked back at me and her lips moved in what I thought were the unsaid words: *I'm sorry*. And then she was gone. The room was deadly quiet.

"What did you do with those coins?"

"I don't know. I guess I spent them."

"What do you mean 'I don't know; I guess I spent them?'" he roared. "Where did you spend them?"

"I don't remember."

"You don't remember; you don't remember. What kind of bullshit are you giving me?"

"I thought you said it would be all over if I just admitted it."

"Never mind that. Where did you spend those coins?"

"I don't know. Maybe I didn't spend them; maybe I lost them."

"What do you mean, maybe you lost them? Where did you lose them?"

"I don't know; if I knew, they wouldn't be lost."

Whap! The pain from the slap was like a branding iron pressed against my face.

"What did you do with those damn coins?"

"I don't know. I think I lost them."

My father took me around to the stores in the neighborhood trying to find out if I'd spent the coins in one of them, but the search proved fruitless.

Marie didn't really feel sorry for me after all. She never forgave me for the missing coins, and I never forgave her for believing I had taken them. Distrust now ruled Marie's relationship with me; hostility, my relationship with her.

As the end of my eighth-grade year neared, I got into trouble again. This time for a theft I did commit. Flynn's Market was a ma-and-pa store a couple of streets up from our house. I'd been successful pilfering candy there before, but it wasn't easy. The candy was at the far end of the cash register counter, in full view of Mrs. Flynn, who was waiting to ring up a customer's groceries. I had to time things right. I had to wait until her back was turned. I'd always been successful, until one day . . .

I busied myself examining the candy bar selection, careful to keep an eye on Mrs. Flynn at the cash register. I picked up a candy bar and examined it, turning it over as if I was reading the ingredients to make sure it would satisfy my sweet tooth. When Mrs. Flynn was busy with a customer, I shoved the candy bar into my jacket pocket and picked up another one to examine. I'd pocketed five candy bars before I uttered a satisfied sigh, indicating I'd made my choice. I went to the counter holding one candy bar, handing Mrs. Flynn a nickel. She smiled at me and started to ring up my purchase.

"What about those other ones in your pocket?"

I whirled around. *Oh shit. Mr. Flynn.*

"Are you planning to pay for the candy bars in your pocket?"

"Ah . . ."

Mrs. Flynn was looking at me, her expression swinging between shock and disappointment.

"Empty your coat pockets, son," Mr. Flynn demanded. I hesitated. "I've had my eyes on you from back there in the meat section while you were stuffing your pockets with candy. Empty your pockets." Two customers watched as I put five more candy bars on the counter. Mr. Flynn threatened to call the cops, but instead he told his wife to charge the extra candy to our family's account and he called my parents.

"Why didn't you call the cops?" my father said when he came to pick me up. "An afternoon in jail would do the little asshole some good."

On the way home my father kept telling me what a stupid little asshole I was. Maybe, I thought, he's right. Prospects for my future didn't look bright. Keith Academy was the boys' Catholic high school in Lowell I was hoping to attend. You had to take a competitive entrance exam to get into the freshman class. Hundreds took the exam each year and only the top fifty were accepted. I took the exam with little hope of being one of the fifty. But if somehow I was able to make it into that group, perhaps I could prove I wasn't that stupid little asshole my father thought I was. A few weeks after the exam, I received a letter that said my scores had not been good enough to get me accepted, but wished me luck in my high school career.

That meant I'd be going to a public school, Lowell High, with over 4,500 students. I'd never been in public school. Besides, I'd be a nobody there; a skinny little runt with big dreams of being a somebody, but with no chance of seeing those dreams realized. Not there. Not in a place bigger than any neighborhood I'd ever lived in.

A few weeks later Father Simeon Heine, a Franciscan Friar of the Atonement, came to speak to the eighth-grade classes at St. Michael's. He was looking for boys who thought they might have a vocation to the priesthood. This was a noble calling for an Irish Catholic boy. Many Catholic families hoped at least one of its boys would become a priest.

Sister Margret Francis took the girls away for "a discussion" about the life of nuns while Father Simeon talked to us boys about the training for the priesthood. If we had a calling, what better place to go than to St. John's Atonement Seminary where, he said, "You can prepare yourself for the priesthood in a new religious order, the Franciscan Friars of the Atonement." He told us the Friars, established in 1898, devoted themselves to missionary work in foreign countries like Japan and China. *Japan, China; they were far enough away.*

I signed up to be interviewed at my house.

Hey, I might even discover I have a vocation.

◆ ◆ ◆

"You want to do what? Are you crazy?"

"Let's hear him out," suggested Marie. "Let's hear what he has to say, Red."

"I don't want to go to Lowell High School; the place is a factory. There are 4,000 kids there. What kind of an education can I get there? Besides, I've been in Catholic school almost all my life; I want to stay in Catholic school."

"Well you should have studied harder for that Keith Academy entrance exam instead of spending your time getting into trouble," my father said.

"Yeah, well, Bobby Cleary didn't ace the exam either, but his father went and talked to the headmaster and they let him in. Why wouldn't you do that for me? Why couldn't you stick up for me like Bobby's father did for him?"

"In this house, you get what you earn. There are no free rides."

Maybe the thought of sending me to a school with over 4,000 city kids where I was sure to get into more trouble affected their decision. Maybe my father felt some guilt about not going to the headmaster at Keith Academy. Maybe it was just that as Marie said: "It will be good to have him away from here for a while."

My father and Marie listened as Father Simeon interviewed me. Then they signed the papers sending me to the seminary.

Chapter Three

John—The Early Years

Someday, maybe, there will exist a well-informed, well-considered and yet fervent public conviction that the most deadly of all possible sins is the mutilation of a child's spirit; for such mutilation undercuts the life principle of trust . . .

—Erik Erikson

"When you were a baby, you had colic. You cried nonstop for six months. I walked around with you in my arms, but you wouldn't stop. Your father was furious at you and me. I felt as if my life depended on stopping your crying. I often walked to the window and considered throwing you out."

My mother told me this when I was a teenager. Since we had lived on the fifth floor of a brownstone in the South Bronx until 1952 when I was ten, she was clearly not suggesting that she was tempted to put me somewhere else, but rather to have killed me. Also, knowing that my mother was not given to hyperbole or whimsical imagery, I understood that killing me had come close to being her decision. Although the details were news to me, I felt no sense of surprise, no disbelief.

I have crib memories, bits and pieces. Nothing good, just fears. A sense of ineffable dread. Despite the fact that I anticipated that my father would kill me almost every day of my life, here I am. So, I worried in vain.

I remember crying in a crib, my father hitting me, shaking me. He stared at me, face red with rage as if he were willing me to silence; daring me to resist him. It worked. I shut up.

Another time I climbed out of a crib in an apartment that was strange to me. I wanted to get out of there—not just the crib, but also the apartment. I crawled to the front door and sat there with my back against it. I knew that, in another room, my father was with a woman who was not my mother. I had no idea what that implied, but I felt upset by it. I would sit there until my mother came in and found me first. I was frightened at what would befall me if he found me. So, I sat there and waited for whatever would happen. I don't remember how that ended.

Infant Johnny with his parents, Jack and Gladys, on the roof of their apartment building in the Bronx.

My father never taught me to fish or catch a ball, although he did criticize me for my inability to do those things. He did teach me to keep my hands up, shoulders hunched, head bobbing, and to trust no one—things of real value to him.

I lived in a working-class neighborhood, full of tough adults and children. I was not tough. Jack Tuohey, my father, was tough. He was a living legend. He was only five-six but weighed 200 pounds and was unbelievably strong and fast. What set him apart from other fast, strong men was his utter unpredictability. What he found amusing one time was an intolerable insult another. A friend one day was an enemy the next, without any perceived trouble between them.

With Jack Tuohey there was no posturing, no chest bumping, no shoulder shoving, no idle threats or warnings. There was also no off switch. Whatever was going to happen was going to happen until he burned out. His opponent's first indication that this was going all the way was that he was on the ground, being mauled by a human Rottweiler.

As the progeny of this wild man, I had a protective shield in the minds of people who knew him or of him. I was walking down the street with my best friend when I was about seven. Two older boys, perhaps sixteen years old, walked by. One grabbed me and slapped me in the face. "Give me your money," he said, gripping me by the front of my shirt. His friend asked him if he knew who my father was.

"I don't give a fuck who his father is," my assailant said.

"His father is Jack Tuohey!"

The first boy looked stunned.

"Is Jack Tuohey your father?" he asked.

When I replied that he was, the kid began telling me that he had just been kidding around, meant nothing by it, did not want my money, and stressed that there was absolutely no reason to mention it to my father.

I agreed, and did not mention it.

If I told my father that someone beat me up, he and I would search the streets for that kid, and I would be ordered to beat him up. That happened once, and I found myself reluctantly pummeling a kid who was too scared to fight back. I would have preferred to just let it go. My second choice would have been for the other kid to give it his best—probably beating the crap out of me, because I was not then, am not now, a tough guy.

My father was evenhanded in teaching lessons. He taught his father that he could no longer discipline him by almost beating the old man to death one night.

My parents, my baby sister Ellen, and I lived in the brownstone with my paternal grandparents. My grandfather had taken a shine to my mother and despised how my father treated her, apparently forgetting he was his son's role model. One night, as was his habit, my father had gone out drinking, fighting, whatever it was that he did. My mother sat in tears waiting for him to return. That, my grandfather decided, was the tipping point. My father needed a lesson.

I shared a bed with my grandfather in the second bedroom from the living room. My parents' room adjoined the living room. I went to bed at my usual 7:30. My grandfather always came in later. That night he waited for my father. Much later I was awakened by shouting and things being knocked around in my parents' room. I slipped out of bed and opened the door between the rooms.

My father was on top of his father on the floor. My grandfather's blood covered them both. My grandfather was not moving, but my father continued to pound his face. My mother and grandmother shouted at him to stop, together trying to pull him off his father. Somehow, he had not killed him.

No police or ambulances were called. I was sent back to bed. Whatever then happened, happened. I have no idea. It was never mentioned. I never again heard the old man voice an opinion, raise his voice, or seem anything more than a shadow for his remaining forty-odd years. The young lion he had routinely beaten was now the beast in this pride.

My father provided the stimulus for his mother to be more religious. She said the rosary nonstop and went to every, and I mean every, Mass. In those days there were many Masses.

He taught my mother the elusiveness of fidelity, and the subtle joys of a life of chaos and fear; taught her that spending her youth in an orphanage was not so bad. He taught her that there are things far worse than having a husband who deserted you while you were pregnant with your first child—such as having him come back.

She was almost free of him twice.

I was awakened by shouting one night. I arose from bed and looked down the hall. I could see my mother at the door to the bathroom. She and my grandmother were crying and talking in some agitated, disconnected way. As I approached, I saw that the object of their concern was my father. He lay unconscious on the bathroom floor. He was lying in a pool of blood, his face covered with it. It was thick and dark, reeking of copper and feces. The alcohol had finally eaten his gut, and he was bleeding to death.

My grandfather came into the room and said that an ambulance was coming. In short order two burly men in white uniforms came in with a rolling litter. They maneuvered my father onto it and headed to the stairs. I found it unbelievable that they could carry him down five flights of stairs, but they did.

We all stood at the stairs, watching him be taken away. He showed no sign of life. My mother and grandmother were hugging each other, which was unheard of. They were crying and saying, "Oh God, he's dead, he's dead." I just thought how wonderful it would be if he never came back, but of course he did. If he learned anything from the experience, he kept it to himself.

My mother's other brush with freedom came when I was eight. It was early in the morning, after my father had gone to work.

"Get up. Get up. Pack your things. We're leaving." My mother was running around, throwing things into an old suitcase. My sister, Ellen, who was four, was crying, probably not because she knew what was up, but in response to this strange mother who was full of anger and rebellion.

"Where are we going?" I asked.

"I don't know, but we are going away. Hurry up." How long does it take to throw some socks, jockey shorts, and T-shirts into a shopping bag?

"When are we coming back?"

"We're never coming back."

"What about Daddy?"

"I don't care about Daddy. We're never going to see Daddy again."

She seemed quite serious. She was obviously very mad. Given all that she had silently tolerated over the years, I can only wonder what he had done that time to push her over the edge. I stood there contemplating the implications of what she was saying, weighing the import of leaving home and never seeing my father again. I cut to the central issue.

"Can I take my baseball glove?"

Alas, we made it no further from our apartment on East 135th Street to the home of my Aunt Alice, my father's sister, three blocks away. There my mother and aunt sat at the kitchen table all day, medicating themselves with strong tea. Ellen and I were sent into the front room to play. The women no doubt did a lot of female bonding over the treachery, uselessness, pointlessness of men, and of my father in particular. No doubt Aunt Alice heard details that we never would. Finally they arrived at "It could be worse . . . At least the kids have a roof over their heads."

The conclusion was, "Get your stuff. It's 5:00 and I have to get dinner started."

So she failed in her escape. In her defense, she was ill equipped to do otherwise.

My mother, Gladys O'Brien, was the fourth of seven children, born to an alcoholic father and a mother who died of pneumonia after the birth of her seventh child. Two of the seven children were taken in by relatives. My mother and the others were sent to an orphanage. She never spoke about that. She had no sense of boundaries, no sense of what she deserved, no idea of what parenting involved.

◆ ◆ ◆

My mother held my sweaty hand in hers. It was the middle of a summer day, sunny and hot. We were walking in a crowd of people. I don't know my age, but I was at the height of their knees. All the legs around me seemed a forest of tall trees. Suddenly I realized that she no longer had my hand. I tried looking around for her, but all I saw was legs.

"Mommy," I began shouting in terror. I was loud enough and persistent enough that many people stopped and tried vainly to console me. After what seemed like eternity but was probably a minute, my mother grabbed my hand and yanked me into the store where she had been browsing. She shook me and told me that I had embarrassed her. What was I thinking, making a fuss like that? Didn't I realize that she had just popped into a store and would return to get me some time?

"Wait 'til I tell your father what you did," which she did, and to which he responded with the only response he knew: beating.

◆ ◆ ◆

I was born very cross-eyed. This enraged my father. It was a blemish on his manhood that he could have fathered such a goofy-looking son. At age five I had corrective surgery. This resulted in an overcorrection, making me walleyed, and in no way improving my standing with my father. I had just transitioned to a new kind of goofy.

I also had to start wearing glasses, necessitating my mother taking me to Manhattan Eye and Ear Hospital at least yearly for glasses. This was a major trip for me. It required that we ride the el, the elevated trains made famous by King Kong.

Once, when I was about six, we were hurrying to make our train. I was a bit ahead of her. I jumped into the car, turned, and saw that she was standing on the platform as the door closed between us. I went berserk. I shoved my hands through the rubber doorstops, trying to force them open. I was screaming in fear. A man came over

Before starting school, Johnny was his mother's daytime companion.

and forced the door open, and my mother got on. She was furious. Why had I created such a scene, caused her such embarrassment? Was I too stupid to realize that all I needed to do was to take the train to the next stop, get out and wait for her arrival on the following train?

"Wait 'til I tell your father how you embarrassed me." No surprise how that unfolded.

◆ ◆ ◆

My mother usually did not work, so I became her daytime companion. She would take me to the movies, generally to grownup movies. I remember three of them. One was a film that involved a young girl, a swing, and ballet slippers. That is all I recall. The second was the very first Technicolor movie I ever saw. It was a western and I think Jimmy Stewart was in it.

The third movie, a life-altering one, was when I was seven. I remember it in great detail. It was entitled *M* and starred David Wayne as a man who went to school yards, enticed little kids to go with him and strangled them. After each kill, he returned to his room, pulled a suitcase from under his bed, removed some sort of figurine, and lopped off its head with a wire around its neck. They had the delicacy in those days to not show the murders, so I was unclear what was going on.

"Why is he cutting the heads off the dolls?" I asked.

"Because he murders those kids and he takes off a doll's head each time he kills a kid. That's what happens to kids who talk to strangers."

I had nightmares for years over that one. I became terrified every time an adult spoke to me. On some level I became afraid of everything. I had been the only kid in my group who could swim, but from then on I was afraid to. I am still amazed that I remember David Wayne, who is not exactly a household name. If you are curious, pick up the film and show it to your grandkids. They won't forget it.

◆ ◆ ◆

My childhood was shaping up as alcohol, violence, infidelity, chaos, lies, insecurity, and terror. And leavening all this was Catholicism, as presented, exemplified, and lived by my paternal grandmother, Cassie, almost six feet tall, rawboned, with large hands and feet and an almost perpetual frown. She was much bigger than my mother, so I christened them "Big Mom" and "Little Mommy." "Big Mom" took, and even her children called her that forever after.

There was a rosary in her hands nearly every minute of every day. She said the rosary while she hung clothes on the line. She said it while watching her very favorite television program, professional wrestling. This gave her prayers a Tourette's flavor, like "Hail Mary, full of grace . . . KILL THAT SON OF A BITCH . . . the Lord is with thee . . . LOOK IN THAT BASTARD'S TRUNKS, YOU IDIOT . . . blessed art thou amongst women . . ."

"You know, Big Mom, no Catholic in the world says the rosary like you do." When I was a teenager, and could provide some resistance, she often leaped from her chair and onto my back, demanding that I wrestle with her. She was pretty good. Often I thought, "Right now, there is no other grandmother in America who is wrestling with a teenage grandson."

God, I loved her.

She was the poster child for Catholic guilt. Since she felt personally responsible for her violent, alcoholic husband, violent alcoholic son, and his alcoholic, gambling brother, she dedicated every waking hour to hurl prayers at heaven's gates, praying that they would all change and that everyone would go together to heaven. Since they all despised one another, paradise together seemed unlikely and unwanted. Nonetheless, that is what she prayed for.

In all of my life, I am convinced, only my dogs loved me as much as she did. As the only person on earth who had any power over my father, she interposed herself between us and did everything she could to protect me and to get me out of there.

"Johnny, the only way that people like us get out of here is through education," she told me often. I understood that by *here* she meant not only our neighborhood and the Bronx, but our home were places to leave, and that education was my way out. She showed me a tender side of herself that she carefully guarded from most people. She was more tolerant of me, more complimentary, more supportive.

She wanted me to be a priest. In her mind, there was nothing greater to achieve. She had had another motive in her be-a-priest drumbeat. She wanted me to go away, where my father could not harm me. She knew she could not protect me all the time.

With that realization, I came to understand why she had sent my father back to Ireland when he was twelve, returning when he was sixteen. She always said that he was in constant trouble, skipping school and hanging out on the docks, and that she thought that he would toe the line in Ireland. I suspect that there was another motive. If family lore is correct, my grandfather was even more violent than my father. Essentially, she had hoped to rescue her older son by sending him away, just as one day she would send me to the seminary. Women like my grandmother, uneducated, poor immigrants, did not think of calling up some social service organization, reporting a husband to the cops, putting everyone in therapy or buying a .357 Magnum.

Those were different times. Children were chattel; expectations were limited; a man's home was his castle; no Catholic divorced; alcohol was holy water.

◆ ◆ ◆

Everything in the world—whatever is and whatever happens—is a test, designed to give you freedom of choice. Choose wisely.

—Rebbe Nachman of Breslov

To live is to feel oneself lost.

—Jose Ortega y Gasset

I really wanted to become a priest. I just had absolutely no idea what that would take, what it would mean. Or cost. What I saw of it, however, was very attractive to me. In addition, I had come to see that I should get the hell out of there before I was devoured.

My father expected me to be a tough guy. Everyone expected me to be a tough guy. I was not. He was a great athlete. I was terrible, fat and asthmatic, in addition to being walleyed. I was that neighborhood kid who always was picked last. Worse yet, with three left, the one whose turn it was to choose would point to me as a throw-in, that is, "I will give you two picks for one, as long as you take him."

I could not run, throw, or catch. I did not know what a foul ball was. I thought the umpire called strikes if the catcher caught the ball.

The kids all said, "You stink."

My father said, "You can't do a fucking thing right; you will never amount to a pinch of shit." The kids said, "We can't believe you are Jack Tuohey's son." My father said, "I can't believe that a man like me could have a son like you."

I said in my heart, *"I only hope you're right."*

The difference between the kids and my father was that they would one day stop saying these things.

As I saw it, I lived with a man who, besides wanting me dead, was offended by my existence, hated my appearance, my voice, my mannerisms, my thoughts, words, and deeds; most of all, my weakness. He felt that I could be toughened up by relentless criticism, epithets, and beatings.

My response was to attempt not to set him off. I began by trying to be absolutely silent. I learned that by applying counterpressure on a doorknob, I could open and close doors without making a sound; that, by walking barefoot along the edges of rooms, I could avoid most telltale sounds of my existence.

I moved on to never making eye contact, inspired by my grandfather, who worked at the Bronx Zoo. He taught me that one should always avoid eye contact with male gorillas, as it pissed them off. The parallel seemed obvious to me.

Gradually I learned to have no opinions, express no personal preferences, state no desires. My goal was to become so small as to be invisible. If I could have stopped breathing, I would have done so.

Jack and Johnny (age 7) in upstate New York. "My father expected me to be a tough guy. I was not."

My father watched me when he assaulted or belittled me, watching to see if I showed any flicker of resistance, a response that called for a harsher punishment than the original issue.

I told a younger cousin, "When they are trying to hurt you, never show them anything. That way they don't know that they found your weakness, and they will move on to something else." I had become so good at it that even I could not tell what my responses were to hurts.

◆ ◆ ◆

Our brownstone apartment was a railroad flat—so-called because of the rooms' configurations—across from the Major Deegan Expressway. In the building next to ours was St. Anthony's Mission. Each morning the homeless men from the hobo jungle under the el by the Harlem River would cluster within the gated front yard for a free breakfast. Their presence troubled the neighbors and my parents, my mother because she did not like "bums" hanging around the neighborhood; my father because the priest who ran it was a "spic."

Each day the large street sweepers found new supplies of vegetables, trash, and dog crap.

Most of the men in the neighborhood had blue-collar jobs, and each day they stopped in neighborhood pubs on the way home from work. They went back to the pubs after dinner, honing their skills at drinking, shuffleboard, fighting, and flirting with the few women who had been smart enough to realize that the only fun they could ever get from these men depended on not marrying them.

Mothers and wives cooked and cleaned, shopped and managed the household. They said the rosary. They prayed that the men would come home intact. They prayed that the rent had not been pissed away. They prayed that the men would not come home angry, looking to even some score on the heads of their wives and children. They prayed that they would not come home at all. It was they who directed our daily lives, fed us, cleaned our snotty faces, got us into school.

◆ ◆ ◆

My mother thought it would be nice if I started school as soon as possible. She thought that I should skip kindergarten, since I could already read and do some math. I am sure that, having had my sister eight months earlier, she figured she could use a break from two kids by sending one to school. She told me that she had spoken to a friend, who worked in the office at St. Jerome's School. That friend saw to it that my age was overlooked.

Thus, in 1948, I found myself in first grade at five years old, separated from my age-mates, in a strange neighborhood, among people who did not know me or my father, guaranteeing that I would always be the youngest, smallest, weakest, least mature kid in my class.

I was quite good at schoolwork. But that made me vulnerable.

"Look how well Johnny Tuohey did his homework. Why don't all you boys do good work like Johnny Tuohey?" did not endear me to anyone besides the nun. I also arrived with all resistance, stubbornness, and rebellion beaten out of me, so I was a model citizen, the darling of many teachers.

"What's wrong with you, ya little faggot? Mama's boy. Ya little sissy." I wished I were dead. All I lacked was a "beat me" sign. Early school years were, at best, a mixed blessing.

Once my pals and I could reliably find our way home, we were turned loose to essentially do whatever we wished. I was not always happy about that because I was scared senseless by the things they chose to do. Nevertheless, I was ordered out of the house to play. I had no choice.

We might form gangs to arm ourselves with broom handles, bricks, and kitchen knives in order to fight like-minded bands of fools from other neighborhoods. We might swim in the Harlem

River, climb bridges, and steal candy. We could—and did—hang out at the hobo jungle, that area under the railroad tracks by the river, where groups of homeless men seemed to live. All was allowed, so long as we were home for supper.

Living in flat-roofed brownstones, we all spent a lot of time on the roofs. Parents and kids hung out there on hot summer evenings. One side of each roof gradually sloped up to a parapet along the front side of the building. When we were five and six, we began crawling up the slope to lie on our bellies and look down at the street, often spitting to gauge wind direction and velocity. Just looking down from that height made me want to puke. Staring down seemed to exert a magnetic pull, and I imagined myself being yanked to my death.

As time went by, the more adventurous began standing up on the parapets, then walking on them, doing little dances. I never advanced beyond peering over the edge.

"You're a chicken," my playmates said.

"Cluck, cluck," I said.

When that challenge no longer seemed brave enough to the risk-takers, their interest turned to the air shafts. These shafts were about three feet square and ran from roof to ground. They were encased by walls that were about three feet high. The risk was to climb onto the protective wall and jump across the gap. In time, this was done by most of my friends almost daily. Never by me, however, and no amount of insults, no matter how vile, could sway me. Jumping across might make my friends stop insulting me, but if I didn't make it I'd fall five stories to a horribly painful death, screaming until the final thud, and making whatever they had to say about me meaningless.

Next up on the fearless meter was to jump from building to building. Most buildings were the same height and abutted one another, but there were the occasionally mismatched ones. The gaps between them were about four feet wide. I never attempted to jump those, either. Others did.

One day as I walked back to school after lunch, I saw a crowd that included lots of kids, some police, and an ambulance. The police were keeping everyone back from something on the ground. Some kids had decided to have lunch on the roofs and some building-jumping ensued. One boy didn't make it. He lay on the ground, a small mass covered by a blanket. I felt dizzy, sick to my stomach. My worst fears were based in reality.

My best friend, Terry Davis, was brave beyond all reason, braver, crazier than anyone. The day I met him, he became my best friend when I tried to intimidate him and he beat the crap out of me. He became my friend when I started crying. Possibly, he felt bad about beating me up. For a little kid, Terry had an impressive résumé. He had been in the hospital for second- and third-degree burns. He used to jump rides on the backs of cabs. One rainy night, his feet slipped on the wet bumper and he fell off, just as the cab stopped. The driver reversed it for some reason, pinning my friend under a tire and with his arm and chest against the muffler. It took a while for the driver to hear his screams.

He was an instant celebrity.

He used to climb the girders to the el tracks and walk along them. He finally got me to do this with him at age eight. He assured me that the tracks we would walk were "dead." They had no trains on them, and the third rail was not electrified. He spoke with such certainty that I believed him. "Don't look down," Terry encouraged me, as I climbed the girder, pulse racing, hoping I wouldn't piss all over myself.

The first suggestion that he had, at the very least, been mistaken was that we had to curl up into balls as a train roared past. There I was, arms wrapped around a steel strut, hugging it as if it were my mother, eyes welded shut. The noise of a train two feet from my head, the vibration of the world falling apart had reduced me to pulp. I would have screamed if I had had some spit in my mouth. I would have crapped my pants if my sphincter had not been clamped. I wanted off those tracks, but was in the grip of my guide, and he was not the least bit daunted by the nearness of death.

He then explained that the track we were on was dead, but the adjacent one was live. I had figured that part out on my own. It did not make things any better. In retrospect, it probably wasn't true, anyway. In short order I found myself sixty feet above the Harlem River in the middle of a railroad trestle.

Johnny (in glasses) with his wild best friend, Terry Davis, years before Terry blew off his fingers with stolen blasting caps.

"Hey, what the hell are you kids doing up there?" We had been spotted by a pair of railroad workers who were on a support island below us.

"Come on, Johnny, we have to run. And don't touch the third rail; it's alive."

Had I heard that right? There was electricity in this third rail? Holy shit. I stared at the rail. It was as if I were being pulled toward it. I needed to lift my foot high enough to step over that rail, but I knew that I would not step high enough, or that my trailing foot would hit it. I was paralyzed.

"Come on, hurry," Terry implored.

"I can't. I know I'm gonna touch it."

"Jump over it." The answer is always so clear to the brave. But three feet past the rail was a small guard rail, well shorter than I was. Beyond that was a long drop to the river. If I jumped too far, or tripped on the landing, I would fall to my death. Suddenly the workman resolved the issue by reaching the track and running toward us. Spell broken, I stepped over the rail and began running with Terry. The worker was a lot faster than we were. He grabbed us by the scruffs of our necks, banged our heads together and dragged us to a utility stairway. When he got us onto solid ground, he and his mate smacked us a few times and sent us on our way with boots up our butts. We cleverly did not complain about our ill treatment to our parents.

That stands as one my most terrifying days. I suppose it was about average for Terry. I lost track of him after he moved to New Jersey and I to Long Island, a few months before my tenth birthday.

The last time I saw him, he had blown off most of his fingers. He had broken into a construction shack and found what he thought was a box of .22 shells. He took them home, sat down at the kitchen table, and poked into one of them with a fork.

Unfortunately for Terry, they were blasting caps. He recounted with some pride that the ambulance drivers dropped him off at the emergency room without realizing that his pockets were packed with the caps he had stolen from the construction shack. It caused quite a panic when the ER staff discovered that they had a load of explosives in their midst. Never a dull day with Terry.

◆ ◆ ◆

My fear of social contact, cultivated under my father's drumbeat of my worthlessness, included school. I preferred sitting in the classroom alone to going out at recess. It included home, where I would often sit, when allowed to do so, rather than play with the other kids. This avoidance crushed me with shame and a sense of failure, but could seldom overcome the dread I felt at participation. There had to be some place where I felt safe.

I found it in church.

The church adjoined the school. It took only a minute to walk there from the schoolyard. Only a minute, and yet it transported me to a different universe. The vastness and stillness of it gave me comfort. The sunlight illuminating the stained glass windows made it appear as if there were a God, and He was there with me. God loved me. The sanctuary light on the altar, signifying the presence of Communion hosts that had been transubstantiated into the body of Christ, was like a warm glow in my heart.

It was clean, quiet, orderly. It stood for values that had nothing to do with being brave, tough, loud, brash. Children from school, elderly men, and women quietly saying their rosaries, all who entered here were well behaved, respectful, awestruck. It was peaceful and promised a doorway to everlasting happiness.

It was everything I wished for and the antithesis of my life. I had no desire to leave this place, and there was a career path ahead of me—the priesthood—that would allow me to spend most of my time there while getting me away from my father. The only question was how to get there.

God began to put some breadcrumbs on my path.

◆ ◆ ◆

When I was in the fifth grade, in September 1952, we moved to Glen Cove, Long Island, where my Aunt Mary and her daughter, Sally, shared a home with my Aunt Sally, Uncle Ray, and their two kids, Maureen and Bobby. My mother had given birth to my second sister, Marie, and the Bronx apartment was strained to bursting. We moved into the house next to my aunts, uncle, and kids.

I was the outsider, joining kids who already had established their alliances and pecking order. Despite that, I found my circumstances vastly improved. I now had a family group of two sisters and three cousins who were all younger than I. I found that I was accorded some primacy based on being the oldest. No matter what the broader world thought of me, I had a little group I could boss around. And I did.

Life in Glen Cove was bucolic. There were fields and trees, ponds, and a choice of rocky or sandy beaches, which we could reach by bikes in half an hour. For another thing, kids in school were far less belligerent than my prior group in the Bronx. There were several, including some of the cool kids, who were actually nice to me. I had friends who invited me to their homes, to the movies. Some of them had paper routes and encouraged me to get one.

Thus it was that, three months before my tenth birthday, I began my work career by delivering *Newsday*, a Long Island daily paper. A boy in my class put me in touch with the man who managed a group of carriers. He took me in his car on a tour of my route, pointing out the fifty-plus houses to which I would deliver. The route described a rough circle, with a few side arms. It was over three miles in circumference.

My first day was a Thursday in early October. Thursday was the day *Newsday* added all its flyers for the week, roughly doubling the weight. It was also collection day. I was required to take my little book of names, addresses, and columns and mark off who had paid me. The book would also be a boon to me, since I could not begin to remember the names and addresses of over fifty homes, which I had seen once from a car.

Johnny in the eighth grade, the year before going to the seminary.

Things would be looking different today, since I had no car. In fact, besides my book and pencil and my blue bag to carry the papers, I had nothing. The manager had never asked how I would get the papers around the route. My parents and I had never asked, either.

I quickly opted to carry the papers under one arm with the strap around my neck on the opposite side. On any other day it would have been a lousy plan. It was especially so on that day. We were in the tail end of a hurricane.

Arriving home after school I found more than fifty newspapers and fifty inserts, bound with wire, on my stoop. I carried them inside with great difficulty. My mother helped me put the inserts in the papers and pack the bag, which was filled to bursting. I was barely able to lift it. As my mother opened the door for me, it flew out of her hands and slammed into the wall behind it. Standing just inside the living room, we were pelted with rain. Grabbing me by my shoulders, she hollered, "You better hurry; it's raining," and shoved me and my crucial news out the door.

Putting the bag on the ground frequently to rest, I bent forward into the wind. There was so much water on my glasses that I had to take them off. I was worried that I would not be able to read the names and addresses in my book without them. No problem. After I reached the second house, the names in my book had been reduced to smudges.

From that point on, I think I delivered papers pretty evenly between people on my route and people who had no idea why they were getting a paper. That probably explains the hostility I received when I asked some strangers to give me money. At some homes they expressed more than a little displeasure that the paper was a congealed lump of wood pulp that would have to be dried for days.

Even in adversity, however, there were traces of humanity. One lady opened her door and exclaimed, "You're delivering papers in this?!" She looked behind me. "Where is your car?"

"We don't have a car."

"Where is your bike?"

"I don't have a bike."

"How are you carrying these papers?"

"Over my shoulder."

"Your mother let you out in this? Come in here and bring the papers."

Despite fewer papers, the bag had been growing heavier from rain. I dragged it into her foyer. She returned with a Red Rider wagon, her son's.

"Put the papers in the wagon. It will make things a lot easier for you. But you should not be out in this storm." She looked worried. I liked her a lot. I put the papers in the wagon and set off again, into the deepening darkness.

I was much quicker with the wagon in tow, but I had such a long way to go. Of the remainder of that circuit, I remember the incredible relief at having that wagon, my utter confusion about which houses were on my route, the angry people—*why didn't you put the paper in a bag, you idiot?*—the soggy newspapers, the fatigue. I arrived home after eight o'clock, exhausted.

"I'm not doin' that again. I'm quittin' this paper route tomorrow," I told my mother as soon as I walked in the door.

"No, you're not," she replied.

"You don't know how awful that was," I countered.

"Quit complaining. If you quit the paper route, I'll never let you watch television again."

I had a hot bath and went right to bed. I would need to be rested for my paper route next day. On the bright side, my mother did agree that I could get a bike to carry the papers. Unfortunately, that was going to come at Christmas, two months away. That left a lot of lugging ahead.

But then God intervened. He did that by making my manager aware of the fact that I was nine years old. The paper had a rule that carriers be at least ten. "Get in touch with me when you turn ten," he said. I had absolutely no intention of doing that, but my mother remembered. When I turned ten, she again drew my attention to the paper route-television conundrum, and I again became a paper boy.

It really wasn't bad after that. There were missed movies and swimming dates, but there was a sameness to the paper route, a pattern to which I adapted, that made it pretty easy, despite my intermittent whining. That, along with spending money, put the paper route solidly in the plus column.

In Glen Cove, I drew closer to the altar and the priesthood.

We were encouraged to try out to be altar boys, and I did so. Those were days of the otherworldly Latin Mass. In the practice of saying the Mass in Latin, a dead language that very few understood, it was clearly stated that what was going on upon the altar was separate from and far above the congregation. It was at one strike both grander and less inclusive. The altar boy, by virtue of being allowed on the altar with the priest and of knowing the Latin responses, was also separated from and elevated above the average parishioner. Heady stuff for a complete loser to anticipate. I could not wait.

Our church, St. Boniface, had the wisdom to have all the Latin invocations and altar boys' responses printed on large laminated cards, which were found on the altar step where the altar boy knelt. Thus, it was possible to be an altar boy without memorizing the incomprehensible Latin.

For the first month of my altar boy career I served the 7:00 A.M. Mass. My mother would wake me early and give me a fried egg sandwich to eat after Mass. It was wrapped in waxed paper and placed into a brown paper sandwich bag. I still can feel the warmth of those sandwiches in my hand as I walked the half-mile in the dark to church, the butter stain on the bag and the smell of the egg almost irresistible. But I did resist, because I could not eat before receiving Communion. Apparently the body of our Savior could not be properly digested if it shared our stomachs with any food.

On arriving at the church, I went to the sacristy behind the altar to don my cassock and surplice, the long black robe and short white overblouse that set us apart. I use the word *my* in the loosest sense, since I never owned a cassock or surplice in those days. My father made it clear that he was not going to "piss away" money on "that crap." I assured him that I did not really need to get them, since there were always spares available.

After putting on the vestments, I would prepare the cruets of wine and water, assist the priest with his vestments, then lead him out to the altar. We would genuflect, he would hand me his three-cornered black hat. I would place the hat on the lower shelf of the stand that held the cruets. When I knelt, I picked up my card with the Latin prayers, the priest intoned the first invocation, and I responded from the card. From that point it was merely required that I be able to read, that I pay attention to his movements, and that I do the appropriate moves when indicated. What could possibly go wrong?

When we went to the altar, it would be covered with a pristine white cloth. Two candles, each about three feet long, would be there, flickering brightly, and at the right-hand corner of the altar would be a large book on a wooden stand. From this book the liturgy of that day would be read by the priest. After a month of 7:00 A.M. Masses, I was assigned to a week of 5:30 A.M. Masses. As I understood it, the only difference between the 7:00 and 5:30 Masses was the time. That was a misunderstanding.

In those days every parish had a dedicated group of church ladies who found some fulfillment in doing things for the priests and the parish. I always felt that they either regretted not having become nuns or had maternal or romantic attachments to priests. Perhaps I was too cynical. Nevertheless, on the day of my first early Mass I was to discover the extent to which I had been in their debt, without yet knowing that they even existed.

There were reasons why I always found my response card waiting for me, why the missal was on the altar, why the candles were already lit. The church ladies had seen to these details. There also was a reason why the white cloth covered the altar: they had removed the thick green Sanctus cloth, which was there whenever no Mass was happening. There was almost no limit to what these invisible angels would do for us.

Almost. For these saints did not get out of bed at 4:00 A.M. to prepare the altar for the 5:30 A.M. Mass. I wish I had known that.

On that terrible day, the monsignor was saying Mass. I had never been close to a monsignor before, and felt quite intimidated.

When he asked if everything was ready, I reflexively said, "Yes." After all, it always had been. So it was that he and I walked out to a totally unprepared altar: no book, no candles, the wrong cloth on the altar. The dozen or so parishioners in the church bore silent witness to the unfolding disaster.

These people all think I'm a complete jerk, running back and forth finding things in the sacristy. Do I hear them laughing at me? What does the monsignor think? Jesus, he must want to kill me. The next time I have to run back to the sacristy for something, I'll just keep going. No, no. The nuns and my parents will kill me.

Thus it was that I had no response card and just stared mutely when he intoned the Latin prayers. He had to say his invocations and my responses. Thus it was that I tripped over the too-long cassock of another student, and fell face-first off the altar. And thus that I ultimately walked on the monsignor's lovely hat, with the purple plume atop it.

After all that went wrong, you can only imagine his expression when I handed him his crushed hat, the plume tattered and dirty, a large footprint imprinted on it.

There was no question in my mind that he was going to beat the crap out of me when we exited the altar. Had he been my father, he would have beaten me to death on the altar, lending a dark poetry to the proceedings.

We walked into the sacristy. He turned to me, hesitated a heartbeat, then said, "Thank you" and began removing his vestments. I assisted him, then removed my borrowed cassock and surplice, ate my egg sandwich and went to school. No one ever spoke about this with me. I continued to be an altar boy. There were no punishments.

I learned some important things: make sure the altar was ready before I went out there; some men exist who, despite enormous provocation, do not resort to verbal and physical abuse with children; some priests, no matter how lofty their position, embrace humility and follow Jesus as their role models.

Despite having been terribly embarrassed, reduced to a sweaty rag, having probably skated on the edge of soiling and wetting myself, that day, too, has to go into the plus column.

◆ ◆ ◆

Give me chastity and continence—but not yet.

—St Augustine

Because we had no car and were now living about thirty miles from New York City, where he worked as a truck driver, my father only came home on weekends. He spent the weekdays at my grandparents' apartment in the Bronx. That was the biggest improvement in my life. We were free of his presence five nights a week. It was wonderful.

My mother still held the "wait-until-I-tell-your-father" card and sometimes played it, always with the same results, but she became more relaxed. She became funnier and more playful. She eased our bedtimes. We became coconspirators in not telling my father what we did not want him to know. It was in this time frame that my father quit drinking.

Sober, he remained a brooding threat. In some ways I liked him better drunk. Drunk, he could be quite affable, talkative, less quick to judge or strike out. Hung over, he was a taut wire, always a threat to snap. Fortunately for us, that was not our problem most of the week. I now had time to discover new problems.

There are certain things we always remember very clearly, like terrorist attacks and assassinations . . . and the way we learned about sex.

After my sixth grade and for the first of several summers, my father invited my cousin Bernard to spend summer vacation with us. Bernard was one of the tough guys in the old Bronx neighborhood, far more worldly and mature than I, and he knew a lot more, as well. He joined our little entourage of cousins and almost immediately pointed out that my cousin Maureen was developing breasts. My response was essentially a combination of "Who cares?" and "Of what interest is that?" He looked at me as if I were pathetic. He asked if I knew anything about sex, and I told him something about different genders. He then described, with remarkable accuracy for a kid one month short of his eleventh birthday, how babies were made. That, I told him, was a lie and it was disgusting.

"Do you know what *intercourse* is?"

"It's some kind of social exchange, like a conversation." He was not dealing with some kind of fool here.

"Take a look in the dictionary," he advised me.

To my horror, the dictionary did hint at something akin to what he had said, although far less graphically. He then got personal, asking how I thought that I had come to be. I was beside myself. I asked if he was suggesting that my mother had allowed my father to do that to her. I was adamant. Not my mother; not with anyone; absolutely not with him.

But some small voice said that this was, indeed, how things happened.

Sometimes when we were playing outside at night on the weekend, I would separate from the others and stand in the dark, looking into the kitchen window at my parents. My mother would be straightening up; he would be wearing his wifebeater undershirt, sweaty muscles shining as he did his crossword puzzles. I found him so awful. Could my mother really have allowed that beast to do something so disgusting to her? A few times I began to retch. I asked Bernard if he believed that my mother had allowed my father to do that on three occasions, accounting for my sisters and me. His response—that they were married, and probably did it all the time—threw me into despair. I fought the idea, but my cousin's confident assertions, supported by the dictionary, wore me down and I began to open my mind to the likelihood of sexual activity.

Bernard frequently brought up Maureen's burgeoning femininity.

"Look at those tits. I'd like to get my hands on those."

"Why would you want to do that?" The whole thing was a puzzle to me.

"Because they feel good." He then told me about how he and some friends had encircled a well-developed girl at school and "felt her up" despite her resistance. That was beyond comprehension to me.

I had never really liked Maureen. She was, after all, a girl. She was eleven months younger than I. She was a good student, and we were academically competitive. I also was troubled that she was more mature and self-assured. I was opposed to finding her attractive, whatever *attractive* meant. And yet there I was, looking at her more and more. I was not conscious of that and would have denied it with a clear conscience if challenged by anyone. But in her presence I found myself zeroed in on her.

By the end of summer, when Bernard suggested that we hide in the dark in bushes outside Maureen's room to watch her undress, I agreed without hesitation. We did that a few times, never seeing a thing. It was very exciting, although I could not say why.

When I returned to school for seventh grade, it seemed every boy in the class had been visited by a sophisticated cousin that summer. All we talked about was sex. A few had already been aware of it, and some claimed to have already engaged in activities far beyond my imagining. They spoke with confidence about how girls looked and felt under their clothing. Sex was a beautiful scent filling the air, but so powerful that it took our breath away, so attractive and scary at the same time.

It was said that the sixteen-year-old sister of one classmate let boys "go all the way" in the back of a car for a modest fee. Rumor had it her brother was one of the beneficiaries. This, too, was beyond my comprehension.

After this year of titillation, Bernard returned for another summer. We immediately organized nightly games of hide-and-seek with a subtext that only Bernard and I knew. Our goal was always to find Maureen, wrap our arms around her and press up against her, trying to feel her breasts. I was always so careful not to make her aware of what we were doing and I tried to maintain an air of false innocence.

One night our parents took us all to the drive-in. I was in the back seat next to Maureen. At some time I felt her breast against my upper arm. I did not move for about an hour. I feared that the slightest movement would cause her to move away. It was amazing. When she finally moved, I discovered that it had been her elbow. I felt pretty stupid, but I can't deny that I really enjoyed touching her elbow.

When Bernard returned in the summer after my eighth grade, things had taken a radical change—not in my desires, not in my behavior, but in my intentions. I was going to be a priest.

◆ ◆ ◆

Forethought is lauded without stint, yet it can give us no guarantee about the slightest turn of events.

—LaRochefoucauld

Still nursing my grandmother's encouragement about the priesthood, I was in eighth grade and twelve years old. We had moved again, one month into eighth grade.

My Aunt Mary and her daughter, Sally, were going out on their own, so my Aunt Sally, Uncle Ray, and my cousins, Maureen and Bobby, were moving to a less expensive house in Central Islip. My mother was about to give birth to her fourth child, my brother, Michael. We needed more bedrooms and less expense. We moved into a three-bedroom house next to our relatives.

I was able to continue being an altar boy, but the paper route somehow disappeared. I certainly made no effort to find another. Apparently my mother had forgotten about it, too.

Once again I found myself in a new class, new school, among kids with friendships and alliances already formed. Without the paper route, I sunk into a lonely torpor, parked on the couch, eating snacks, and watching TV.

I had made no movement in the direction of the priesthood, never read anything or talked to a priest about it, had made nothing but the most superficial mention of it in my parents' presence.

Then one day our class went to a religious fair, something akin to a farmers' market, college expo, or job fair, only it promoted a future in Catholic religious life. Booths were arranged in the gymnasium featuring convent or missionary life as nuns for the girls and, for the boys, a life as brothers or priests who vowed never to marry. Options included contemplative living, teaching, nursing, missionary work, and preaching orders. One might be interested in being a diocesan priest, those assigned, mostly, to parishes. They had their own cars, dressed in black suits, lived in big houses called rectories with one or more other priests, and were usually supported by a housekeeper and a cook, often the same person. When they weren't being fed at the rectory, they were frequently dinner guests in people's homes. In parishes where churches were associated with schools, diocesan priests lorded it over the teaching nuns, who showed them great deference.

There was an array of religious communities, or orders, at the fair: Dominicans, Trappists, Jesuits, and several different orders of Franciscans, familiar for their Dark Ages brown habits. I knew nothing about any of these and had no conscious intent to join anything. I knew nothing about where any of their seminaries or training schools were located, whether they were strict, whether they were good schools, what they cost, or what their rules were.

For no particular reason I stopped at only one booth, The Franciscan Friars of The Atonement, also called The Graymoor Friars. I took a postcard with a few questions on it from the booth, filled it out that evening at home, mailed it, then forgot it. Several days afterward my mother told me a priest was on the telephone asking for me. He introduced himself as Father Simeon and asked if he could come to my house to interview me about going to the seminary. I told him that would be fine.

Not for a second did I think that my parents would say no to a request from a priest to visit our house, and I was right. When I sat down to eat, my mother asked me what the phone call was about. Having not thought to mention it before, I explained that I had filled out a card at the religious fair, and that the priest was coming to see me next week. It was so perfect that I may be making this up, but their responses were "Oh" from my mother and "Pass the gravy" from my father.

The following week Father Simeon came to our home. He took me off to the living room and interviewed me. He said that my being an altar boy was a plus, and that he would check with the nuns about my grades and behavior. I knew that would go well. He talked about the life of seminarians. They rose early, went to Mass, made their beds, did chores, attended classes, exercised, went to chapel, studied, spoke only when allowed to do so, ate only when food was provided, and watched no television.

It sounded pretty good to me, although I had some reservations. I had done minimal exercise in over a year, spending my time eating and watching television. How could I exercise and how could I live without television and snacking? Additionally, there was my asthma, which often woke me at night. It flared when I exercised and whenever I was asked to do something that I feared, did not like, or might embarrass me. I was troubled by frequent headaches, some of which lay me up all day. I was a weekly visitor at the doctor. How was that going to play out?

I did not mention my concerns to the priest.

Father Simeon then had a conversation with my parents, probably including a discussion about the cost. There were no snags. It was decided that I would be going, pending the nuns' recommendation.

Perhaps the most gratifying thing was the joy my grandmother expressed. "You'll make a lovely priest, Johnny. And don't let your father make you feel guilty about the money. It's only thirty dollars a month, and I'm paying it."

Chapter Four

Ollie—Deep Catholic Roots

There's more beauty in the truth even if it is a dreadful beauty. The storytellers at the city gate twist life so that it looks sweet to the lazy and the stupid and the weak, and this only strengthens their infirmities and teaches them nothing, cures nothing, nor does it let the heart soar.

—John Steinbeck

My world back then was very Catholic. That I left home in 1956, at fourteen, to become a priest, while remarkable, was not unheard of for a kid like me, educated in the Roman Catholic Archdiocese of New York City's school system. My mother was not there when I left home for St. John's Atonement Seminary some 260 miles away in Montour Falls, New York. However, her Irish roots and Catholic practice, drawn from immigrant parents from County Sligo, helped chart my course.

St. John's was a forty-two-month retreat from the chaos and anger that I carried. Just four percent of my life, give or take. But it saved my life.

We lived at 1505 Metropolitan Avenue in Parkchester, a housing development of more than 12,000 units in the Bronx. When built in 1940, Parkchester was reportedly the largest housing development in the world, an oasis of well-manicured lawns, tree-lined sidewalks, playgrounds, and a fenced-in expanse large enough for three softball fields. At least one encyclopedia heralded it as the ideal urban living setting for middle-class families. More specifically, middle-class white families. The rigidly enforced policy of Metropolitan Life Insurance Company, Parkchester's owner, barred people of color from residency. St. Helena's elementary school, situated on the eastern border of Parkchester, was as segregated as the housing development. During the nine years I attended from kindergarten through eighth grade, I never saw a black student among the thousands enrolled there. The only black face was painted on an Irish classmate who parodied Al Jolson singing "Mammy" in a fourth-grade school musical.

Parkchester had a lot of first- and second-generation Irish, Italians, Germans, and European Jews. Some, including the adults in my own family, casually referred to other groups as "wops," "krauts," and "kikes." It got uncomfortable for us kids when such comments went public—like a mother leaning out of her window and yelling at a neighbor, "Tell that guinea kid of yours to keep his greasy hands off my son"—because even though we argued among ourselves and sometimes fought, we did not resort to nasty racial epithets; we needed each other for street games.

Given the virtual absence of any black child or adult in our day-to-day lives, the use of racial slurs about them was extremely rare, usually coming from some white adult. Even when using "eeny, meeny, miney, mo" to settle who was it for hide-and-seek, we'd say "catch a tiger by the toe" as directed by most of our parents. This was a small sign of evolution from the crass reference to a black person's toe chanted to us kids by my grandmother and others of her generation.

Born in 1942, I was the firstborn of Bob and Florence Oliver. Susan and Rosemary were four and nine years younger, respectively. We were all baptized within weeks after birth. As I got it from the Dominican nuns in school, Baptism was to make sure an infant would not be exiled to limbo for eternity if, God forbid, it died before receiving the sacrament. Limbo was pleasant enough, but God didn't live there. This didn't seem fair. After all, they were only babies. Besieged for sensible explanations, the nuns eventually ended the discussion with that's-just-the-way-it-is conclusions or diverted our attention to another subject.

The whole family dressed up for Sunday Mass, then stayed in their Sunday best for the rest of the day. My father and I wore suits and ties with shined shoes. Susan, my older sister, had an ironed dress with patent leather shoes and a bonnet. My mother, who always wore dresses or skirts like they did in those days, did extra gussying up.

To qualify for Holy Communion at Mass you had to stop eating or drinking anything at midnight Saturday except for water. For

Summer, 1942: Ollie's mother strolls with Ollie, her firstborn, past St. Helena's Catholic Church.

me the fast was even longer because I had to be in bed by 9:00. So breakfast the next day was a big deal because, by then and after church, it was around 11:00.

Sunday dinner, usually served around 4:00 P.M., was special, often roast beef or leg of lamb, with enough leftovers for one or two more meals and sandwiches for school all the way to Wednesday.

The whole neighborhood was quiet on Sunday. Some candy stores, bakeries, and Jewish delicatessens were open, but everything else—grocery stores, department stores, etc.—were closed. There were fewer buses. There were no express trains in the subway system and there were five cars instead of the normal seven in each train.

Before evening meals, no utensil was touched before we finished grace by saying, "May the Lord provide for those in need." Susan and I had to eat everything on our plates, urged on by a parent saying something like, "People are starving in Hungary," which made perfect sense to me. Friday was no meat. The reason: that's the day Jesus died, and if he could allow himself to be whipped and nailed to a cross for us, the least we could do is not eat meat one day each week. I could not make the connection. So supper on Friday could be scrambled eggs, frozen fish sticks or crab cakes—all stuff that needed help from ketchup.

St. Helena's was a fifteen-minute walk away. Almost everything we got about being Catholic came from the nuns. Covered head to foot in starched, neatly pressed black-and-white habits that always smelled like they were fresh from the laundry, their only visible body parts were hands and face. Huge beads featuring all fifteen decades of the rosary clicked from thick black belts around their waists. Anticipating that their children would need help overcoming the initial shock of encountering nuns, most mothers took their kids to school on the first day. I stuck close to mine when I saw

Christmas 1951: Florence Olive, Richard (9), Rosemary (4 months), Susan (5).

other kids clinging to their mothers' legs in stark terror. Did they know something I didn't? One kid was screaming like he was being held over boiling oil while the nun motioned with an index finger, "Come with me, dear."

A single nun had no trouble handling a class of sixty kids, especially in the early grades, when most of us were still compliant and fearful. As each nun stood in front of the classroom, a towering black-and-white presence over our little desks, we followed her with anxious eyes. On their ring fingers they wore gold bands. Some would rap them on the blackboard loudly when they wanted your attention. The ring, one said, was a sign of their "betrothal" to Christ, a vow they would never get married. I had trouble imagining any of them married, what with all those clothes and big rosary beads.

In second grade we started learning about the sacraments, especially Holy Communion, which we would be receiving in the spring. We learned that this sacrament started at the Last Supper, when Christ gave the apostles bread and wine and told them it was his body and blood. Today, the nun said, the priest changes bread and wine into Christ's body and blood and, as Catholics we get to eat his body, which tastes like bread. But we can't drink the blood, which tastes like wine. Only the priest can do that. We had a lot of questions about this, but you could tell Sister was getting upset and frustrated about all the raised hands. Eventually, she would tell us to turn the page in our catechism.

Before Communion, we had to go to Confession, which is another sacrament. By confessing your sins, your soul would be clean to receive Jesus. For our First Confession we had to think of all our sins from as far back as we could remember. Being eight, that was a tall order. But they also said if you couldn't think of every sin, tell the priest the ones you could think of. That would be a good confession as long as you were truly sorry for them, even the ones you couldn't think of. The First Confession erases the stain of sin, which everyone was born with because of Adam and Eve, who didn't know a good thing when they had it. They called the first sin "original." Who could argue with that? It turns out that disguised as a snake, the devil tempted Eve to eat an apple she wasn't supposed to. Then she talked Adam into doing the same thing. Because of them, every baby in the world from then on starts life with that sin from a million years ago.

On the big day for First Communion all of us boys wore navy blue suits, white shirts, a high starched white collar (the kind rich kids wore in olden times), and another huge white bow around our necks. Girls wore white dresses and veils. My mother took a picture of me and Judy McPartland in our Communion clothes that day. We look like a child bride and child groom in some exotic arranged marriage. Walking down the aisle to the altar I was in a procession with some 250 other second graders, hands clasped, fingers pointing prayerfully skyward. I was thinking about the nun's warning to keep my teeth off the wafer, afraid I might damage some divine body part. I was also thinking of something that happened to a classmate a few days earlier during a "practice run" when they gave us unconsecrated hosts—ones not yet changed into Christ's body. The nun rapped him on the back of the head with her ring finger because he was chewing the host.

On the day of First Communion I knelt at the altar railing and the priest said stuff in Latin and put the host on my tongue. I said, "Amen," and returned to the church pew, where I knelt and squeezed my eyelids tight for the greatest possible holiness while making sure the host did not touch my teeth. Suddenly, panic. The host, thin as light cardboard, was stuck to the roof of my mouth. I tongued at it as secretly as possible while it slowly dissolved. Small pieces of Christ fell to the back of my tongue, cleared my teeth, and were safely swallowed.

When it was all over at the church, I got a lot of cards and forty-five dollars, even five dollars from the pharmacist at Liggett's Drugstore. I had never gotten that much money. My father said he would hold it for me. I asked him for it once and he said they had never charged me for food, rent or my clothes. I didn't ask again.

Only Catholics could get into heaven. I felt bad for Protestant and Jewish kids, especially some friends. I didn't have the heart to tell them they were going to hell. Take a kid like Stanley Alper, Jewish, who lived upstairs in our building. He spent so many hours studying at temple after a full day at PS106 that he had no time to play with us. And for what!? Stanley was a lot smarter and a lot more polite than I. But I was the one who'd be going to heaven. That was pretty confusing.

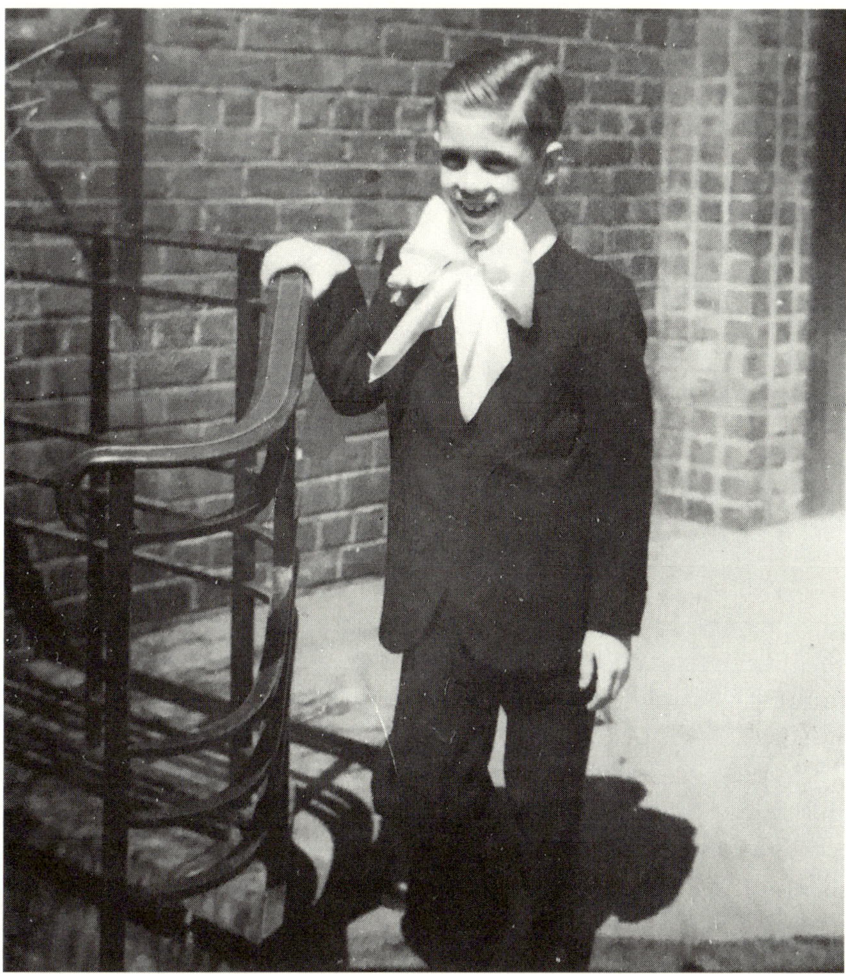

April 1950: After first Holy Communion, on the stoop at 1505 Metropolitan Ave., Parkchester.

I was average academically. My only distinction in school came in the fifth grade when I got into the children's choir. That was after I flunked in tryouts for altar boy because I couldn't get all those Latin responses. Choir was a good deal. I got out of class early once every week for practice and I didn't have to sit with my class at the children's Mass, where a nun might rap you on the head for talking or chewing the host. Best of all about choir was Christmas. One year we sang "Silent Night" on WOR-TV. We also got to sing at the Christmas Eve midnight Mass. We wore rented black cassocks like the ones priests had and starched white surplices like the altar boys had. The way my mother fussed over my hair made it clear this was huge. I watched her proud face in the bathroom mirror as she pressed a soap bar to the front of my pompadour to make sure every hair would stay in place.

The choir took the lead in the church vestibule for the procession. Opening with "O Come, All Ye Faithful," we walked slowly to the altar between rows of beaming adults. I floated down the aisle under the strains of booming organ music, our voices, the smells of incense and melting beeswax from candles we carried. Kneeling across the front of the sanctuary with the rest of the choir, I was hypnotized by the hot wax running over the shallow cup onto my fingers, where it quickly congealed. Christmas midnight Mass was the most magical and joyful moment of the church year. I loved it and all the church stuff.

I went to confession a few Saturdays every month. Confessional booths were lined on both sides of the church. You would stand in line next to one and wait your turn. Sometimes there were eight or nine people ahead of you. When it was your time, you went into the booth and dropped to a soft kneeler facing a closed sliding window. The priest was seated in an adjoining booth and you could hear mumbling between him and the person in the booth on the other side. Try as I might, I could never make out what they were saying. When the sliding window at the other booth closed, you knew it was your turn. I would close my eyes and take a deep breath and suddenly the door would open and there was the priest leaning toward me, his ear inches from my face.

"Bless me, father, for I have sinned. It has been (whatever period of time) since my last confession." Mostly I'd go to the standards, like "I was mean to my sister and stole (whatever number) of candy bars from the corner store," which was usually the case. The priest would say something like, "For your penance say three Our Fathers, three Hail Marys, and three Glory Bes. Now, say your Act of Contrition."

Then he'd start talking in Latin, "Ego te absolvo . . ." while I'd start,"Oh my God, I am heartily sorry for having offended thee . . ." After about four minutes from the time I started, he would give me a blessing, tell me to sin no more, and I would go kneel in the church and say my penance. As I saw it, the best time for dying was right after Confession, when the priest had wiped away your sins. Otherwise, you could screw up your clean soul pretty quickly—like disobeying your mother or something—and if you died before getting back to Confession, you would wind up in purgatory, which was a holding pattern where you paid for new sins before going to heaven. Purgatory was about as bad as hell, but at least you'd be getting out of there someday. However, if you committed a mortal sin before getting back to Confession—say, for example, you killed somebody—you'd go straight to hell. Case closed.

At the center of church life were the priests. At Mass they wore a lot of different-colored vestments: white or gold for celebration; purple for sacrifice, like during Lent; bright red at Pentecost, when the Holy Spirit came to the apostles like tongues of fire; black for funerals. All the parents and nuns—everybody—was in awe of the priests.

My mother saw me in my bedroom playing church one day when I was ten. She watched, smiling, from the doorway. My older sister, playing the altar boy, knelt behind me as I did priestly things. Eyes closed, I genuflected before the altar, a little table covered with a lace doily from the living room couch. My sister raised my bath towel-turned-vestment and rang a bell while I hoisted a white Necco candy wafer to heaven. I was every bit the priest.

◆ ◆ ◆

Florence Neary Olive was my North Star, a nurturing, vigilant, mother hen to my sisters and me. Everyone in the neighborhood knew Flo, and I proudly soaked up the fame that held her in the social limelight, whether among family, friends, or neighbors. Outgoing, wisecracking, and comic, she also was tuned into the needs and concerns of others. One lady upstairs in our building, Helen Pritchard, who had one kid and was about Flo's age, came down with cancer. After she got sick, Flo spent a lot of time with Helen, visiting in her apartment and having her down for lunch.

Our kitchen was set immediately off the main entrance of our building, and you had to walk within four feet of the window to leave or enter. Flo spent hours every day there, preparing meals, washing dishes, shelving groceries, or doing laundry with the manually operated Thor washing machine—enough time day in, day out to be the unofficial greeter for virtually every one of the tenants. With ten apartments on eight floors, there were a lot of them. "Hi, Flo"—I heard that all the time. Some neighbors would linger for a brief chat. As tired as many were returning from work—their day made more exhausting by the round-trip subway ride downtown—Flo often gave them something to chuckle about as she went about her tasks.

Reenacting First Holy Communion picture 48 years later. (The two windows behind Ollie are part of the apartment where he lived, including the kitchen window, to the right, where his mother was "unofficial greeter" of tenants returning from school and work.)

At five-foot-ten, blonde and athletic, she was an especially strong swimmer. And a baseball nut. During the season, a glass of Rheingold beer often within reach as she ironed clothes, Yankee day games blared from the radio, which made her a reliable source for score and game details. Before Mel Allen's play-by-play crackled at 1:00 P.M., the top forty hit tunes, or one of the day's soaps, like *Our Gal Sunday* or *The Romance of Helen Trent*, drifted from the kitchen window.

Five days a week during the school year she had the same exchange with Stanley Alper as he schlepped home from school and temple with his massive book bag.

"Hello, Mrs. Olive."

"Hello, Stanley."

He was a big kid who had a problem with his right foot, which he dragged. When she said "Hello, Stanley," I could feel her affection for him. I loved the way Stanley and other kids in the building related to her.

Gatherings of family and friends often went way beyond my 9:00 P.M. bedtime. As drinks flowed and guests became more raucous, hand-clapping signaled the call for Flo's Irish jig.

There was considerable frivolity and joshing between my mother and me, but she stood firm about her rules.

There was the Saturday I watched from the window as my friends left the building to go to the Palace Theater to see *Mighty Joe Young*, a King Kongish movie that was playing with a Lash LaRue western, plus the news, a Flash Gordon serial, and eight cartoons. Flo wouldn't let me go. The night before Skippy O'Connor's mother had taken a bunch of us to the Loew's American theater for his birthday, and Flo had a rule against more than one movie in a week. I panicked as the guys were almost out of sight.

"Please, Mom. Pleeeez. How about I don't go to the movies for three weeks?"

"Sorry, Rich. You know the rule. One movie a week."

"But Mom, Skippy's thing was a party. I didn't know they were going to a movie. And it was a dumb movie."

"Sorry."

I could no longer see my friends. But if she gave in now I still could catch them because I had my coat on. "Mom," I said, wailing now. "*Mighty Joe Young*! This is the last week."

No response. It was over. My sobs turned into anger. What was I supposed to do all day?

No point in asking. She'd say, "Why not go out and play? Or do some reading."

Nah! I'll just hate her and be miserable.

Once when she was punishing me—something serious because I was sent to bed without supper—I sat at the window at the head of my bed to watch the kids play. Paulie Medaglia spotted me and came over to the window.

"Are you sick?"

"No."

"How come you're in your pajamas?"

"I'm being punished."

"Who punished you?"

"My mother."

"Ahh! Your mother's a fag."

I jumped out of the bedroom window and beat the crap out of him.

Flo was the family's only match for Nana, my father's mother, an intimidating, cranky wisp who sometimes reduced other women in the family to tears with her sharp tongue. I heard my Aunt Virginia say once that Nana slapped Flo when I was a toddler because she didn't like the way my mother whacked me on the butt, and Flo slapped her back. Still, their bond was firm, and Nana came by many evenings to sit at the dining room table for a couple of glasses of port.

One day my mother asked me what I thought about our family having another baby. "We don't need any more girls," I said jokingly, not understanding her question was serious.

"What do you mean? You only have two sisters."

"It would be nice to have a brother."

"Well," she said, "maybe this time you'll have a brother."

◆ ◆ ◆

Before turning twelve, I did not get into much trouble. Fear of my father helped. His anger would erupt in loud yelling that would freeze us. The worst thing my mother could say was, "Wait till your father comes home." Indelibly etched was the whipping I got the day Flo gave me thirty-five cents, specifically for spending money for a fourth-grade outing to the Bronx Zoo. The trip was canceled because of rain and we were let out of school early. Unconsciously, I spent thirty cents on candy for me and a friend and a kiddy merry-go-round ride. Approaching home the thought occurred to me that my mother would be asking for the zoo money.

Already informed by the school of the canceled trip, Flo casually inquired about my day.

"The zoo was a lot of fun," I said.

I was given one chance to recant. "I thought they canceled because of the rain."

"It wasn't raining at the zoo," I said. "I got some soda and stuff. I have five cents left."

She ordered me to bed to wait for my father. It was early afternoon. Waiting anxiously over the next few hours, I looked out the window, picking absentmindedly at a fragment of loose plaster around the windowsill, watching kids playing on the street. I saw my father coming up the sidewalk and grew more nervous as he entered the building. The apartment door opened and closed, followed by my parents' muted conversation. Then, to my horror, I noticed the gaping hole that I had dug into the wall, some eight inches across and two inches deep, reaching to mesh lathing. My bedroom door suddenly opened and he stood there, filling the entire door frame with his muscular six-foot self.

"What are you doing sitting up? You're supposed to be in bed," he asked.

My back to the hole in the wall, I shrugged.

"Lie down. You're being punished."

I stayed against the windowsill.

"Lie down. NOW!"

I melted slowly onto the bed and watched his face turn crimson upon seeing the hole.

"Get into the bathroom."

I pleaded for mercy all the way down the hallway, even as I pulled down my pajama bottoms and exposed my butt while bending over the bathtub. He pulled his electric razor cord from the medicine cabinet as he repeated a familiar claim that I never believed: "This is going to hurt me more than it hurts you."

I gritted my teeth through the first two or three lashes but could not resist screaming when the third stroke whipped across one of the earlier welts. Several more reduced me to snotty-nosed sobbing before he ordered me back to bed. Whether the beating was because of the unauthorized expenditure, for lying, for digging a hole in the wall, or because he had had a bad day, I never knew. However, I never misappropriated funds from my parents again and I never dug another hole in a wall.

I was not, however, ready to give up lying. My batting average lying was abysmal, but it was still worth the risk. Odds were I'd get spanked, whether I fessed up or lied, but there were those rare occasions when lying worked. It became such a part of me that I lied when it was pointless.

◆ ◆ ◆

Sunday, March 14, 1954, was a quiet, relaxed day. My father was asleep in the master bedroom, having worked a midnight shift as a New York City motorcycle cop. On the kitchen wall was a calendar with three circles around days in February, predictions by my father, sister Susan, and I for when the baby would be born. One date early in March, my mother's guess, was circled.

More uncomfortable with each passing day, she didn't go to church that day. She moved slowly to an easy chair in the living room, holding the small of her back with both hands and breathing with difficulty. Rosemary, eighteen months old, was at the living room window babbling about a passersby outside our building. Susan was in bed with chicken pox. I was sprawled on the living room floor in front of our TV, mesmerized by the flashing screen, ominous orchestra music, and an urgent voice-over. *Victory at Sea*, a weekly documentary about World War II, was showing the U.S. fleet under attack from relentless waves of Japanese kamikazes, anti-aircraft fire blazing away. Thud-thud-thud, interrupted by periodic explosions that literally shook the whole pictured image. My mother broke the spell. "Go wake your father, Rich."

Exasperated at the interruption, I jumped to my feet to complete the task as quickly as possible. I opened the door to the darkened bedroom. "Mom . . ." was barely past my lips when my father bounded to the floor, almost bumping me over.

"Turn that thing off," he said, pointing to the TV and walking across to my mother. "Take the baby into the bedroom, shut the door, and stay there until I call you." It felt like punishment, what with the TV turned off and being sent to the bedroom in the middle of the day. But this was different. His urgency told me something was wrong. The bedroom door closed, I pressed my ear against it to hear what was happening. I thought I heard my mother sobbing softly. Yes. She was. I had never heard her cry. I was stunned.

Suddenly, I heard an agonizing, frightening scream.

My nose to the door, I stared at it, paralyzed, then turned toward the girls. Susan had bolted upright in her bed clutching a doll, looking to me for an answer. Rosemary stood frozen, her gaze on the door as if she was trying to see through it. Cautiously, I dropped to the floor to look through the narrow slit above the door sill.

"What do you see?" Susan asked.

"Shut up!" I hissed, fearing my father would hear her.

I could see down the hallway to the living room, through the dining room and to the apartment door. My parents were not in sight. Panic climbed with a mounting sense of helplessness as her crying and moaning continued amidst gentle murmurs from my father. I had never heard her cry. *Do something! Help her!* I whimpered silently. There came a deafening silence. Then he called me. "What, Dad?" I answered.

"Call Nana and tell her to come right away. Leave the front door unlocked for her."

Slowly, anxiously, I opened the door and started toward the telephone, which was in the dining room. They were in the bathroom, and as I passed it I was startled to see that the door was open. I quickly averted my eyes, but try as I did to shut them out I could see that she was on the toilet and he was straddling her. I hurried to the phone.

"Nana is coming, Dad, "I said as I hung up.

"Okay," he said. "Go back to the bedroom and stay with the girls."

Holding my breath I rushed past the bathroom, back to the safety of the bedroom and closed the door. Her sobbing continued, though more softly. Rosemary's attention had turned to some toys. Susan sat in stony silence against her bed's head board, straining to hear. I sat on the floor by the door, bobbing periodically to the door sill for information while feeling guilty about spying on the adult world.

My grandmother lived about fifteen minutes away. Upon arrival, she took control: "We've got to get her to the bed." From under the door I saw three sets of feet, my mother's in the middle, slowly negotiating the narrow hallway. As they approached to within inches of my face to turn the corner into the master bedroom, I quickly sat upright, afraid my father would open the door and find me snooping. They closed the other bedroom door and their words became indistinguishable.

The doorbell rang. I dropped to the floor again and saw my grandmother admit two sets of white shoes and pants, which followed her to the bedroom. There were sounds of men struggling and, again from the floor, I saw those in uniform, one set of feet going backward, carefully turning into the hallway. As they approached the front door I could see the gurney, my father and grandmother walking alongside. The door slammed shut. Except for my breathing and pounding heart, there was silence.

Suddenly I realized I was the oldest person in the apartment. Nothing was said, but, clearly, I was left in charge. And overwhelmed. Turning the knob, carefully to be quiet, I slowly opened the door.

To horror.

A trail of blood on the parquet floor, some of it spattered on the white walls, stretched from the bathroom to the master bedroom. The bedsheet and the mattress were saturated with a massive red circle. I followed the trail into the bathroom. The water in the toilet was crimson and blood had coagulated on the sides of the bowl. My eyes roamed over a scene that blotted out all thought and feelings, except for suffocating numbness.

I was standing stock-still in the hallway when my grandmother returned. We looked quietly at each other for a long moment before she said, "Go back to the bedroom and stay with the kids while I clean up."

◆ ◆ ◆

Nana fixed dinner and brought a tray to Susan. We ate in the dining room without speaking, except for my grandmother coaxing Rosemary to eat. Sometime in the middle of the night my father woke me and told me to go to the 6:00 A.M. Mass. "Ask the sisters to pray for Mom," he said. "I'm going to the hospital now and I'll see you later." He kissed me and quietly closed the bedroom door behind him.

My grandmother awakened me in the dark and I arose to dress and walked to church, where about ten parishioners were scattered among the pews. The first few rows were filled by nuns. After Mass I approached my sixth-grade teacher and relayed my father's request.

"What's happened, Richard?"

"My mother's in the hospital."

"We will pray for your mother," she said with a pained expression, and I headed home.

My father was turning around the corner as I approached our street. I called to him but he drove on, giving no indication that he saw or heard me. Within ten minutes I rang our doorbell and my father opened the door. His eyes were red; his face, contorted.

He choked out one sentence: "God took Mommy to heaven."

A howl erupted from me and I pitched forward into his chest, wailing and throwing my arms around his waist. We cried together—for the first and only time in our lives. I pressed my face into his chest, trying to escape. His arms were a shelter from reality and, for a brief moment, I felt a flash of mutual grief. Much too brief. His body tensed and his hands reached to my arms and gently pulled them from his waist. Nodding toward my grandmother he blubbered, "We need to talk. Go to the bedroom with your sisters." I stifled my crying, shifting into dutiful obedience. Zombielike and feeling disregarded, I walked to the bedroom. Susan was propped against her pillows, trying again to listen to events elsewhere in the apartment.

"Mommy's dead, isn't she?" she asked.

"Yes."

She stared at me blankly. No expression. No reaction. Rosemary was sitting on the floor playing with toys. The three of us were alone.

◆ ◆ ◆

Anger and confusion began a slow boil in my guts, then erupted later in the morning when my grandmother sent me for groceries. An elderly woman from our building stopped me on the way and asked, "How is your mother, Richard?"

"SHE'S DEAD!"

I glared at her with a hatred that might have been reserved for someone responsible for the death. At the same time I was befuddled, knowing she was a kindly neighbor who knew my mother well. She looked at me in shocked silence and I turned and ran to the store.

The following days were a blur of suffocating relatives and family friends, bombarding my father and grandmother with the endless question, "Is there anything we can do?" I wandered about in a nightmare that looped with the same ending.

My father said, "Go out and play."

The only kid not in school, I went to the empty playground. I punched a tetherball around its pole and sat, barely moving for long minutes, on a swing. Grief sucked me deeper into its dark hole as my mother's last words, the only ones I could remember from nearly twelve years with her, echoed in my head: "Go wake your father, Rich."

Then the funeral home. I had seen a dead person once before, but not the whole body. A guy down the street had killed his wife and two kids, then shot himself. I went down there when I heard all the sirens and saw the cops carry out the lady's body. But it was under a blanket and I only saw her feet sticking out. My grandmother and I walked into the funeral home and there was something in a raised casket that bore no resemblance to my mother. The body was in an ugly puffy pink gown. Shoulder-length blonde hair was swept strangely above an atrocious, frozen waxen face. A sweet smell of floral arrangements was sickening. I sat in the back of the room, as far away from the casket as I could, and watched a parade of gawkers shuffling past, staring down at her and moving on, shaking their heads, some whispering, "How beautiful."

I hated them.

Some approached me to say they were sorry, that my mother was a wonderful woman. I felt like part of an exhibit, not knowing my role or what I was supposed to say.

My father was inconsolable. He looked much older than his thirty-five years, much smaller as he followed the coffin from the church, supported on either side by two hulking partners from Motorcycle 1, his precinct.

A long line of cars, led by the motorcycle cops, crept to Gate of Heaven Cemetery in Westchester County. Family, relatives, and friends stood around the open grave as the priest prayed, then nodded to some workers who began lowering the casket into the ground. My father, who'd been sobbing quietly, suddenly became hysterical and pulled violently against the cops beside him, like he was intent on jumping into the grave. I froze in fear. An arm from nowhere went around my shoulder and pulled me into a hug. Aunt Dorothy, my father's cousin, continued squeezing me to her side as she led me down a hill through the tombstones, back to the parked cars lined along the driveway.

◆ ◆ ◆

With Susan and me back in school, a strange calm settled over our lives. On the streets neighbors nodded pitifully when they saw me. None of my friends said anything, like they knew they weren't supposed to. My father, grandmother, and uncle were having trouble figuring out what to do about us kids. Nana had hurt her back—either helping my mother to the bedroom or pulling groceries up some stairs in a shopping basket, she wasn't sure—and Uncle Bill said, "We'll have to bring somebody in. An Irish woman or a colored." They hired an Irish lady. Nana didn't like her, so she was fired and Nana started spending more time with us. Our apartment became eerily quiet. No more mornings-long music or lunchtime soaps.

One evening my grandmother and her sister, Aunt Loretta, came to pack up my mother's clothes. I could hear them in the master bedroom telling my father, "You have to find a mother for these kids." Aunt Mae, my mother's sister, also came and took away a lot of stuff, including a bunch of photographs. Page after page of our albums now had blank spots where my mother's pictures had been lifted from their four-cornered black holders. Any trace of her in other pictures was removed by a razor blade.

Susan and I were sent away for a few weeks that summer, twice with relatives and once to a Catholic Youth Organization camp upstate, where I received a letter from my father. He wrote that he had attended a men's religious retreat.

"While I was there I prayed to Mother that she would look after you, from Heaven. I know you will be a good boy and not disappoint her, nor make her unhappy. The baby and Nana miss you, and so do I. However, it will only be a short time and we will all be together again. Love, Daddy."

It was the only time he ever mentioned my mother to me.

Susan and I were in separate areas for boys and girls at the camp. One day we saw each other when our groups went to a creek to look for polliwogs. "That's my brother," she squealed, jumping and waving to me from the opposite bank.

Meanwhile, evidence of my mother's existence continued to fade like disappearing ink. No one talked about her, not until the day I overheard Nana on the telephone sobbing softly. I rushed quietly to within better earshot when I heard her mention Flo, and she was saying, "I could touch the baby." I knew that the baby we had waited for had died; too, but in short order my curiosity prompted me to ask my grandmother, "What did they do with the baby?"

"They put it in the casket with your mother. It was a boy."

Before long I could find nothing that was my mother's. With one exception. On the parquet floor between the bathroom and the bedroom I discovered on one of the small brown tiles a single drop of blood that my grandmother had missed in her cleanup. Occasionally I retreated to it—secretly, lest my grandmother remove it. I would sit on the floor, holding an index finger on the waxen droplet. Three months after my mother died this last physical vestige was lost to me when we moved to a larger apartment to be shared with my grandmother and Uncle Billy, my father's crotchety older brother.

◆ ◆ ◆

Frail, cantankerous, and seventy-five, my grandmother moaned endlessly about the pain in her back. She also complained to my father about not getting enough help from "these kids," which meant Susan and me. In response, that summer we were assigned to four-hour shifts to babysit Rosemary. Our primary task was to keep our sister out of the apartment during the day because my uncle, like my father, a New York City cop, was sleeping after a graveyard shift. The worst possible scene for all of us, including my grandmother, was for my crotchety uncle to be awakened from his sleep.

Having to drag a two-year-old around the neighborhood for four hours was hell. I waged futile warfare with my grandmother about the injustice. Other kids didn't have to babysit.

"All you ever think about is play, play, play," she'd reply, exasperated and leaving me to wonder what it was I was supposed to be thinking about.

I decided to run away and took the subway downtown. After wandering around Rockefeller Center, I went into St. Patrick's

Cathedral. Pausing at the altar dedicated to St. Veronica, I studied the facsimile of the cloth they said she used to wipe Jesus' bloody face while he was carrying his cross. Even though it looked like cracked glass, I assumed it was the very one on which Jesus left the miraculous imprint before going on to his crucifixion. I marveled at the coloration and detail of the bloody face—right down to the crown of thorns—that I assumed had stood the test of time for almost 2,000 years. He looked like I felt, alone and, come to think of it, hungry. It was dinnertime, so I went home. There was no sign anyone noticed I had been gone.

On another occasion I told my father I was leaving, but changed my mind when he offered to lend me a suitcase.

His work hours continued to vary—days one week, evenings and overnight shifts at other times—so, when he was home, either he or we kids were asleep. This had its benefits. I had greater freedom and there was no more "Wait till your father gets home." With my mother gone, I think parenting was overwhelming for him. He had no father figure to copy because—this was the big family secret—his father had committed suicide when he was five, a fact I would not learn until well into adulthood.

◆ ◆ ◆

Johnny Barbera, a classmate at St. Helena's, was my best friend. I was so taken with him that I took "John" as my middle name when confirmed as a Catholic in the second grade. In fourth grade Johnny introduced me to hitching rides on the back of delivery trucks and jumping off before they accelerated on wider streets. By the time we were twelve, we had ratcheted up our adventures to skipping school and jumping turnstiles to explore New York in the interminable subway system. We became blood brothers by cutting our forearms with a pen knife and rubbing the gashes together. All kinds of juvenile stuff—like slapping the rear panel or fender of a car turning a corner and screaming in mock pain before fleeing.

Pushing the envelope led to joy-riding at 2:30 one morning in his uncle's car. With my Uncle Bill awake in the living room reading, I quietly lowered myself with sheets tied together from the window of the third-floor bedroom I shared with my father, who was working a graveyard shift. Johnny, his cousin, and another kid—each of them, like me, thirteen—were waiting near my house in a new Pontiac. We were impressed when his cousin peeled away from the curb, fishtailing wildly down a series of side streets before accelerating for a high-speed run along several miles of Bronx River Parkway. Heading home with dawn breaking, it struck me that I was locked out. Apprehensively, I rang the doorbell and held my breath.

"Where were you?" asked my uncle, awakened from his sleep.

"I went to an early Mass to . . ." before I could continue my head snapped to the right from the sudden, stunning force of his open-handed slap across my head.

"You're a liar," he bellowed.

I was also a thief, a practice that had begun about four years earlier by stealing candy bars when I went to the corner. Next came snatching cookies after Sunday Mass from behind the counter at Pakula's Bakery. The penance of three Our Fathers, three Hail Marys, and three Glory Bes seemed a fair exchange. Petty thievery morphed into riskier heists, like the theft of several quart bottles of Rheingold beer from a grocery store shelf, which some of us smuggled out a side door to the loading dock. We carried them to a train yard alongside Tremont Avenue and drank warm beer while sitting on shadeless tracks under the summer sun. An elderly woman who later spotted me staggering down the sidewalk asked, "Little boy, are you all right?"

"Fuck you," I said, frightened somewhat by my own outburst toward an adult, a kindly old lady no less. Panicked, I ran away, thinking I might be arrested for this and, God forbid, my father being called.

I did not take that encounter or my more ambitious thefts to Confession, thinking the priest and God had their limits.

By seventh grade, some of us started getting into trouble at school and we were getting detained after classes for misconduct. One would get detention for any of a wide range of infractions: talking or fooling around in class, failure to do homework. Before being sent home with a note for our parents citing our violation, we had to write a hundred or so "I shall nots . . ." on loose-leaf paper. During one detention a student hit me on the back of the head with a paper wad. I turned and said, "You son of a bitch," not seeing the nun from another class who heard me from the hallway while passing our classroom. Enraged, she ordered me to my feet. Then came a vicious slap to my left cheek, followed in rapid succession by a series of rotating slaps across both sides of my face. She drove me backward between the desks, coordinating each slap with a cadenced demand: "Don't you . . . ever . . . ever . . . ever . . . let me . . . hear you . . . speak like that . . . again." As the assault continued, I looked defiantly into her face, determined to show she could not crack me, which further fueled her rage even as she gasped for breath.

Johnny, one or two other boys, and I were summoned with our parents one night to a meeting with the school principal, Sister Mary Richard. "These boys," she said, with a tremor in her voice, "have been shooting water pistols at their teacher. Sister discovered this because of wet spots she found on her habit while ironing. Each boy is to be suspended from school for three days. If there is a repetition of such outrageous behavior, anyone found responsible will be expelled."

Looking at each other with surprise and relief, we quickly copped to the charge because, in fact, the wet spots were spit, projected as the nun wrote on the blackboard. We never learned how this turned into a tale of water pistols or how our names got linked to it, but the relief for dodging that bullet— more seriously, the degree of my father's wrath— was indescribable.

Our little gang loved to stump the nuns, especially the older ones. We would tell them how the polluted creek that ran under the Cross Bronx Expressway near the school was packed with migrating "white eels."

"White eels?" the sisters would say. "How big are they?" Failing miserably in suppressing laughter, we'd hold up two hands about five inches apart—the approximate length of a used condom floating down the waterway. Some of us may not have known what "rubbers" actually were—I didn't—but we knew it went on a man's penis, and having the nun engaged in a dialogue about it was a crack-up.

Relishing our mounting reputation for outlandish antics, Johnny and I grew bolder. Our attitude was arrogant, a declaration of immunity to consequences. We had a motto: "I care. I really care"—which meant exactly the opposite. It was a message aimed at adult authority: "You can't touch us." We sneaked into our classroom early one morning and vandalized it, overturning desks, tossing papers about and snapping the flagpole, leaving it dangling over the bulletin board.

Then there was the incident on the busy Cross Bronx Expressway. We carried a cobblestone onto an overpass, pushed it over the side onto onrushing traffic below—and suddenly struck by fear or conscience or reality ran from the scene without waiting to see the results.

A lot of the stuff we did, we laughed and bragged about.

We never said anything about the cobblestone. Or laughed. Not even between each other.

◆ ◆ ◆

From the time we were in kindergarten at St. Helena's, boys and girls were equally represented in each classroom. Until seventh grade there was virtually no social interaction. In the schoolyard and in the neighborhood most of the boys played all kinds of ball—stickball, softball, punchball, basketball—and marbles, hockey on roller skates; we flipped baseball cards and traded comic books. Girls played with dolls, jumped rope, and seemed to mostly stand around talking.

In the fourth grade they started bringing us to the auditorium for square dance and foxtrot lessons. Since they matched boys and girls according to height, my partner most of the times was a fat girl with blackheads around her nose who was notorious for her body odor or another who routinely picked her nose and ate her findings.

I was kissed for the first time by a girl not my sister when I was thirteen, the summer of 1955. We were at a lake cottage near Patchogue, Long Island, and I was coming from the garage with my bicycle. Linda, a sister of my friend, Georgie, who lived across the street, suddenly appeared at the garage door and blocked my exit. I tried to get the bike around her, but she quickly stepped across my path.

"What are you doing?" I asked.

She stood there with such resolve, her eyes locked onto mine, as to fascinate me. Then she stepped up to me, moved slowly and close to my face, put her arms around my neck and kissed me passionately on the lips. I looked around frantically. Where was Georgie? Was anyone watching?

"Come with me," she said, taking me by the hand.

I let the bike drop and she led me across the street to her backyard, where there was a miniature house that replicated her parents' New England cottage. "We're going to play house," she explained as we approached the house's door, which was large enough to crawl through. "You go in first."

Curiosity, mixed with some inexplicable surging anticipation, made me comply. Too tall at five feet to stand, I positioned myself cross-legged in the middle of the tiny house and looked around at painted furniture on the walls and a faux kitchen in one corner. Linda crawled to me and, with hypnotic eyes, said, "You're the father and I'm the wife. Lie down and take a rest while I fix dinner."

"Okay," I said, stretching out. She went to the "kitchen," which was about three feet away, futzed around for a few seconds, then crawled back and lay down alongside me. Reaching across to my face, she turned it toward hers and began to kiss me.

"Dinner will be ready in a little while," she said.

I was in no rush.

She climbed on top of me and I put my arms around her. She pressed her lips to mine and I closed my eyes dreamily. My body was beginning to tingle with newfound sensations when I opened my eyes to see four faces, including my sister's and Linda's older sister, peering into the window over the painted living room couch. Horrified, I pushed Linda off and bolted from the dollhouse and the backyard.

Besides the humiliation of being caught playing house, I knew I'd been caught doing something over the line, although I could not have said what that was. I avoided Linda like poison ivy after that and at summer's end, greatly relieved, left Patchogue. Georgie never said anything about me playing house with his sister. Neither did I, my sister nor, to my knowledge, the other two kids at the window.

◆ ◆ ◆

There was a cataclysmic change in the social order soon after school started for our last year in elementary school. While I was playing punchball one afternoon Johnny and a couple of boys in my class came running through my neighborhood like a pack of wild stallions. They were in hot pursuit of three girls from our school who, judging from their giggling, were complicit.

"C'mon, Ollie!" Johnny yelled.

Curious, I ran after them, following them into the stairwell of an apartment building. The girls went to the third-floor landing and were unscrewing lightbulbs there and on the fourth floor as the guys stopped on the second-floor landing and started unscrewing its lightbulb. "What are we doing?" I asked, and then felt stupid because everyone else seemed to know. Johnny told me I was number 4 and when the girls called out my number, to go up to the third floor.

This was the game. When called, you went upstairs where a girl would reach out for you in the dark, put her arms around you and kiss you on the lips. You were to guess who the girl was.

I went upstairs. Like venturing onto thin ice, I felt my way along the walls, lips pursed and hands tentatively reaching out, concerned I might touch something improper. A girl's hands touched my chest, then went around my neck. I felt her breath against my face and her lips gently settled on mine, shooting electric currents through my chest into my limbs.

"Who am I?" she giggled.

"Maureen?"

"No."

There were only two other girls.

"Kathy?"

"Yes, how did you know?"

"You smell nice," I said, hoping that was a good answer.

The game marked the beginning of hanging out a lot in mixed company. Things continued to pick up in the eighth grade. Erections, for one. They would occur at the weirdest times, like right before recess or when I was sent to the blackboard to work out a math problem. None of the other boys ever mentioned this problem, so I assumed it was mine alone.

The eighth-grade nun made an interesting change in seating. Instead of girls in separate rows, now a girl was in front and behind every boy. Lorraine Sarrubo, amazingly well endowed and dating a boy in high school, would casually, yet discreetly, drape her legs around my seat and rest her feet on my lap. I would respond by gently stroking her nylon-stockinged calves, occasionally to her lower thighs, about as far as I could reach without falling out of my chair. For reasons I could not quite understand, this became another occasion for hard-ons.

Then came coed birthday parties. There was spin the bottle and, in some cases, parents would permit one or two slow dances with lights low at the end of the party. Young pelvises would rub gently to strains of the Platters' "Great Pretender" or the Penguins' "Earth Angel." Amidst this raging chemistry, girls would sometimes plop on boys' laps and sing along with the music while pivoting their hips and—yes—bringing on the predictable development, which I hoped they could not feel.

About this time there also was a change in fashion that focused breathtaking attention on the busts of such movie stars as Jayne Mansfield, Marilyn Monroe, and Jane Russell. At the same time, teenaged girls adopted a shift in dress that delighted us boys. Away from school and the dress code of modest jumper uniform over white blouse, some girls wore their cashmere sweaters backward, buttons down the back, prominently displaying developments previously concealed. Other girls, particularly those lagging in development, took a pass on the new fashion.

As elsewhere, Johnny was the trailblazer with the girls. One time we went to the apartment of a classmate, Hillary, whose parents were gone. Hillary invited us because, like a lot of other girls, she was crazy about Johnny. I was part of the package, which, for Hillary, was apparently tolerable. But to Hillary's dismay, we showed up with Maureen, Johnny's girlfriend. Given this, I thought that maybe I could be Hillary's boyfriend.

We sat around listening to records, then Johnny led Maureen into a bedroom. Hillary and I sat in the living room as the music continued, but she was much more interested in what was happening in the bedroom. I followed her down the hallway as she opened the door where Johnny and Maureen were making out on Hillary's parents' bed. Johnny looked annoyed and being a loyal friend I felt it would be helpful if I kept Hillary in the living room.

"Let's go listen to the music, Hillary," I said. Johnny smiled approvingly. I put my hand on Hillary's shoulder and she dropped like a limp protester. "C'mon," I repeated, and took her by the ankles and dragged her to the living room, feeling very uncomfortable all the while about it. I tried making light of it but Hillary was not amused. She stormed around me and back to the bedroom, where the door was now locked. She started pounding on the door and screaming, "All of you, get out of my house!"

Scared about the neighbors, the three of us left hurriedly. On the ride in the elevator I told Johnny and Maureen, "I was going to ask Hillary to be my girlfriend." They were not encouraging about any chance of that happening.

◆ ◆ ◆

One bright, warm spring day my father brought a familiar, attractive young woman to our apartment. Eileen Ryan lived upstairs at 1505 Metropolitan Avenue. She was one of the really good-looking working women who turned my head each day when she returned from work in midtown Manhattan. With our reintroduction she reminded me that she once babysat for us when my parents went out.

From the moment my father and Eileen arrived at our apartment he was acting weird. Just much more nice and polite, introducing her around and all, like she was some kind of celebrity. I knew this was not about babysitting.

For several weeks after that visit there were no more Eileen sightings, but my grandmother started talking about her—how "she can't hold a candle to your mother; probably doesn't know how to sing; doesn't even know how to cook or keep a house." For me, such comments were welcome cracks in the code of silence about my mother. Also, the periodic verbal barrage was having a negative effect on my own feelings about Eileen. Like my grandmother, I began to view her as something of an interloper.

In time Eileen began showing up, sometimes for dinner or brunch at our apartment after Sunday Mass. Despite my grandmother's palpable disapproval and my passive hostility, Eileen was ever gracious. The announcement of their engagement came about three months before my graduation from elementary school.

◆ ◆ ◆

Virtually everyone in our eighth-grade class was anticipating going to St. Helena's High School. As graduation approached, there was a religious "vocations fair" in the auditorium. Tables were arrayed throughout the space with literature and posters about the religious life—priesthood and brotherhood for the boys, convents for the girls. Representatives of various religious orders were at each table to describe the mission of their organizations and to answer questions. Manning one of the tables was a young, outgoing priest of the Franciscan Friars of the Atonement, Father Simeon Heine.

I paused at his table and he started talking baseball, which proved easy for us, two Yankee fans. In time he tapped into my childhood fantasy and asked whether I had ever considered the priesthood. If qualified, he said, I could be eligible for admission to St. John's Atonement Seminary as a high school freshman. Father Simeon was, by far, the most energetic and friendly priest I'd ever encountered. He showed more attention to me and my interests than I had ever experienced. He liked sports and I thought maybe I could be a priest like him—a priest who has fun. The seminary, he told me, was in far upstate New York and he showed me some pictures of the grounds, surrounded by beautiful rolling hills. Going away to school, especially as described, sounded like an attractive alternative to life with a stepmother. I filled out an application and later pointed out Father Simeon to Johnny.

The priest sought a visit to our home soon afterward and was invited to dinner. Astonishingly, my father recognized him immediately as "Buzzy" Heine, a boyhood friend from their old neighborhood off Fordham Road in the Bronx. Buzzy, my father gushed with an enthusiasm I had never seen, "was the greatest stickball player ever. He could crush a Spaldeen into the next block."

"And your father," the equally animated priest said, "could kick a football about as far."

I enjoyed listening to them carrying on with their boyhood memories throughout dinner. Then they turned attention to me. My father had no objection about me applying for the seminary and he filled out the paperwork. Parental permission cleared, Father Simeon said the rest of the process, assuming a favorable recommendation from the school, appeared favorable for my admission to St. John's.

He asked if I knew Johnny, noting he had a meeting scheduled that week at the Barbera home. This was a total surprise to me. The thought of Johnny and I going away together to school was beyond my imagining.

Within weeks after Father Simeon's visit, the Franciscan Friars of the Atonement invited me into St. John's freshman class in Montour Falls, New York, commencing in September, 1956.

Johnny received an identical letter.

◆ ◆ ◆

The summer of 1956 was a time of major change. My father and Eileen were married at St. Helena's on August 25, two years and five months after my mother's death. An eight-millimeter camera captured them stepping from the church to the applause of family and friends and a shower of rice. In the film I can be seen emerging from one side of the crowd, an assassin in a powder blue suit, winding up and, from a distance of about seven feet, side-arming a handful of rice into the bride's face. She flinched and bowed over as the celebration continued around her.

My father, stepmother, and my sisters moved to Putnam Valley, fifty miles north of the city, where my father was building a home. I would be more than 250 miles away with my best friend. My grandmother and uncle moved to a smaller apartment.

The church bulletin listed some fifteen eighth-grade and high school graduates from St. Helena's bound for seminaries or convents. There were our names side by side, John Anthony Barbera and Richard John Olive, headed for study for the priesthood with the Franciscan Friars of the Atonement. To our friends, the idea was nothing short of crazy.

With the newlyweds honeymooning in Miami Beach, my grandmother helped me pack. We checked the seminary's list to ensure I had everything they prescribed and jammed it into a brown leather suitcase, which was my eighth-grade graduation gift. We placed the suitcase on the floor and had to sit on it together until, just barely, I was able to click shut its two latches.

It was 7:45 A.M., September 8, 1956, the Saturday after Labor Day, and it was almost time. Johnny's parents would be downstairs in fifteen minutes to drive us to the seminary. Suddenly, as if for the first time, the magnitude of the moment hit me. I'm leaving home. I choked up, but held my emotions in check. My sisters were asleep in the bedroom they shared with my grandmother. My father was gone, not to return until days after I was gone.

I stole a glance at my seventy-seven-year-old grandmother as she stretched, trying to diminish the familiar pain in her lower back. Things, I realized, would no longer be the same, like sitting with her before bedtime when we shared her favorite cookies, Social Teas, she slurping some tea from the saucer while I dunked cookies in warm milk.

. . . or hearing her cheer as the likes of Carmen Basilio and Tony DeMarco battered each other to pulps in the Gillette Friday Night Fights.

. . . or seeing her sitting on the edge of her bed every night in an old, ratty nightgown wheezing through her rosary.

I would not be around to provide my penmanship, which she admired so, for addressing her Christmas cards. I gently took her wrist as she bent over to lift my suitcase. "Nana, don't. You'll hurt your back." I kissed her goodbye.

"Be a good boy, Richard."

She watched me labor down the hallway to the elevator, straining with the valise that was half my weight. "Goodbye, Nana," I said, stepping onto the elevator.

I tugged the suitcase onto the street to the Barberas' green Plymouth sedan, parked curbside. Mr. Barbera stepped out and placed the luggage in the trunk as I slid into the back seat with Johnny, which helped to blunt my twinges of melancholy. As I greeted Mrs. Barbera, who paused in sorting some road maps in the glove compartment, Mr. Barbera glanced over his left shoulder and pulled from the curb. I looked out the back window at our apartment building, then continued stealing sights of the familiar red brick buildings of Parkchester, my lifelong home, as they slipped into my past. The car went under the noisy IRT el on Castle Hill Avenue and turned onto the Cross Bronx Expressway.

Chapter Five

Leaving Home

I travel not to go anywhere, but to go.
—Robert Louis Stevenson

John

Hoboken in 1956 was heavenly. Well, in truth it was pretty slummy, but it seemed great to me. It was the home of the *Phoebe Snow*, queen of the Erie-Lackawanna Railroad, the train that carried St. John's Atonement Seminary students from the New York City area through the Pocono Mountains to Elmira, New York. My father and mother drove me to the Hoboken station. I was scarcely aware of the ride because, for the only time in my life, I had a bout of hay fever and was blind with itching eyes and water running constantly from my nose.

As directed by the packet of introductory materials mailed to us, I was dressed in a dark suit. I had a beige cardboard suitcase with some sort of diamond pattern encircling it, apparently intended to make it seem less cheap. When we arrived, the station seemed packed with teenage boys in dark suits and hovering parents. Mothers were teary, while fathers maintained their manly stoicism. My mother gave me her spare handkerchief for my runny nose and ten dollars, a fortune to me. She kissed me on the cheek. My father said goodbye and they left.

The engine and cars were unbelievably high to a boy like me, accustomed to stepping onto the subway. Smoke from the engine made me think of British films with Lawrence Olivier and Greer Garson. It was otherworldly and overpowering. I was beginning to feel frightened when a tall boy with thick black curly hair said, "Hey, kid, are you going to the seminary?"

He was Jerry Waters, and he was to become one of my heroes in the next two years. He led me into a car filled with cigarette smoke and seminarians. It seemed as if everyone was smoking. Jerry offered me a cigarette. Not wanting to seem square, I took it. I asked if everyone smoked in the seminary, and he informed me seminarians were not allowed to smoke, but that it was standard practice to smoke on the train since we would not be able to do so again for months.

Until then, I had probably stolen a few drags in my life, but there I was, puffing away like a chain smoker, desperate to get every lungful possible before we arrived. Oddly, considering the fact I was in a carcinogenic torture chamber, my sniffling, sneezing, and itchy eyes had cleared.

Along the way, Jerry introduced me to Richard Basch and others, and they told me all I should know about life in the seminary. There were many details, but once they said I would be getting up at 5:40 and exercising for an hour and a half every afternoon everything else was "mumble, mumble, mumble." Father Simeon had said much the same, but I apparently thought there was some wiggle room. There was not.

I said I had never gotten up without my mother making it happen; that I had only risen that early for the rare 6:00 Mass I had to serve; that I had asthma and could not run to the door if the place was on fire.

Basch said, "This stuff isn't optional. This is what you have to do. If not, you'll be gone." I did not want to be gone.

We went to the dining car. I had never seen anything so elegant, except in movies. Black waiters in red livery; tables with white linen tablecloths, napkins and heavy silverware that matched. They served water in thick, fancy glasses that did not have the name of a jelly or peanut butter company embossed on them. Each table was positioned in front of a large, clear window, wondrous views of mountains racing by.

The waiter asked what I would have. Stumped for a second, then, no doubt influenced by my Irish roots, I ordered tea.

"Would you like milk or lemon?"

I had never heard of such a thing. Lemon? Like my grandparents, I had always had tea with milk and sugar, served in a cup with a saucer into which you could spill your tea for cooling and from which you could sip it. I ordered tea, at least in part, because its rules were carved in stone. So simple. I could not possibly say something that would make me appear foolish. Now this had become complex. How could I regain momentum and appear to be the *bon vivant* I wished to seem?

"Both," I replied.

"Both?" His surprise, the arched eye, should have stopped me. But it did not.

"Both."

Was that a little shrug he gave? If so, what did it mean? A small voice told me to cry out to stop and change the order to "make that just milk." I didn't listen to that voice. He returned with the tea and milk in lovely silver pots. The lemon was a wedge on a small plate. I put a couple of teaspoons of sugar, some milk and the *coup de grace,* squeezed lemon juice, into my tea. Then I watched in startled silence as multiple small lumps floated to the surface like grains of rice.

"Your tea has curdled," said Richard Basch. "The acid in lemon curdles milk."

Tick, tick, tick; the longer it takes to respond, the stupider I look. So . . .

"That's the way we drink it," I said.

"What?"

"In my family, that's how we drink tea." Matching deed to word, I then drank my curdled tea. It was awful.

Perhaps attempting to save the moment or to buy friends, I offered to pay for the refreshments of the other three boys at the table. Immediately and emphatically, Jerry Waters said, "No. Hold on to your money. You'll need it."

"What do you mean? My mother gave me ten dollars."

He laughed. "Ten dollars, huh? How long is that supposed to last you? Listen, kid. Ten dollars is not a lot of money. You are going to need things like paper, ink, pens, pencils, soap, candy, soda. Stuff. Don't spend your money on people."

He could sense what I had come to realize, that I was over my head.

I would ride that train back and forth several times a year, yet I only remember that trip. Why? All the other trips were transportation. That one was transformation.

Mike

So, here I was, thirteen and getting another chance to run away from home.

"What have I gotten myself into?" I wondered. *"In the name of the Father, Son, and Holy Spirit: Please Jesus; don't let me be a failure at this too."*

My last escape attempt had been a miserable failure—a three-day stint at summer camp. I was supposed to stay for two weeks—maybe the whole summer. But I hated camp; I missed the chaos of the city streets. I called home every opportunity I had. I complained about the food, the dormitory, the bed I slept in. "There are more sick kids here than in the whooping cough ward at St. Joseph's Hospital," I told Marie. "The counselors are cruel. They insult us every day."

Finally, they had had enough. Marie and my father came and took me home. My father was angry. "Do you ever finish anything?" he asked. We drove the rest of the way home in silence.

And now I was running away again, and they were driving me to my new hideaway, St John's Atonement Seminary in the Finger Lakes Region of Upstate New York, some 400 miles away.

"Him, a priest?" I heard my father say to Marie as I lay in bed the night before we were to leave.

"Never mind; it will be good to have him away from here for a while. And who knows . . . ," Marie said.

"Yeah for a while, three more days maybe—if we're lucky. If he thinks I'm driving 400 miles up to Montour Falls next week to bring him home, he's got another think coming."

"Let's just see what happens."

Our '55 Chevy moved along the steamy roads through upper New York. The countryside was beautiful, a green quilt of pastureland and cornfields. Occasionally, in the distance I could see the outline of one of the area's many lakes. So different from the city I was running away from. "Wow!" Paul said, "Look at all those cows and horses."

In the front seat, my father and Marie talked about the rest of the trip and what they would do after they left me. Our destination was the Greyhound Bus Station at Elmira. There a charter bus would be waiting to take seminarians, new and returning ones, on the final fourteen-mile journey to Montour Falls. I wondered what my father and Marie would be talking about once they dropped me off.

The Chevy inched into a tight parking space in front of the Elmira terminal. I saw a group of boys milling around in the afternoon heat of September. I felt tightness in my throat and sweat starting to dampen my clothing. A few adults outside were saying hurried goodbyes to their sons and climbing into their cars. There was an uncertain expression on some of the boys' faces as they waved goodbye.

"Are you ready?" my father said. My sister Carol began to cry.

I opened the car door and stepped out. I was having trouble focusing; my eyes were moist. *It's the heat, right?*

"Don't leave. Don't leave," my sister sobbed as I moved to the back of the car where my father stood with the trunk open. She was old enough now to understand what losing someone felt like. My father stood there smoking as I struggled to pull out my two suitcases. Then I walked to the front of the car stumbling under the weight of the suitcases to say goodbye to Marie. She reached out, pulled my head down and gave me a kiss. "Make us proud, Michael," she said.

I kissed my sister on the forehead and whispered: "Don't worry. I'll be fine and I'll write you every week. And I'll be home for Christmas," I added as an afterthought. I shook my brother's hand. He didn't look particularly unhappy about my departure; he was already talking excitedly with Marie about what they would do on the trip home.

I walked with my father to the group of boys waiting outside the station. When I put my bags down, my father shook my hand and pressed a twenty-dollar bill into my palm and said: "Try not to mess this up, too." I watched as he walked back to the car. They pulled away, my sister waving frantically from the back seat, the others looking straight ahead. I retrieved a handkerchief from my jacket pocket and found a spot behind a group of boys where I hoped I'd be invisible and no one would see me crying.

Soon a forty-five-seat red-and-white chartered bus pulled into the station. There was a general rush toward the bus as its door swung open with a whack. Standing in the doorway was a tall figure in a brown Franciscan robe. The onrushing herd stopped, the clamor subsided. The friar greeted a few boys by name. Then he became very businesslike. "Boys, every year we try to get this right and every year it seems to still go wrong." A group of boys beside me snickered. I flinched. "Now let's try to get it right this time. When I call your name, hand your bags to the bus driver and then get on the bus. Take the seats in the back first and work on down toward the front. Got it?"

"Roulliard, Richard; Dwyer, Dennis; Dever, Thomas; Basch, Richard; Connolly, Michael . . ."

When the bus was finally loaded, it headed down the quiet streets of Elmira and onto a highway. I heard one of the boys say this was part of the Watkins Glen Grand Prix race route. I was seated next to a boy who reminded me of Orson Wells. In a slightly exaggerated, deep-throated voice, he introduced himself as Richard Basch, a sophomore class member. I told him my name. He began a conversation with a group of boys he knew. His comments were short and swift, like a boxer's jabs. Most of them had to do with "newbies" and the problem of BO. To Basch, a new boy seemed like a booger hanging on a finger, needing to be flicked away. I wanted to change my seat, but there was no place to go. And besides, I felt it would only add to his disdain for another new boy.

Basch told one of the boys listening to him: "If you don't attend to it (hygiene) properly, you will be the butt of many unflattering comments. Pun intended," he declared with a smirk. After a while I stopped listening, my head began to bob from side to side as the bus wound its way along Route 14 toward Montour Falls.

Bending over the chalice the priest says: "And taking the cup he blessed it and gave it to his disciples saying: 'Take this all of you and drink from it for this is my blood, which will be shed for you and for all mankind for the forgiveness of sins. Do this in memory of me.'" He lifts the chalice high above his head and the bells begin to chime. I watch him genuflect and feel a sense of contentment.

The bus lurched to a stop. Startled, I was instantly awake. *Had we arrived?*

Photo credit: Franciscan Friars of the Atonement, Graymoor Archives

Seminarians from the New York metropolitan area and New Jersey traveled by way of the Lackawanna Railroad to Elmira, then were bused to Montour Falls. On this trip students were met at the station by Father Simeon Heine (far right, second row), who recruited Mike, Ollie, and John.

Confusion and noise. Boys scrambled from their seats and began to rush toward the door, which slapped open. I got out of my seat. Out the window I could see an imposing red brick building with a circular staircase leading up to an entrance. Dozens of figures in back cassocks or brown Franciscan robes lined the stairway. My chest began to tighten and heave; it was difficult to breathe. "Well, are you coming?" Basch said as he headed for the door. My throat felt like it was filled with dry sand; I couldn't reply. I glanced again at the figures in black and brown.

The Inquisition?

I slid back into my seat pretending I'd dropped something and was looking for it. I hoped no one would notice and the bus would leave before anyone realized I was not with the group.

Take me back. Take me back.

Ollie

I loved the country. Maybe because ninety-nine percent of my life till then was on sidewalks and cement playgrounds in the Bronx. My ultimate adventures in those years were periodic weekend drives across the Hudson River to Rockland County. My father was helping his brother, Jack, build his home on fifty wooded acres purchased with seven other rapidly growing Irish Catholic families who were determined to escape the city. A small gang of us kids were free at those times to roam the woods, hunt polliwogs, climb trees, and, in the summer months, go swimming.

Now this, riding with my best friend and his parents through sweeping expanses of the Catskill Mountains on Route 17, skies so alive with blue. Barns, horses, and grazing livestock on both sides of the highway. Everything was in raging Technicolor. It was my longest journey ever, so much further than when my parents rented a cottage two different summers sixty-three miles away in Milford, Connecticut, on Long Island Sound.

Mrs. Barbera, sitting in the front seat, did a lot of reading. Every once in a while Johnny's father asked her to check the map. Deeper and deeper, hour after hour we rode next to fields and green mountains that Mr. Barbera said were hills. To me they were mountains. At every town's approach Mr. Barbera cut his speed to thirty-five while Mrs. Barbera put aside her book and grabbed the map. In many of the villages and towns people were lounging on benches in pocket parks or squares or in front of stores. In the Bronx only old people and women with baby carriages sat on benches. I wondered what it was like at our destination.

A sign said, "Hancock 5 Miles." Mrs. Barbera said, "It's about time for lunch."

Like many of the other towns we rode through, Hancock was a few blocks of storefronts on both sides of the street. Except for peoples' clothes and the cars, it was easy to imagine what it was like in Colonial times. Stopping in such a quaint place was an adventure, but I was restrained in my excitement because Johnny was being his usual cool self. I wondered if the Barberas would let me get a Coke or a cream soda with lunch. I didn't have to ask. Everyone was picking what they wanted from the menu. When it came to me I ordered a cream soda and a chicken salad sandwich—and felt so grown-up in the process.

Back on the road, the car grew quiet, except for periodic static from the radio as Mr. Barbera tried to stay in touch with local radio stations that seemed to fade in and out in the hilly countryside. Mrs. Barbera continued reading. Johnny nodded off, and I fell to daydreaming, gazing out the side window as billboards, signs, and eastbound cars zipped past.

Another sign: "Elmira 75 miles." As I got drowsier, the thought crossed my mind prompting a small wave of anxiety: *this is really far away*.

"Fourteen miles to go," Mr. Barbera announced, waking me from a deep sleep. In Horseheads, just north of Elmira, he turned right onto Route 14, a narrow two-lane blacktop with signs periodically advertising the annual Watkins Glen Grand Prix. Johnny and I perked up as the car came around a bend that opened to a wide field. Off to the right was an earthen levee and a sign: "Catherine's Creek." Further ahead alongside a small hill was a red brick building, at seven stories much taller than anything we had seen for miles. Closer, we saw a sign on the expansive front lawn:

"St. John's Atonement Seminary."

Mr. Barbera parked in the driveway as two young men approached the car.

"Is it okay to park here?"

"Yes, sir," one of them said. "If you would give us the luggage we'll show the boys where to check in."

Denny Walsh and Ron Nickel, two seniors, introduced themselves and led us up curving steps to the entrance. We passed under a framed portico into a high-ceiling circular rotunda. At its center was a statue of St. Francis wearing a brown, velvety habit, a bird perched on its shoulder. Two men walking through the rotunda wore habits like the statue's, with hoods hanging from the back of their necks. We stepped into an office off the rotunda where another monk, a metal cross hanging from a red string around his neck, asked for our names.

"How was your drive?" he asked the Barberas as he consulted his list.

"Very nice. Beautiful," Mrs. Barbera said.

"Good. We're happy to welcome John and Richard. I see you're from the city. Will you be staying in the area overnight?"

"No," Mr. Barbera said. "We may make a few stops, but the plan is to head back today."

"Very well. The boys will be shown to their dormitories, then they will be welcomed by the rector in about two hours."

Mrs. Barbera appeared a bit taken aback by the sudden finality of the moment. "Okay, boys, be good now," Mr. Barbera stammered, turning to shake our hands.

The transition struck me with suddenness, as well. We were staying and the Barberas were returning to Parkchester. Thoughts of my father, sisters, and grandmother brought a twinge to my chest. A slight quiver in her voice, Mrs. Barbera said goodbye to me and turned to Johnny. She hugged him and kissed him on the cheek. I wanted her to do the same to me, but, of course, she was not my mother.

"Okay," said Johnny, ever cool, as Mrs. Barbera whispered something in his ear. He picked up his bags and I followed suit. The Barberas watched as Walsh led us, lugging our stuff across the rotunda, to the elevator. They were still watching as the elevator door closed.

◆ ◆ ◆

"The elevator is only for the priests," Walsh explained as we rode to the second floor. "The only time we're allowed to take it is when we're moving our luggage to the attic or getting it down." The elevator stopped just off a rotunda that bisected two long hallways.

"Wait here while I show your friend his dorm," Walsh told me.

Johnny and I looked at each other, confused. Being from the same school and all, we never considered that we would be separated. My heart rate accelerated as I watched Walsh and Johnny go to the end of one hallway. Back with me, Walsh pointed to the other end of the hall and said, "Your dorm is this way and I'll be your dorm senior for the first half of the year."

"These are the barracks," he said as he opened a door, using the school's name for the largest dorm. There were twelve beds and narrow closet doors along three walls. Several tall windows faced west. Walsh pointed out my bed and clothes closet, which included five drawers.

"You can unpack now, but you have to leave the dorm once you unpack. The rector will be welcoming everyone to the new school year at supper."

"Can I go down and see my friend?" I asked.

"We're not allowed to visit other dorms."

Walsh asked if I had any questions, but my thoughts were on Johnny—and me being in a dorm with eleven boys I didn't know. Somewhat in a daze, I began unpacking.

A bus pulled into the driveway and I went to the window to see scores of chattering boys piling out and retrieving their luggage. In time a number of boys, bantering excitedly, hauled their luggage into the barracks and claimed their beds. Two of them moved tentatively. They looked like I felt and, as I suspected, they, too, were new. I wanted to get out of the dorm as soon as possible to see if I could find Johnny, so I unpacked quickly. Relieved, I found him in the recreation room and we went outside for a walk before supper.

"I thought they'd put us in the same dorm," I said.

Johnny shrugged without a word. I never knew what he was feeling.

A loud bell went off signaling the call to the refectory, where all the day's meals were served. We followed others into the spacious dining area and copied the example of upper classmen by standing quietly facing the crucifix over the head table. Three-quarters of the student body, those in high school, were on one side of the refectory. On the other side were about twenty-five men, all wearing black cassocks. I thought they were priests but was to learn they were in their first two years of college. One had gray hair and two, we later learned, were Korean War veterans.

Suddenly and with no little drama, three priests in brown habits, all looking very serious, marched through the doors in single file. The leader, hands tucked under a triangular section of habit covering his chest, had an odd twist to his mouth and meticulously combed gray-white hair. He had the bearing of a general reviewing troops. Behind him was a quick-paced, balding priest with an intimidating scowl. The third, a curly crop of red-brownish hair topping his slender frame, was much taller than the other two.

His long, almost languid strides, which would become the target of much of our secret mimicry, easily kept pace with the more intense marchers before him. They took positions behind their chairs. The leader, with clear deference from the other two, scanned the assembly.

"Welcome to St. John's," he said. "I am Father Wilfrid, the rector." He nodded toward the balding priest standing to his right side. "This is Father Owen, the prefect, and to my left is Father Alban, the assistant prefect.

"Please be seated," he said, and the three priests pulled back their chairs, which was a further invitation for everyone to sit.

The upper half of the kitchen's Dutch door swung open and a small band of students assigned as servers lined up to receive trays of food for the tables. The silence was striking, consistent with the refectory decorum prescribed in a pamphlet mailed to our homes. It was entitled "Rule and Regulations of St. John's Atonement Seminary," which implied that "the Rule," as opposed to the many and more detailed regulations, represented the total order of things:

> *Silence must be kept in the refectory unless talking is permitted. All noise, such as that caused by moving dishes, shifting benches or walking too heavily, must be avoided. When talking is allowed, it shall be carried on in moderate tones. Loud laughter, shouting . . . are forbidden.*

As a hundred forks tapped away on thick plastic plates, a college student at a podium began reading a scriptural passage. After about a minute, Father Wilfrid interrupted him and said, "That name is pronounced Her MAH jo nees."

"Thank you, Father," the reader said before repeating the passage from Paul's second letter to Timothy:

"You know that everyone in Asia deserted me, including Phygelus and Hermogenes . . ."

After some five minutes, Father Wilfrid rang a bell and a gentle buzz of conversation arose across the tables. Unaccustomed as we were to such restrained exchanges, which were just above whispers, Johnny and I nevertheless complied and reservedly introduced ourselves to those sitting near us. The rector rang his bell again after dessert, restoring the silence.

"We want to welcome everyone who is new to St. John's. These are the first steps in training for the priesthood." I hung on to every word, but noticed that older students were not so engrossed—like they had heard this before.

"Father Owen and I, and the rest of the faculty are here to guide you on this journey. For some of you, it may take thirteen years until your ordination in the Franciscan Friars of the Atonement. Some of you will leave us in time with the knowledge that the priesthood was not your calling."

I glanced around the room, wondering which of the students would be leaving.

At 8:40 P.M. the entire student body filed into the chapel for the regularly scheduled night prayer. Except for the large main altar in the front, flanked by two smaller altars, the chapel was different from any church I had ever seen. Seminarians sat in three tiers of seats facing each other from opposite walls, separated by a large open space of shiny terrazzo flooring. Chapel was for being in communion with the divine, so even though one's gaze would naturally be toward seminarians across the floor, eye contact was avoided.

After night prayer, we filed from chapel in total silence to prepare for bed. In the dorm everyone avoided eye contact. I took my first stab at undressing "modestly," as the Rule prescribed, which meant following others' examples and putting on my bathrobe and, with the closet door shielding me, removing my pants and slipping into pajama bottoms.

Some in the barracks were already settled in their beds and had turned over to sleep. I stared at the ceiling and thought of home. My grandmother, I thought, was probably having tea and some Social Tea cookies about now. I could see her at the dining room table slurping from the saucer with little painted flowers around the edge.

I looked around the dormitory. It appeared only one other student, our dorm senior, Denny Walsh, was still awake, propped up on his pillow and reading, waiting to turn lights out at 9:30. I picked up the fifteen-page pamphlet detailing the seminary's Rule and Regulations and turned to the preface, which said the Rule helps the seminary "by preserving order" and also serves "to sanctify the students . . ."

I blinked several times to refocus on the script, but it was getting blurry.

John

All things change; nothing perishes.

—Ovid

The chartered bus that picked us up at the Elmira railroad station turned into a long, wide drive, lined with cathedral elm trees in Montour Falls. Perfectly centered ahead of us was what seemed the biggest brick building I had ever seen, with sweeping granite stairs that rose to large double doors of oak on the second floor.

In retrospect, perhaps one of my grammar schools was that large, but those schools were part of a background of similar buildings, while this stood alone on a slight rise, surrounded by fields and trees with a background of low-lying mountains. An observer

Period postcard (circa 1950) of St. John's Atonement Seminary, originally Cook Academy, built in 1862. Over the years it also has served as an orphanage and a private boarding school. The seminary operated from 1950 to 1969 before it was purchased by the State of New York in 1970 and renovated as the state Academy of Fire Science.

had no choice but to single this building out as the focus of the tableau. I found it wonderfully beautiful.

The day was perfect; the sky clear blue with bright sunshine, the temperature, warm. It was, in fact, so lovely that it seemed that God had painted it just for us. We retrieved our luggage from the undercarriage of the bus and were directed by the welcoming senior students and priests to climb impressive steps to the rotunda outside the chapel. We freshmen did not yet know that our arrivals and departures were the only times we could use that entrance.

The first-floor rotunda had beautiful terrazzo floors, a high ceiling, and ten-foot oak double doors to the chapel, where we would spend much of our time. As we filed into the rotunda, we were asked our names and given dormitory assignments. Dormitories ranged in size from four to twelve beds.

I was assigned to a six-bed dorm at the front right corner of the building on the second floor. The dorm had three windows. Two looked out across the lawn directly onto Route 14; the side window showed the slope up to the gym. The room was filled with light and the views were a panorama of wooded hills on the other side of the highway.

Our beds were old-style army metal cots. They were neatly made (thanks to the seniors), each with a single, white-cased pillow, each with a green woolen blanket, again of the World War II variety. One entire wall was taken up by oak wall lockers, with one assigned to each student.

Richard Basch, whom I had met on the train, was one of my dorm mates. I would learn that besides seeming very bright and very much older than he was, Basch was one of the most sarcastic, clever boys I ever knew. He was obsessed with cleanliness and believed most of us freshmen were wanting in that. Verbal exchanges with Basch left me checking myself for bleeding.

Another dorm mate was Joe Timson, a freshman with whom I would become good friends and with whom I would battle academically, consistently finishing two tenths of a point below him.

My dorm senior—the guy in charge of my dorm and my orientation—introduced himself as James Barry Lonergan. Barry was formal in demeanor and exquisitely neat. He never had a hair out of place, no matter the activity. He walked with a bounce in one foot. I don't mean a figurative bounce, but rather a sort of bounce when he stepped off on one foot. He attributed that to an Achilles injury sustained years earlier. I always thought it was put on for effect.

Barry took his dorm senior responsibilities very seriously. He assigned me a locker, told me to unpack and put everything away, explaining that everything had to be put away at all times that we were not in the dorm.

Barry told me that the next day, Sunday, we would be having a picnic/swim party at a nearby park. I was excited at the prospect of the picnic. It somehow seemed magical that our first full day should be given over to fun. I expressed my fear of being unable to get up at 5:40 in the morning. He explained that I had nothing to fear, for on Sunday we got to sleep until 6:30. I did not see that as a big improvement then, but over the years it would come to mean a lot.

Barry's orientation covered just about everything in St. John's rulebook. We were not allowed to have radios; there was no TV. There was a music room on the fourth floor, where we could listen to the hi-fi at free times. There was no rock and roll. There was classical music, folk music, show tunes, and some jazz. We could send letters, but the envelopes had to be left open. The priest in charge of discipline, the prefect, could read them if he saw fit. Incoming mail was opened and could be read. Any packages were checked; boxes of candy or cookies had to be opened in the day room and shared with everyone.

Barry told me that, upon awakening, we would go to the "jakes" (seminary lingo for the bathroom), attend to our bodily functions, brush our teeth, comb our hair and, if at that point in our puberty, shave. Then we would return to our dorms, flip our mattresses, make our beds, get dressed, and get to chapel for Mass—all within twenty-five minutes after rising.

The part about clothing our bodies required added explanation.

None of us was ever to be undressed in front of anyone else. Living together as we did, this meant going to unusual extremes. Every time we undressed or changed clothes, we were required to put our bathrobes over our clothes. Then we were to open our closets, stand facing the closet while shielding ourselves with the closet door as we stripped off pants and underwear, put on pajama bottoms or other pants, and only then remove the robe and swiftly change shirts.

When taking a shower, we were to step into the shower stall with robe on, close curtain, remove robe; chastely reach out blindly to hang robe on nearby hook. After showering, reverse the procedure.

In four years of living together, I would see one other boy naked, and that was to happen on that very first day.

Barry also told me that we could wear no bright colors. We were not there to be peacocks. Calling attention to oneself was hubris and detrimental to the functioning of the Order. For the same reason, he said, we were not to wear leather soles or heels on our shoes. These would make a lot of noise on the terrazzo floors, thus causing others' attention to be drawn to us. We were also to walk as closely as practical to the walls in the hallways and when mounting or descending stairs. Walking in the middle called attention to oneself and bespoke a vanity that was discouraged. We were not to converse in hallways on the dormitory floors, although we could speak in the dorms.

In the free time after dinner I encountered a naked guy walking down the hallway to the shower with a towel slung over his shoulder. Someone caught him at the shower door and clarified things for him. Clearly he did not have a dorm senior of the James Barry Lonergan variety.

I then heard the approach of what turned out to be another freshman. Clearly someone had been deficient in filling him in, because he was wearing leather heels. In addition to the loud noise he made, he was dressed in a pair of the brightest blue pants imaginable.

Armed with my abundant knowledge of the rules, I told him that both his shoes and pants were in violation of the rules. He apologized and headed off to his dorm. I saw him later that evening and he struck up a brief conversation with me, indicating that he found the place intimidating.

The next morning at Mass, I saw him again, for the last time. Unlike the rest of us, he was dressed in a suit and was seated in the back of the chapel, in the area reserved for those not of the Order. I asked an older boy why he was back there and he told me that the boy was leaving.

Leaving! After one day this boy was going home? I asked the older boy why, and he responded that he had heard that the boy was homesick.

I could not believe that someone would leave here to go home.

Mike

We entered a dorm that Denny Walsh announced to me with a smile as "your dorm—shared with eleven other boys, of course." I liked Denny. He was the one who found me hiding behind a seat on the bus. He spoke in a friendly, confident voice that finally convinced me I should get off and at least give St John's a try. "It really isn't a bad life," he said. "You'll find people here who care about you. The priests here aren't just teachers and spiritual guides; for some of us they're stand-in fathers. And it's easy to make friends here."

Denny was a high school senior who had been at St. John's for three years. He would be my dorm master. He stayed with me, my guide and protector, as I walked the gauntlet of boys and friars on the stairway. He took charge of introducing me to them, and as if to prove his comment that it was easy to make friends here, he asked a couple of boys to carry my suitcases up to the dorm and they easily agreed. I glanced around the room.

My dorm? I've been drafted.

The bunks were aligned side by side, twelve in a row. Across from them were twelve closet spaces standing at attention, doors open as if saluting the bunks. Denny led me to a bunk. The boys put my suitcases at the foot of the bed, and Denny told me I'd have time to meet my dorm mates and get settled in later, but now we had to get downstairs for dinner in the refectory and be welcomed by the rector. My bunk was by a window. Outside I could see the highway I'd traveled to get here, the same one that would bring me back home if I failed to adjust to my new life here. *Not if. When.*

Once inside the dining area, everyone was standing in silence as the doors behind us swung open and three priests dressed in brown robes with ropes around their middles entered. They were smiling, but they looked serious—imposing. My fists began to tighten again; my chest, too. I felt sweat start to run down my left

Photo credit: Franciscan Friars of the Atonement, Graymoor Archives

Dorms at the seminary ranged in sizes accommodating four to twelve students. Storage space allocated to each student provided a narrow closet to hang clothing and store shoes; an accompanying section had three shelves and five drawers.

side the way it does when I'm expecting the worst. Beyond some welcoming remarks, I didn't hear much after that. I looked around the refectory while the voice of the rector, Father Wilfrid Brennan, droned on. Tables lined up cafeteria style, three chairs on each side. The rector and the other two priests sat at a slightly raised dais that dominated the refectory. I was startled by the sound of banging trays coming from the kitchen and snapped back to attention.

What am I doing here? What have I done?

And then, a familiar smell—Toll House cookies. I felt myself begin to relax.

That night as I lay awake in bed, I was overwhelmed by a rush of doubts: *Do I really have what it will take to become a priest? Isn't this just another attempt to escape from the frustrations at home?*

And there was a more immediate uncertainty: *Do I have the ability to master the course of studies I will be taking here?*

My father's words came back to me—this time with the sting of truth. "Well, you should have studied harder for that entrance exam for Keith Academy instead of spending your time getting into trouble."

Father Simeon had said in the conference he had with me, my father, and Marie: "If a young man doesn't work hard and apply himself to his studies, he will be asked to leave St. John's. You understand that, Michael, don't you?" I nodded even though I wasn't sure I knew how to study hard. I'd read in the literature he'd given me that, as a freshman, I would be taking classes in English, math, history, general science. Math in particular worried me. I hated it, with its strict rules you had to follow to be good at it. Then there was the Latin. I hadn't been able to master even a tiny bit of it when I tried to become an altar boy.

And speech? The only time I'd come close to giving "a speech" was in eighth grade when I stood up to tell a joke during a classroom Christmas party. That experience made the thought of giving a speech as appealing as dinner with lima beans. Facing my classmates, I shifted from one foot to the other, impatient for Sister Catherine to give me the signal to begin. Finally, it came just before I was about to ask if I could go back to my desk and tell my joke some other time.

"What is the difference between a baby and a soldier?" I asked, chomping on my lower lip to choke back my nervousness and inclination to laugh at my joke even before I'd finished it.

"A soldier's a lot older," one of the girls in the class answered.

"No," I replied. "A soldier loads his gun and a baby loads his pants."

No one laughed but me. Everyone turned to look at Sister Catherine as I hurried to my desk.

I had made it through supper and the evening with Denny's support. He seemed to me everything that I was not, but wanted to be: calm, confident, and as I would learn, studious and devoted to a life of prayer. He was handsome and witty, too, qualities that I much admired.

I listened to the sounds of sleep around me and of crickets drifting up through the window above my head. Somewhere in the distance a night bird sang what I tried to imagine was a lullaby. But it couldn't lull me to sleep. The doubts that plagued me refused to let me rest. I reached under my pillow and pulled out the only photo I had of my mother. I'd put it there before going to bed, being careful to make sure other boys didn't see. I pressed the picture to my chest.

Please Mom, ask God to not let me fail at this.

Chapter Six

A New Reality

Mike

The next morning I was startled awake by a loud knock on the door and someone shouting something in Latin. It was still dark, but boys started to roll out of their bunks and head for the "jakes" with their toiletries. I followed, unsure of myself. Later, dressed in black cassocks and sitting in choir stalls, we attended Mass. I found the celebrant—offering prayers in Latin and boys responding in Latin—strangely comforting.

At breakfast, after the scripture had been read and Father Wilfrid had rung the Communion bell, freeing us to talk, lively chatter arose across the refectory. The atmosphere was very light, no doubt brought on by the day's scheduled picnic at Havana Glen. I sat mostly in silence.

Heading upstairs to the dorms to change out of my cassock into casual clothes, I was troubled by my silence and feelings of insecurity. While lost in these thoughts, a muscular boy in jeans and a T-shirt was coming down the middle of the staircase rather than to one side as instructed by the seminary rule book. He looked supremely confident, arrogant even. My mind flashed back to Richard Killick, a bully I'd challenged in the schoolyard in the eighth grade. Killick and his two buddies used to prowl the schoolyard pushing other boys around when the nuns weren't there or weren't looking. One day he pushed my friend Bobby Cleary; I pushed him back. Killick was a boxer. His picture appeared regularly in the *Lowell Sun* when the Golden Gloves Tournament was being held. He had beaten me senseless that day in front of a whole group of other kids. Now, as I looked up at the boy approaching me, I thought, *There he is, another Killick.* "Hey Samson," I said, "Who do you think you are? You gonna hog the whole stairway?" I felt the adrenaline rising. My hands folded into fists. I was ready. *Let's do it.*

The seminary chapel was integral in the seminarians' lives during six years at St. John's. Students attended Mass and night prayers there every day and mid-day spiritual readings were scheduled five days a week. In the picture above, seminarians listen to a spiritual reading and reply with a responsorial prayer.

"Oh, I'm sorry," the boy replied, moving aside.

I passed by and walked to my dorm in disbelief. What had just happened? I had challenged one of the biggest, and I was sure, strongest boys in the school, and he had apologized and moved aside to let me pass. I didn't know it at the time but I had just introduced myself to John Tuohey, a classmate who would become a lifelong friend.

Ollie

Roused from a deep sleep at 6:30 A.M. by a student pounding on doors in the hallway, I saw others in the dorm scrambling into bathrobes, grabbing towels and toiletry bags, and rushing to the door. I arose and stood alongside my bed in a stupor. By the time I got to the bathroom, called the "jakes," all the sinks were taken and about fifteen other students were waiting their turn. When I returned to the dorm, others, already in their cassocks, were heading to the chapel. I got there with two other stragglers about twenty-five minutes from the time we were awakened. Father Owen and two altar servers were beginning the celebration of Mass:

"Introibo ad altare Dei" (I go to the altar of God), Father Owen intoned.

After Mass, there was a festive atmosphere fueled by anticipation of the annual picnic as students filed into the refectory. I looked hungrily at the pancakes, eggs, and bacon being passed down the table, the kind of morning feast we freshmen would come to appreciate as a Sunday tradition.

Though temperatures were cool and the sky overcast that day, the conditions could not detract from the excitement in the air or the beauty of the picnic site, Havana Glen, one of numerous spectacular sandstone and limestone gorges in the Finger Lakes. It had towering cliffs that had been carved for millennia by rushing, spring-fed waters that continued their geologic processing unabated.

Johnny and I hiked upstream, struck dumb by nature's splendor all around us. We came around a corner and there, right before us, was a wide sheet of water coming off a smoothened limestone table between two high walls, plunging sublimely in a narrow ribbon some twenty-five feet into a deep pool. The cool wind coming off the falls and the mist in my face were coupled with the fragrance of pine. We got close to where the falls pounded into the water below. I stood mesmerized by frothing green reflecting the dense vegetation and moss-covered rocks. It was the first waterfall I had ever seen. This, I thought, is heaven.

Some of us were anxious to go swimming. "I think it's too cold, boys," Father Owen said.

Anxious to demonstrate what a good swimmer I was and hoping to dive off one of the cliffs, I was with about four other students who pressed the case. "C'mon, Father. We're okay."

Our pleadings, coupled with those from some older students who, it became apparent, had no intention of swimming themselves, made him relent.

I jumped off a rock ledge into a state of shock from the frigid spring-fed waters. There was a special impact in my groin, where I felt I'd been punched and while swimming underwater my mind screamed, "Holy crap!" Gasping, I hauled myself from the swimming hole. As I reached, quaking, for my towel, several upper classmen were standing atop a small bluff over the swimming hole, laughing. Determined to squelch my humiliation and to demon-

Photo credit: Gerry Whitfield

Shequaga Falls at the foot of Main Street in Montour Falls regularly froze in the harsh Finger Lakes' winters, tumbled in full force throughout the spring and maintained lighter, but steady flows in summer and fall.

strate that their enjoyment at my expense was misplaced, I turned back to the water and, with as much nonchalance as I could muster, dove back in.

That second night at St. John's I was tired before night prayers and, once again, was asleep before lights were out.

John

On my first full day at the seminary, after discovering that I would have no trouble waking up and that staying with the herd got me in and out of the jakes on schedule and to Mass at the ordained time, I got to experience my first seminary picnic. I would attend four of these, and I thoroughly enjoyed them all. This first one, however, was especially vivid.

Before leaving for the walk to Havana Glen, the picnic site, there was an unsettling encounter with another student. I was walking downstairs from the second floor. Despite my self-appointment as arbiter of the rules, I was walking in the middle of the stairwell and coming up was a little kid who appeared to be about eight years old. With surprising boldness, he called me "Samson" and asked if I was going to take the whole stairway. I assumed that, despite his waifish appearance, he must be a sophomore, and I apologized and moved over as he brusquely shoved by me.

In the ensuing days, having discovered that he was also a freshman, I was embarrassed at having been cowed by him. I decided then that I did not like him, not realizing what an acquired taste he was.

At Havana Glen, there was a pool, several feet deep, even deeper at the base of the waterfall. I had never seen a waterfall, other than in movies. It was perhaps twelve feet high. I thought it was majestic and perfect.

The water was icy cold and as clear as I could have hoped. I stayed in the water for as long as I could, but at some point I developed a cramp in my calf and began flailing. An upper classman pulled me out telling me that I cramped up because I had been eating. I filed that piece of information away in my "taken-as-universal-truth, but-ultimately-bullshit box." God knows how many years I thought that was true.

Jerry Waters asked if I would like to accompany him and some others on a hike. We asked Father Owen if we might follow the water back some distance into the gorge. He said okay, and we were off on my first woodland adventure. We climbed the falls and followed the stream. It was amazing. In places there were more pools, more waterfalls. The stream became wider, then narrower, deeper, then shallower to a minimal trickle; then over a falls to another big pool, and on and on.

Finally we arrived at the widest, deepest pool that we had encountered. We would need to cross to the other side in order to continue. That place was so completely still, the only sound the water. It appeared untouched. I had the thought that we might be the first people to have ever come here. But that thought evaporated when Jerry, who was leading the way, holding his sneakers above the water, wading chest deep across this pool, screamed in pain. He had stepped on a broken beer bottle, unseen on the rocky bottom, and was bleeding like crazy. We helped him out of the water, tied someone's T-shirt around his foot, then started to make our way back.

We took turns supporting Jerry over the uneven terrain, one supporting one shoulder, another, the other. With Jerry, about the tallest person in the school, the challenge intensified. We had to scramble away from the stream in some spots, and then back to the water where the going was easier.

From my point of view, this adventure had been as full as I might have dreamed. I had had a sweet illusion of virgin exploration and had had it destroyed by a broken beer bottle. I had walked over more varied terrain than I'd ever encountered; had walked farther than I had in years, if not ever. I had kept up with everyone, and I was not wheezing or quitting. Nothing more needed to be added to make it more interesting.

That's when one of the other boys stepped on a bees' nest. I didn't know that bees nested on the ground. In cartoons they are always hanging from trees. These lived on the ground, however, and they did not tolerate being stepped on. We suddenly were navigating a steep, slippery slope, while carrying a guy and being attacked by bees, leading to much screaming, swearing, sliding, and swatting.

Jerry was taken for stitches and recovered. The next day classes would begin, and we neophytes would see the seminary when it was not all about fun.

5:40 arise
6:00 chapel for Mass
6:45 breakfast
7:45 study
8:15–9:00 first class
9:05–9:50 second class
9:50–10:10 recess
10:10–10:55 third class
11:00–11:45 fourth class
11:55–12:10 spiritual reading
12:15 dinner
1:25–2:10 fifth class
2:15–3:00 sixth class
3:20–4:30 sports
5:00–6:10 study period
6:15 supper

6:45–7:25 free period
7:30–8:40 study period
8:45 night prayers
9:30 lights out

John

"We don't want boys who like boys."

Father Owen Murphy

As freshmen, we were required to take Latin, English, history, algebra, religion, and elocution. Religion was Catholicism, taught in far more depth than we had experienced in grammar school. Although we would not realize it, this was taught with an eye to apologetics—arguments designed to bolster the primacy of the Catholic Church and arm us with appropriate responses to beliefs of heretics and other nonbelievers. The final course, elocution, was a cornerstone of the Franciscan Friars, a preaching order. From day one, we would be shaped into men who were comfortable and able to get up in front of a crowd of people, have an impact on their minds, and move their spirits. Success was, of course, quite variable.

At the end of each year, we would be expected to not only have achieved good grades within the school, but to have taken the New York State Regents exams and The Catholic University of America exams in the disciplines chosen for that year. If, at the end of four years, we had passed all of our internal courses, all the Regents Exams, all the CU exams, we would be given three graduation certificates, one from each entity. That was the goal before us.

The seminary did not encourage mediocrity. It was possible to achieve a passing grade in a course and still be required to take it again the following year. We had, in fact, two sophomores in our algebra class who had passed the preceding year, but not with the grades required. Then there were those who passed, but did badly in several studies. They were dropped, often to great disappointment. Some boys quickly found that they could not keep up academically and chose to leave.

In obedience, as in academics, there was minimal tolerance for those who did not fit. There was no three-strike rule, no accepting lame excuses. Small infractions yielded cleaning duties. Big infractions, like being caught smoking a second time or leaving the grounds without permission, merited a bus ticket home.

Father Owen, an omnipresent entity in our lives, held meetings with the freshmen every week. Right off the bat, he told us, "You want to be here more than we want you to be here. This is not a prison. The doors are not locked. If you want out, come and tell me, and you will be out of here the next morning." He could not have been more right. I wanted to be there more than he could have dreamed. I was never going to be in danger of failing, never anywhere close. They were not going to opt me out.

Father Owen took us all completely by surprise in one of these meetings.

"How many of you like girls?"

We all sat there stealing looks at one another. We sensed a trap. If we a acknowledged liking girls, we might be thrown out. Not a hand was raised.

Well there seems to be a problem here. We don't want priests who don't like girls."

What? We're supposed to like girls? Every boy raised a hand.

"That's more like it. Every one of us is designed to like someone. We don't want boys who like boys. Our vow of chastity has value because we are giving up something that we really want, not something we don't want. That would be no sacrifice. This is a life against the dictates of nature. It starts out difficult and it stays that way."

So, it was okay to be interested in girls. What a relief.

Another time he said something that seemed to look into my mind.

"You all probably think that we go overboard in our constant cleaning, putting clothes away. Many of you never used a linen napkin before; never saw a napkin ring. It all seems silly to you. Let me point out that we are men who live without women. Men who live without women quickly degenerate into living like pigs, unless they follow strict schedules."

So he was telling us that the priests realized what a civilizing effect women have on us. He was acknowledging the respect in which they held women. It was a good thing for us to hear. Women were not the enemy. The enemy was the devil.

Photo credit: Franciscan Friars of the Atonement, Graymoor Archives

Father Owen Murphy—disciplinarian, mentor, and role model. Some seminarians sought ways to break the rules and not get caught by him, most times unsuccessfully.

There were thirty-one freshmen. We were the largest class. This was always so. Each year more would fail, or opt out, or be dropped for bad behavior or marginal grades. Each year we might pick up one or two newbies, but the overall number always decreased.

From the first day I began making the acquaintance of my classmates, most of whom would leave before I learned much about them. A few, however, would be around long enough to make sufficient impact on me—good or bad—to always be remembered.

Joe Timson, my competitor for top grades, was a pleasant, quiet kid with a good sense of humor. We hung around together quite a bit. I was stunned when he failed to return for sophomore year.

There was Mike Connolly, a tough street kid from Lowell. His size belied his fierceness.

Fred Delcimento was like a full-grown man at fourteen. He weighed about 260 pounds and was six feet tall. He could produce on demand farts lasting up to twenty seconds, which was impressive and disturbing.

Kevin Kristoff was the smallest kid in the class and was uncannily irritating, especially to Delcimento, who would scoop him up like a bear and threaten to pin him down and fart on his head. There came the day that Kristoff stopped annoying Delcimento. Some said they had witnessed the threat carried out.

There was Tom Dever, a very intense guy, full of energy, very bright, interested in everything. He immediately began to learn to type (the only one of us to do so) and take organ lessons.

Mike Hunter was an oddity. He was very big. He was a good athlete, a good student. One day he and I would be good friends, but, for the most part, Mike had no friends. He was too intimidating. He was very tough and loved to fight. He needed to establish the pecking order right off the bat.

Johnny Barbera and Richie Olive need to be described as a unit, because, as freshmen, no one ever thought or spoke about one without the other. They had been best friends since grade school in the Bronx, came to St. John's together, and were inseparable. Barbera was very handsome, almost six feet tall, husky, confident, sarcastic. He had black hair in the duck's ass style made popular by Elvis. Like Fred, he was a very talented farter. Since I sat behind him, I was frequently the first to suffer.

Richie was much smaller than Johnny, but he was the only person to whom Johnny was at all deferential. He emanated an air of confidence and generated a force field that told people to stay away. Together they were crazy. They chased each other around, threw things at each other—occasionally desks. They jumped out windows, tore their clothing. They were as close to wild as was possible in that place. No one was ever invited into that dyad; the doors were quite clearly shut. I, for one, wanted to be invited in. It seemed to me that they were free and fearless, and I would have liked some of that.

Other names and faces have faded over the years. How little I actually knew these people with whom I lived, studied, played sports.

Mike

When classes began the day following the picnic, I was pleasantly surprised by the quirky personalities of some of our teachers. Most of the nuns in grammar school, with the exception of a couple who were noted for their abusive discipline, had been bland and boring.

Father DeSales Standerwick, our English teacher, was a tall, skinny figure whose buck teeth and long neck brought to mind Walt Disney's Goofy in a Franciscan habit. He had, I would soon discover, a passion for literature, grammar, and especially vocabulary that would infect me and many of us before the year was over.

Father Edmund Delaney, our history teacher, would share his own particular, often humorous, version of historical events. His lesson on the 1898 Battle of Manila Bay ended with the tongue-in-cheek comment that practically the entire Spanish navy was destroyed and "perhaps one American sailor was wounded by a flying Coke bottle."

Father Alphonsus Hoban was a relentless pacer, back and forth, back and forth in the rear of the classroom whenever he was our study hall monitor. The rumor was that he had been chaplain for the crew of the *Enola Gay,* the B29 that dropped the atomic bomb on Hiroshima, and that he had never recovered from seeing the images of the death and destruction.

Photo credit: Gerry Whitfield

First-year classes were generally larger, with class populations numbering more than twenty students. Classes gradually diminished over the years as students chose to leave or were not invited back. By senior year, they were as small as five students. White shirts and black ties were mandatory dress for all classes.

As quirky and entertaining as they were, none of those teachers had quite the mystique for us as Father Owen, whose responsibility was to ensure that the school's disciplinary code was obeyed and to dole out consequences to those who violated it. He had the uncanny ability to materialize out of nowhere and catch a seminarian in any misdemeanor. Some claimed he could detect misbehavior even as it was forming in the mind of the transgressor.

Stories were told of a time when the sacristy was raided by boys late at night in quest of some unconsecrated wine for a dorm party, and how Father Owen emerged from the darkness and apprehended the would-be thieves. Students had also raided the kitchen freezer at midnight for some cake and ice cream, only to be foiled by the prefect as they emerged with armfuls of booty. He'd copy their names into his little black book and tell them he'd see them in his office in the morning.

Despite the school's tight regimentation, what surprised me most about this new life was how easily I settled into it. By the end of the second week I was feeling that I belonged here. I didn't have any real friends yet, but I hadn't made any effort to welcome friendship. I had heard boys talking about how one day a classmate might be sitting in class or chapel next to you and the next morning you might see him sitting in street clothes in the back of the chapel with his suitcase, preparing to leave.

Nothing is permanent. Best to keep from getting too close to anyone.

Still, I hadn't made any enemies, either. Even after my encounter with John Tuohey, he didn't appear upset with me. And Denny Walsh continued to look after me as if I was his younger brother.

The routine of early morning Mass, then breakfast, followed by classes, after-school sports, study hall, supper, a half hour for evening recreation, study hall again, nighttime chapel and then lights out was oddly comforting—but at the same time puzzling. Why didn't I miss the chaos of the city streets the way I had when I'd gone to summer camp?

Most challenging of all was my growing anxiety about getting passing grades. I'd heard boys talking about their fear of flunking out, and although I never joined that conversation, flunking out was a real concern of mine. Where would I go if I did? What would I do if I had to leave? The image of me sitting in street clothes at the back of the chapel with my suitcase tormented me.

But studying was easier here than it had been in grammar school. We had organized study periods, proctored by priests who monitored them while they read their prayers. There were no distractions; everyone was studying at the same time. Even so, I was worried. I had never applied myself to studying in grammar school. And study skills? Although I'd heard teachers mention them, I had no idea what they were talking about. How would I ever pass algebra or geometry, or even Latin? I began to spend much of my free time studying. Fear was a great motivator.

Ollie

Day three, beginning at 5:40 A.M., the first day for class and a prelude of every weekday routine at St. John's, was a cold-turkey experience into responsibilities previously unimaginable. There was no adult hounding or pleading for me to get out of bed. There was no one to make my bed or pick up my clothes. My dorm senior gave me a crash course in folding my sheets into hospital corners and demonstrated the precise way one towel and one wash cloth were to be hung neatly over my bed's bottom railing. The brief lesson, coupled with the sight of every other bed in the barracks uniformly arrayed, was all that was necessary for my instant compliance.

"You put your dirty clothes in your laundry bag and keep it in your closet," Walsh said. "On Saturday mornings we strip beds of the sheets and take the sheets and all the laundry to the basement. But not socks. You wash them every day or, at least, every other day. Any questions?"

The clock was relentless as the day's schedule ticked from 5:40 A.M. to lights out nearly sixteen hours later. On Friday there were stations of the cross, a half hour for reflecting on Christ's crucifixion, and on the first Fridays of every month, known as "days of recollection," silent meditation, and reflection from 1:45 P.M. until supper at 6:10 P.M. There were free times on Wednesdays and Saturdays from 1:00 to 6:00 P.M., and on Sundays after lunch.

Daydreaming was a rare luxury; punctuality, paramount. If you arrived late for chapel or any meals, you had to kneel in the entranceway and wait for a signal to proceed to your seat. Being on time was considerably easier than the humiliation of kneeling in plain view of more than 100 high school and college students.

There was forty minutes for relaxation after supper. Lying down was not an option. We were barred from our dormitories much of the time. If a student wanted solitude, he could walk around the building or go to the chapel or the library. Many played table tennis, shot pool, or strolled in pairs or groups.

On Saturday mornings students cleaned virtually every corner of the building or worked on the grounds. I was happy to be assigned to tasks outdoors, where, except for the winter months, the air was rich with the smell of fresh-cut grass. In the fall we also cleaned up endless piles of leaves from the towering elms whose limbs stretched over the main driveway.

My favorite parts of the week were the free times on Wednesday, Saturday, and Sunday afternoons. Depending on the season and the weather, these periods meant basketball, touch football, or softball.

Photo credit: Gerry Whitfield

Saturday morning until lunch was time for the entire student body to do chores, including housekeeping in the dorms, bathrooms, classrooms and hallways, grounds keeping, and sorting clothes in the laundry.

Some other students, despite thirty-three scheduled hours each week for classes and study periods, used their free time for more study, which I found mystifying.

I quickly and enthusiastically acclimated myself to this tightly regimented lifestyle.

There was a clearly defined social order, with freshmen on the lowest rung. Compared to us, the older ones were so much more mature, self-assured. The collegians were in a separate universe beyond my imagination. They were adult men much closer to ordination and involved in such esoteric studies as philosophy, Greek, German, and theology. Once finished with their second year of college at St. John's, they would advance to the novitiate at Saranac Lake, New York, where they would receive their brown habits, delve more deeply into theological studies, and take first vows of poverty, rejecting material ownership; chastity, disavowal of sexual pleasure; and obedience to the Franciscan Friars of the Atonement. College dorms and classrooms were in separate parts of the building, consistent with the Rule that "high school and college students are to keep to their own group." The only times we shared space were meals and at chapel. Collegians also were entitled to smoke breaks, whereas high school students caught smoking faced expulsion.

The brothers were another stratum of the seminary's social order. Like the priests they took vows of poverty, chastity, and obedience to the Franciscan order, but they were not ordained, so could not say Mass. Their jobs included cooking and doing the laundry for the student body and faculty.

The teaching faculty was made up of eleven priests, including the rector and the prefect.

The pecking order was further defined by dress.

Priests and brothers wore brown habits. Students' clothes and appearance were prescribed by the Rule:

> ***Excessive care for one's external appearance is to be avoided, but the moderate concern befitting a Christian gentleman shall be cultivated . . . College students wear cassocks as their normal seminary attire and are not to take them off unless recreation or work demand it. High school students wear cassocks on Sundays, at daily Mass, and at the more solemn religious functions. When not at outside recreation or work, high school students are to wear a clean (white) shirt and black tie. Clothes of very bright colors and those that attract attention are not to be worn.***

Ultimate power rested in the rector, Father Wilfrid, and his next-in-command, the prefect, Father Owen. Each stressed at various times that we were at St. John's by our own choice. There was no mollycoddling here. From the time Father Wilfrid said that not everyone would make it to ordination, there were many signals that no one was forced to stay—like Father Owen periodically reminding us about the open door. It sounded harsh and threatening. But these guys were serious about personal responsibility.

It was curious arriving at the chapel in the morning for Mass to find a student sitting in the entranceway in traveling clothes, his suitcase on the floor alongside him. Unless there was a death in the family and he was going to the funeral, you had no idea why he was leaving. One day he was part of the student body and the next morning he was an outsider, sitting alone like an injured football player at the end of the bench. The former student would pick up his luggage about ten minutes into the Mass and slip quietly out the door for a 6:30 A.M. bus to Elmira, and from there the Erie-Lackawanna train ride home.

The message of personal choice was made pointedly even before we arrived. One of the recruiting pamphlets listed a typical day at St. John's beginning at 5:40 A.M., and said, "Look it over. If it scares you, then you're not the type we want." The schedule did not scare me, but I had only the vaguest idea of what it would take to become a priest. I knew this: I did not want to be asked to leave.

◆ ◆ ◆

One section in the seminary's fifteen-page Rule encouraged students to be "friendly, cheerful, and neighborly to all" and warned against "picking anyone as a constant companion to the exclusion of others." It sounded threatening to my friendship with Johnny Barbera. Father Owen eventually cautioned me about this. As we were filing into the chapel one evening, he summoned me: "Olive, I know that you and Barbera are friends," he said. "But I want to see you cultivating other friendships here."

"Yes, Father."

"When you're out walking around the building during free time, invite some other classmates to join you or join other groups."

"Yes, Father."

"Any questions?"

"No, Father."

With the reputation he had for knowing what every student was doing, I wondered if Father Owen's warning was prompted by some of the juvenile things Johnny and I did. One was retreating to our hideout, hollowed-out bushes in a windbreak at the southern edge of the seminary's property line. We would just sit there reveling in secrecy and obscurity, confident and secure, observing the seminary and the grounds while other students went about, not knowing they were being watched. Another was placing huge logs across some old, abandoned farm machines and imagining them, with their huge wheels, to be Civil War cannons, the "barrels" pointed over a valley below frustrating the advances of Confederate troops. While we didn't go so far as to feign the sound of cannonade, we took special delight in our created imagery.

But I took Father Owen's warning seriously. It encouraged me to venture beyond my dependence on Johnny.

John

"I began adjusting to my new surroundings almost immediately." I loved the orderliness and exotic nature of marching to meals from chapel, all the while saying the rosary in Latin. Each week one boy was assigned to call out the first half of the *Our Father,* followed by ten *Hail Marys* and a *Glory Be* as we hauled our endless appetites to the refectory (as we called the dining hall). The rest of us replied with the second half, the sounds of thousand-year-old prayers in a dead tongue echoing with our footsteps in the halls.

I loved all our courses, except elocution. I was not eager to talk in front of the group. We had no choice, though, and it became easier as we all grew to know each other.

My favorite subject was English and my favorite teacher, Father DeSales, who taught it. He also made me crazy. I had been a stellar English student, getting top grades in the grammar school Regents exams. On my final English Regents exam, my score was 99.5. The nun had subtracted a half point for my handwriting. I never anticipated anything but A's in English.

Father DeSales told me that my writing was very good. He often read my papers aloud to the class. When he handed them back to me, though, they had scores of eighty-eight or eighty-nine, B's. Basch told me that Father DeSales was the strictest grader in the school, but that did nothing to placate me.

Still, he was a great teacher. He was about six-two, weighed about one-thirty, had buck teeth and thick, horn-rimmed glasses. He was a gold mine of information, as well as fascinating mannerisms. Initially, before we caught onto his ways and wishes, some unwary student would find Father DeSales holding four fingers in the student's face, staring him intently in the eyes. The culprit would be totally frazzled. Father DeSales would look around at all of us until someone realized that the one under the microscope was sitting back on two legs of the chair, and the helpful student would shout, "Sit on four legs." We would all laugh, even the culprit. In short order, everyone knew what was meant by four fingers, which, eventually, were no longer required.

He would stroll the aisles, abruptly ordering, "To the board, to the board, to the board," selecting the chosen with each exclamation to diagram sentences, write definitions, spell words, whatever was on the agenda. If you gave a monumentally dumb answer, he threw a piece of chalk at you underhanded. The guy was a born entertainer. He never raised his voice. He never belittled anyone. If you disagreed with him about a meaning or use of a word, he would say, "Someone, get me Merriam." Now, really, he knew he was right; he was never known to be wrong. Nevertheless, he always showed you the courtesy of looking in the Merriam Webster dictionary. Only then did he move on.

It was Father DeSales who held up Sir Walter Raleigh as a model to us. The epitome of the Elizabethan man: Raleigh was courtier, essayist, poet, swordsman, explorer; a man in full. We could never consider ourselves really cultured, he said, until we had written poetry, learned a foreign language, visited a foreign country, and learned to play a musical instrument.

He also told us that you have not truly lived until you have smoked corn silk and chewed road tar; that you have never lived until you have received rejection slips from a really good magazine.

He was deeply Franciscan, deeply Catholic, but there was an impish little boy in there. For all his wit and erudition, he could not do simple math. When he added numbers—a rare enough event in English—he never got the right sum. Once he handed me back one of my tests. At the top he had written 100 – 2= 88. After class I brought it to him, pointing out that 100 – 2= 98. He told me that the ability to add does not correlate well with intelligence. I said I knew that, but it did correlate well with my grade. He laughed.

He told me once that the problem with my writing was that I believed that each word from my pen was a piece of genius that deserved no editing. For the life of me, I could not understand his point.

I also loved Latin, taught by Father Romanus Dunne. For the first two weeks of class, he actually did almost no Latin. Instead, he focused almost entirely on English parts of speech and sentence structure. I had considered myself an excellent English student, but he made English make sense. He stressed that we would never grasp Latin if we did not fully understand our own language. When we finally dove into Latin it came to me easily and it was consistently my best subject for four years. I also felt that I had dramatically improved my English.

I enjoyed algebra, too. It was so logical that the main problem I had was attending to it as often as I should. It was, in that sense, too easy.

History was a pleasure, due mostly to the instructor, Father Edmond. He injected humor into history with gently subversive asides and comparisons, forcing us to think in nonprescribed ways about American interventions in far-away places. He pointed out that we were the recipients of Native American largesse, while doling out genocide; that we manufactured the very one-sided Spanish-American War, not to free the Filipinos, Puerto Ricans, and Cubans, but to replace the effete Spanish empire with our own.

He suggested that textbooks failed to accurately reflect the true reaction of these newly "emancipated" American colonies. He was the first person to suggest that the reality of colonialism is not dependent on the use of that word. He tried to give us some perspective. Once he said to us—all Catholic, all Caucasian, mostly from Northeast cities—"It's easy for you little Irish Catholic boys to look down on slaves, but let me ask you a question. When the bales of cotton were brought to the river, to be placed on barges, the bales were slid down steep ramps. They were very heavy, and they picked up a lot of speed. Unimpeded, they might have gone over the other side of the boats. Bales of cotton were worth a lot of money, so the owners had no intention of letting that happen. So they had people catch these fast, heavy bales. That was very dangerous, sometimes crippling or killing the catchers. Who did they have catch the bales?"

"Slaves," answered several of us, setting the trap.

"No. Bales of cotton were valuable, but so were slaves. The owners used Irish day laborers. They had very little value." Trap sprung, leaving a lot of little Irish heads saying, "What?"

Another time, someone asked him if it was a mortal sin to let the host touch one's teeth at Communion.

"Where did you hear that?" Father Edmond asked. The boy replied the nuns taught that in grammar school. Father Edmond tipped his head back and chewed on that for a few seconds, apparently mulling over a tactful answer.

"Well," he finally drawled, "nuns are wonderful people. When asked, they will answer almost anything. Unfortunately, they are often wrong. Fundamentally, the host is a piece of dried toast. You have to swallow it. Whatever you have to do to get it down is fine."

We were stunned. He had just told us that we could chew the host. Until then, unheard of. He had just said that nuns were often wrong. I personally had had my mouth washed with soap by my grandmother because nuns were never wrong. Next he'd be telling us that men would walk on the moon. Well, perhaps nothing that ridiculous.

As Father DeSales threw chalk for really stupid replies, Father Edmond awarded "Clyde Awards." He never explained the derivation of the award, but one never wished to be a recipient. One also enjoyed the hell out of someone else getting one. Fred Delcimento got one for telling us that the author of *The Caine Mutiny* was "the same guy who wrote *The Diary of Anne Frank*."

The religion course was, well . . . religion. There were no new revelations. We had the ONE TRUE RELIGION. There had been no Protestant Reformation; there had been a Protestant Revolution, the progenitor of all the heretical sects that surrounded us. These sects were filled with poor souls, deprived of the light of truth, to which only true Catholics were exposed. It was sad, but most of them would go to hell. Thank God that there were missionary orders, such as ours, that were out laboring in the field, trying to bring souls into the fold in time to save them from the devil.

In elocution class, I learned that I did not pronounce my R's. I also received my first intimation that it was not only non-New Yorkers who had accents. I must confess that it took several years to accept the idea that I truly had an accent. The lesson about the R's, however, began to take hold immediately. Once I grasped the fact that I said, "The stahs at night ah big and bright," I found it sounded really uneducated, and I focused a lot of energy on verbalizing my R's. It was important to change this very evident proof of where I came from, and change became the central item of focus in almost every sphere of my life. Since I had always hated myself, I would try to become someone else.

◆ ◆ ◆

What started as a few boys with colds in the fall suddenly morphed into avian flu that was part of a worldwide pandemic. The three-bed infirmary was quickly overwhelmed so that several dorms were converted for quarantine. I labored with fevers, sweats, crushing muscle aches, constant thirst, and loss of appetite. There were times I stood to walk to the bathroom and, sweating, achy, and weak, fell back on my bed.

In the midst of the misery there was Father Owen. To us he was the most powerful priest in the world. He struck fear in all our hearts. I thought of him as a complete hard-ass.

I was in a room with five others. We didn't know that it was not only we six who were ill, that our scene was recreated in many other dorms. As we lay there, soaked in sweat, Father Owen came to our dorm several times a day and at night, took our temperatures, gave us aspirin, washed us, dried us, wiped us down with alcohol. He brought us food and water, and did his best to have us take it.

Who was not sick? How many priests and brothers were ill? Was Father Owen sick himself?

This was God's love made real by a Franciscan priest, not talking about it, but doing it.

What relief those priests must have felt when, within two weeks, we all recovered. All the while we were happily unaware that millions were ill and many thousands were dying.

Mike

For the most part, I found the sermons during Sunday Mass inspirational. They usually focused on a Christian's and a priest's duty to develop discipline, holiness, self-reflection, and a commitment to service to others. Most were about Jesus and his willingness to sacrifice himself for our salvation. But one Sunday Father Peter Rudden, one of the younger priests and one I would grow to deeply admire, delivered a sermon that disturbed me. It was about God the Father. How we should seek to know him as a loving father, the depth of whose love for us had led him to sacrifice his own Son for our salvation.

Confessions were heard each morning before Mass and I waited for the day I saw Father Peter enter the confessional. When he opened the sliding door to the grill that separated us, I didn't even bother with the traditional, "Bless me Father for I have sinned." Instead, I told him that it was impossible for me to imagine God as a "loving" father. I told him I didn't even know what a loving father was. I rattled off all the failures of my father: his drinking, his insensitivity, how he had all but abandoned me, my brother, and sister after my mother's death. "How do you love a father like that?" I asked.

Father Peter took a deep breath. He began talking about how it is often difficult for us to understand the motivation of other people, especially when we are younger. He talked about how forgiveness is often the first step on the road to understanding. He asked me if I had ever tried to put myself into my father's shoes and tried to imagine what it must have been like for him losing his wife and facing the prospect of raising three young children alone. He told me to take some time and pray that I might be given the grace to forgive and perhaps then come to understand my father better.

I was shaken. I sat through the Mass that followed barely hearing a word that was said. In classes that morning, I wasn't much better. I kept thinking back to an incident before my mother died. My father had come home with a bellyful. He was belligerent and abusive. Usually when he was in that condition my mother handled him with the delicacy of a midwife delivering a baby. She'd speak to him softly and shuffle him off to the bedroom, get him settled into bed, wait until he fell asleep, and then lock the bedroom door. But on this particular night he was unusually aggressive and refused to be calmed. For some reason I couldn't understand, I was the object of his wrath.

"Yah self-important little shit, get out from under your mother's skirt and get over heaha."

"Red, leave the boy alone," my mother warned.

"Get over heaha, mama's boy." I moved toward him, but my mother grabbed me and held me back.

"Red, I'm warning you: if you don't leave the boy alone, I'll call the cops."

"Get over heaha, yah sorry little bastard. Yah gotta learn to be a man soona or latea. Get over heaha and get your goddam dukes up."

"I'm warning you, Red, leave the boy alone and go to bed or I'll have you in jail."

"Let the little bastard go, Ruth; he's gotta learn to be a man soona or latea."

"I'm warning you, leave the boy alone and go to bed."

It went on for a while like that before my father passed out. My mother had me help her pile him into the back seat of our Chevy. Then she had me wake up my brother Paul. She drove directly to the police station while Paul and I sat beside her keeping an eye on my father in the back seat. When we arrived at the police station the policeman behind the desk tried to convince my mother to take my father home and put him to bed. "He doesn't look like he'll wake up until morning," he said. "And if he does, he won't be in any condition to do anyone any harm. I'll get a few officers to follow you home and help you get him into bed."

"No, goddamn it," my mother said in a tone I'd never heard her use before. "He stepped over the line. I've never seen him like this; threatening a seven-year-old." She put her arm around my brother and me and hurried us to the station door. "Let him spend the night in jail. It will teach him a lesson."

One day a few weeks after this incident, I confided to my mother how much I hated my father. "You ought to be ashamed of yourself for saying something like that," she said. "You have no idea what he and men like him have been through to protect you and me and this country from the Germans and Japanese."

She had forgiven him and loved him, and she expected the same from me. But I resisted.

Christmas that year I unwrapped my presents to find the popgun I'd coveted when my brother and I walked through the Bon Marche department store with my father and mother in October, the two of us pointing to toys we hoped that Santa would bring.

"Remember boys," my mother had cautioned, "Santa has lots of boys and girls to take care of on Christmas; you might not get everything you want."

But there it was when I tore away the Christmas wrapping: a beautiful new popgun with a stash of six ping-pong balls for ammunition. I was so proud Santa had deemed me deserving of such a great gift. I broke open the package of ping-pong balls and loaded up the gun. I spent the rest of Christmas morning shooting at our dog, Limpy, and my brother. I was so absorbed in my happiness with my new toy that I almost missed the look of satisfaction on my father's face and the smile he exchanged with my mother.

It was on a Wednesday morning that I made my confession to Father Peter. On Wednesdays, as usual, we had classes for only half a day and had free time in the afternoon. I walked to a hill behind the seminary. From where I sat, I could look across Catherine's Creek to a field where some of my seminary mates were playing touch football. This time, I had no desire to join them. I sat there thinking about what Father Peter had told me about forgiveness and how it was often the path to understanding. Could I ever forgive my father? Would I ever be able to understand him? Accept him?

But there was that other thing that Father Peter had said just before he had sent me off to pray for the grace to forgive and seek understanding. It bothered me even more than my confused feelings about my father: "You know, Michael, it sounds as if you're not just angry with your father, but with our Heavenly Father as well." I wasn't ready to accept that. Not yet.

John

It is often a comfort to shift one's position and be bruised in a new place.

—Washington Irving

At home I had become a frequent visitor to our family doctor. I seemed always to have asthma, headaches, rashes, sore breasts, athlete's foot, thus confirming my father's contention that I was damaged goods. I was living out his prediction that I would never be a real man, never be capable of working like a real man, that I did not deserve to be his son.

The seminary had a contract with a local physician who came every Friday. I immediately lapsed into my old behavior and signed up to see the doctor every week for the first month I was there. There had to be something wrong with me. Like original sin, I had been born with something wrong with me. One day Father Owen materialized beside me.

"Tuohey, why do you keep signing up to see the doctor?"

"Because I don't feel well, Father."

"Tuohey, we don't want priests who are sick all the time. If you keep needing to see a doctor, you have to go home."

I was stunned. Go home! There was no way I was going home.

My headaches stopped. My asthma stopped. There was nothing wrong with me, nothing at all. The next time I saw the doctor was almost three years later, and they made me go.

The first two weeks in the seminary did give me discomfort because I was forced to exercise. My pudgy breasts were chafed, as were my armpits, crotch, and thighs. There was a lot of sweating and rubbing going on. With all that sweating there came a lot of body odor. I was completely oblivious of that reality. I entered the dorm one day and found a small package on my bed. I unwrapped it to find a bar of soap wrapped in two pieces of paper. One piece was a map to the shower; the other was a diagram of how the shower knobs worked. Richard Basch had struck.

And then the aching, rubbing, chafing—and the stinking, to a great extent—stopped, just like magic. A few weeks of no snacks, no TV, daily exercise, early to bed and early to rise, and I had stopped being fat. My clothes no longer fit me. My pants sagged down at the waist, which was okay. I had grown about four inches, so they stayed an acceptable length by hanging down.

Throughout the fall we were made to play touch football. Everyone in the school was on a team and everyone played, every day. When the bell rang at the end of last period, we ran upstairs, changed into play clothes, and ran across the bridge over Catherine's Creek onto St. John's vast fields that had space for three or four concurrent games to be played.

It was amazing to me, but the act of putting on sneakers compelled me to run. To my amazement, in short order I could run as fast and as long as anyone else. I could make good plays, along with the more accustomed bad ones. I was not the last one picked. I wasn't wheezing or in pain.

In time I lived to play basketball. Whenever we were not otherwise engaged I went to the gym, often seeking out Jerry Waters and Denny Walsh, who were the stars of our team. Because of my walleyes, I lacked depth perception, making catching footballs or softballs problematic. But the basketball was a ball so large that I could consistently catch it. I loved dribbling, passing, and shooting. I loved the running, the stopping, the cutting. I could have played basketball all day, every day.

After weeks of playing as much basketball as time would allow, Jerry and Denny encouraged me to try out for the basketball team. It seemed ridiculous to me, but I gave it a try. To my utter amazement and joy, my name was on the list of those selected when it was posted. There were some boys not selected whom I was sure were better than I, but there I was. In the case of one, Brian Clendenin, a junior, there was no question that he was much better, but he was having a tough time with his grades that semester, and the administration decided that he should focus on his studies.

So through a convergence of grade issues and the fact that it was a small school, I was on the basketball team. Two months earlier I couldn't get out of my own way.

◆ ◆ ◆

Nothing succeeds like success

—Alexandre Dumas, père

Father DeSales told us one day about a forthcoming "Know English" contest. There would be two teams, each consisting of one freshman, one sophomore, one junior, and one senior. I was to be the freshman for one team. I felt blessed beyond reason.

The contest took place on the gym's stage in front of all the students and staff. It worked this way. As moderator, Father DeSales, called a student front and center, then said a Latin word. The student had to identify the part of speech; whether it was masculine, feminine, or neuter, if a noun; identify the conjugation if a verb; give the masculine, feminine, and neutral forms; if an adjective give the meaning; then name an English word derived from that word and spell and define the English word.

I sailed along until I was given the Latin word *pes*, meaning "foot." I sailed through everything until I said that an English word deriving from it was *pediatrician*, which I correctly spelled and defined as "baby doctor." How I concluded that "baby doctor" derived from "foot." I will never know.

The student body clapped like crazy, and, all full of myself, I sat down. Then I noticed Father DeSales reading Merriam. That could not be good. He held up a hand and interrupted the applause, then told us that *pediatrician* derived from a Greek work. If I had picked *pedal* or *pedestrian* or *moped* or anything that had a foot connection I would have been fine.

I was crestfallen, but in this humbled state I was surprised. Several students, including some of the older ones, congratulated me on doing so well. They focused on the words I had gotten right, and even complimented me on knowing, spelling, and defining *pediatrician*. They focused on what I had done right, not what I had done wrong—a complete reversal of my life experience to that point. Amazing, one error did not negate everything else.

Mike

During the second week of October excitement began to build throughout the seminary about the coming parent visitation weekend and first family reunions in some six weeks. I was ambivalent about it. The routine of seminary life was getting familiar and comforting and I didn't want it disrupted. I was worried that my parents might embarrass me by making comments to my teachers about my history of bad behavior and irresponsibility. On the other hand, I wanted to see my parents' reaction to the new me, my new home, and my new life. My failure to get into Keith Academy had made me a failure in their eyes—and my own. But this place, I was sure they would see, was better than Keith Academy, much better.

Friday evening before the weekend I sat silently at supper as others at my table talked about family reunions and getting off campus for good restaurant meals. I just kept pushing my food around my plate, occasionally taking a bite, but most of all pretending I was listening to the conversation, even though I wasn't looking at anyone. Richie Roulliard, who may have read me, asked, "Are your parents coming, Mike?"

"Yeah, I guess so."

"You don't sound too excited."

I'm not excited; I'm worried.

"I am," I said, "I'm a little tired tonight." Then I filled my mouth, hoping he would talk with someone else.

"I wish the weekend was longer," one of the others was saying.

Yeah, that would just be great. More time with my parents.

At chapel on Saturday morning, I prayed that the visit would be uneventful—and brief. *Lord, don't let them be fighting when they get here. Don't let my father be hung over.*

The family, including my brother, Paul, and sister, Carol, arrived at 9:00 A.M., having spent the previous night in a motel in Watkins Glen. I ran to meet them when I saw the Chevy pull into the seminary driveway. I adopted the posture and look that I had practiced in front of the mirror in the "jakes" on Friday, hoping that it wouldn't betray my concern and lack of enthusiasm about their visit. When they got out of the car, the tension escaped from me like air from an inflatable mattress. They weren't smiling but there was a look I took as admiration on their faces.

"Wow," Paul said, "this is your school?!"

Carol rushed to me and threw her arms around me. "I missed you so much."

Even Marie gave me a hug and said she'd missed me. My father and I shook hands. My enthusiasm increased as I led them around the campus and building. I introduced them to Father Wilfrid in the front corridor. "We're really happy to have Michael here," he told them. "You've sent us a very fine boy."

Wow, I wonder how they will react to that.

But they didn't betray me. "He *is* a fine boy," Marie replied.

I showed them the chapel, the classrooms, the school library, our rec room, and cafeteria. My father's reaction when I brought them to my twelve-bed dormitory didn't surprise me. "Looks like an Army barracks," he said. I smiled as I thought of my own reaction when I first saw it.

We took a few pictures in front of the shrine of the Blessed Virgin Mary, the statue of St. Francis of Assisi, and the St John's Seminary sign. I introduced them to a few of my classmates and dorm mates and to Father Owen and some of my teachers. All of them were very polite and had nice things to say about me. Then we went off to dinner in Watkins Glen.

On Sunday the family returned for morning Mass. It was the only time I'd ever seen Marie or my father in a church. Later we drove over to Havana Glen and I told them about our hikes there and the first picnic when some of us swam in the ice cold waters of the glen's basin.

By early afternoon my father announced it was time to leave.

"It's a long drive back and we have to work on Monday."

"We're proud of you, Michael," Marie said.

My father looked at me with an expression I had never seen before. It seemed to be a combination of respect and envy. "You look like you're settling in here nicely," he said.

"Thanks, Dad. And thanks for letting me come here." My throat was dry and my chest was heavy.

"Keep up the good work," he said holding out his right hand. I took it.

"I will." My voice was beginning to crack. He hesitated like he wanted to do more, say more. But he let go of my hand and walked to the car. Marie, my sister, and my brother gave me a hug. Then they climbed into the car and waved as my father drove off. Still choked up a bit, but mostly relieved, I watched the Chevy turn onto Route 14.

Thank you, Lord.

The car disappeared behind the first hill south of St. John's and I turned to the building.

Go shoot some baskets.

After changing clothes I went to the gym and heard the echoes of one basketball bouncing. John Tuohey was there, alone.

"Hey, John!"

"Hi, Mike. Good visit with your parents?"

"Yeah. You?"

"Okay . . . Wanna play some one-on-one?"

I took one long jump shot with my ball and then rolled it off to the side. John tossed his ball to me. "Go ahead," he said. "You take it out."

Ollie

Parent visitation was scheduled twice yearly, in mid-October and in the spring, usually around Easter. I had not seen my father and Eileen since they left their wedding reception to honeymoon two months earlier, so I had some anxiety as my father's shiny 1949 Cadillac, striking with its outside windshield visor and whitewall tires, turned onto St. John's driveway and inched to the front of the building.

Over the previous few weeks, despite some lingering reluctance, I had warmed to Eileen. She had undertaken regular correspondence with me, periodically sending packages with cookies and other treats. The letters were water in the desert because they carried the only news from home—about life in the family's rented cottage in Putnam Valley as construction proceeded on the new home. Susan was now ten and Rosemary, five, and Eileen reported about their experiences at St. Columbanus, their new school in Peekskill, about ten miles from home. She apologized that my father was not writing, telling of his grueling commute to New York City. No longer a cop he had returned to his trade as an electrician and was taking advantage of every overtime opportunity to address the mounting expenses associated with the new home. And when he wasn't working he was busy completing the house at the earliest possible time before winter set in.

In our correspondence I had addressed Eileen as "Mom." Something of a tentative step for me, it was more easily done in writing, but it was also a response to my own hunger to once again have a mother. Mothers of other seminarians were stepping from their cars as I wrestled with myself over my first physical encounter with a stepmother.

"Hey, Rich!" my father said excitedly. My joy brimmed over even as I tried to maintain a certain nonchalance at the reunion. Eileen stepped from around the passenger side looking genuinely happy to see me. I stepped over to hug her and almost unconsciously said, "Hi, Mom."

The visit was outstanding, highlighted by a long stroll into the breathtaking gorge of Watkins Glen at the foot of the equally spectacular Seneca Lake. We feasted on a few dozen raw clams for lunch and had a prime rib dinner Saturday evening at the historical, stately Watkins Hotel.

Seeing them leave Sunday afternoon was tough. There were signs my family was being reconstituted for the first time in nearly three years, but their departure—and my being left behind—suggested that I was not part of it.

John

For the only time in my four years, my parents came to visit me on visiting day that first October. It was a shock for all of us. In less than two months I had grown four inches and was taller than my father. I weighed about the same, most of my fat gone, replaced by muscle. Pictures my mother took showed a long thin-faced boy with no double chin, no gut, beside his shorter father. I wonder what he thought.

Jerry Waters' parents did not come to visit, so I asked my parents if we could take Jerry out with us. They agreed, as did Father Owen. This was monumental to me. I had had the temerity to ask the coolest guy in the place to spend the day with me, and he had agreed to do it. My parents took us to a restaurant, where I ordered a ham steak and asparagus with Hollandaise sauce. That was my first experience with asparagus and with Hollandaise sauce. We went back to my parents' motel and watched the Yankees and Dodgers in the World Series on television. My father gave us cigarettes, which annoyed my mother.

The next morning my parents came to the seminary and said that they were leaving right away, since it was a long drive. I said goodbye, changed my clothes, then ran to Father Owen's office to check out a basketball.

"Aren't your parents here, Tuohey?"

"They were, Father, but they just went home."

"So they just left, and you want to play basketball? A lot of the boys are very sad when their parents leave."

There was an unspoken question there, something evaluative. It made me wary.

"Of course I feel bad, Father. I figure I could lie on my bed and cry over missing them, or I could occupy myself with something distracting. I figure basketball is a good distraction."

"That's true, Tuohey. That's a mature way to look at it." He gave me a ball.

Alone in the gym shooting baskets I thought about my exchange with Father Owen. I realized that I had been completely deceptive. I wasn't sad to see them go; I was happy.

As a freshman, John (right) was delighted when his teen hero, Jerry Waters, accepted his invitation to go to Watkins Glen with his family on parents' weekend.

Not for the first time, and definitely not for the last, I wondered at my detachment. I thought that there was some element that was typically found in sons that was completely absent from me.

That realization caused me no distress.

◆ ◆ ◆

Turning seasons in the Finger Lakes were a flip chart of masterpieces. Fitting to the region's name, a series of spectacular elongated lakes stood as marks of deep gouges of glaciation. They all bore the names of bygone residents, the most prominent among them Oneida, Canandaigua, Cayuga, Keuka, and Seneca.

Seneca, deepest among them at more than 600 feet and well below sea level, was standing testimony to the awesome power of an ice age. Like its sister lakes it stretched north and south and was sandwiched between rolling hills that featured pastures, woodland, and vineyards. Never wider

Photo credit: Franciscan Friars of the Atonement, Graymoor Archives

Seneca Lake, largest of the five predominant Finger Lakes and stretching northward forty miles from Watkins Glen, is also the deepest at more than 600 feet. Catherine's Creek, which flowed through the seminary grounds, meandered northward three miles before emptying into Seneca Lake.

than three and one-half miles, it was, at forty miles in length, the center finger among the namesake lakes, with Watkins Glen at its southern tip.

Catherine's Creek, one of thousands of feeder streams into the lake, empties at Watkins Glen after a northward flow that carries it through the grounds of St. John's Seminary and Montour Falls. Depending on the season, St. John's students regularly crossed the metal cable-trestle pedestrian bridge over Catherine's Creek for softball or football games in the expansive fields behind the seminary. Underneath the bridge redwing blackbirds lived out life among the cattails on both banks, filling the valley with their endless daytime chatter and trills.

The tranquil comfort of Indian summer subtly shifted to fall's pleasant briskness and the hills on either side of the watershed exploded into ridiculous color. Oranges, reds, yellows, pinks, golds that shimmered from maples, elms, and oaks were more Disney cartoonish than true. This annual display marked its absolute peak of colored intensity in mid-October. Then, quickly and with startling suddenness, usually prompted by season's first freeze, it all faded into dull gray. Perhaps there would be a holdout tree here or there in the hills, stubbornly clutching its rouge. But you would look the next day and it, too, had given up the ghost to winter's march.

Before arctic blasts settled in, there were a few more football games—freshmen against sophomores, freshman and sophomores against juniors and seniors—and maybe a day hike around the hills led by one of the priests.

Mike

By the end of October, I didn't have any real friends, but I hadn't made any effort to encourage friendship.

Nothing is permanent. Best to keep from getting too close to anyone.

But my determination to remain detached was doomed from the start. We ate, prayed, and went to class together. Likewise, we were required to play touch football, basketball, and other games. We went on group hikes and watched movies on Saturday nights together.

One Saturday, while working in the school's laundry, sorting and folding clothes that would be delivered to their owners later in the day, I spotted a sweatshirt among the unclaimed clothes with "Earlham" on the front. I had no idea that Earlham was a famous liberal arts college in Richmond, Indiana. All I knew was I didn't own a sweatshirt and I liked this one. The first time I wore it out to a touch football game, my fate was sealed.

"Hey look, here comes Earlham," Richie Olive shouted, laughing as I came onto the playing field.

"Wow, I thought that was little Mikie Connolly," John Tuohey said, a big grin on his face. "So he's Earlham in disguise. Hey, Earlham."

I gave them my best *I care* look—our way of saying: "Do you actually think you can bother me?"

All afternoon it was "Earlham, you block Dever; Earlham, cut across the middle for a pass; Earlham, keep an eye on Barbera; he's going long." After a while, seeing how taken everyone seemed to be with the name, I began enjoying my new name. By game's end I had become Earlham (the Earl of Ham), fitting for a short, skinny runt who acted like a tough guy he wasn't, but wanted to be. Most importantly, I was no longer little Mikie Connolly; I was Earlham and felt

Photo credit: Gerry Whitfield

Wednesday, Saturday and Sunday afternoons were free times, when many students engaged in sports, including indoor and outdoor basketball, football, softball, tennis, handball, and table tennis. In the winter the tennis courts were frozen for ice-skating.

like I'd gained a small measure of prestige. The name stuck and my grip on detachment started loosening. Like an anxious hermit crab peeking out, I began connecting with those who were kidding me.

Still, I was haunted by fear of failure.

Every time I sat for an algebra or Latin test it felt like I was heading into a minefield, where one false step could kill any chance I had of staying in the seminary. Where could I go if I was asked to leave? Back to where I had come from, back to where I had already proven myself a failure? I buried myself in study, a practice I'd never considered committing to before. Now my dreams—night dreams and daydreams—were overrun by an image of me sitting in the back of the chapel with my suitcase.

Organized study periods proctored by priests made studying easier than it had been in Lowell. No street games to distract me; everyone was studying at the same time. When regular Saturday morning work details were finished and lunch was over, I'd go to the library with a pile of books while other boys were playing sports or relaxing. Sitting alone, I'd pull at my hair and swear under my breath as I struggled to understand algebraic algorithms and Latin declensions. I'd spend Sunday afternoons the same way. Occasionally, I'd slip off into daydreams of touch football on Myrtle Street. Ray Coleman, dancing and dodging around boys trying to tag him, me leaping for a pass. Touchdown! I would jerk awake, angry for having wasted time.

One Saturday afternoon as I sat studying a Latin assignment I was startled by a voice behind me.

"What are you doing here, Michael?" It was Father Peter, dressed in sweats and sneakers, a basketball tucked under one arm. He didn't look much older than many of the college students at St. John's.

"Studying, Father."

Little Mikie (far right, aka Earlham and later Rick Savage) on the bridge over Catherine's Creek with (from left to right) Joe Silvia, Mike Taylor, and Joe Timson.

"It seems that every time I come by here on a weekend you're here."

"I don't want to flunk out, Father."

"Listen, Michael, all work with no rest isn't going to make you a better student; all it's going to do is exhaust you. Go upstairs and get into gym clothes and meet me down here."

We played basketball that afternoon, Father Peter and I. Other boys who were playing invited us to join them, but Father Peter told them, "Another time," and took me to a side court and began teaching me how to dribble and shoot. That was my introduction to a game I would come to love and to a priest I would never cease to admire.

Ollie

Capping the fall season was apple harvest, its fruits bound for the cider press and the Halloween party. Father Ralph Thomas was the harvest's driving force. Slight, taciturn, soft-spoken, and ever toting a book, he was held in awe as the resident intellect. Father Ralph taught on the college level, which made him even more remote to us high school students.

But with the harvest he burst onto the scene as a gleeful participant, all professional and scholarly decorum left back at the seminary door. He would steer the seminary's big dump truck into the driveway and as many students as could be accommodated clambered into the back and onto the running boards for the short ride to the orchard on the hill behind the building. Except for his position at the wheel of the truck, he was as much one of the seminarians as anyone else, delighting in the annual harvest adventure.

There were only four old, motley trees, but their branches drooped with a bounty greater than the whole seminary population could consume in one setting. Back at the kitchen, the brothers pressed most of the apples and used the rest for Brother Dennis Stennert's special apple betty. Even though many students picked up the term *apple crud* that was coined by Tom Dever, a fellow freshman, there were never any leftovers of this creation of baked apples and sweetened crumbs.

Soon after the pressed cider had taken on a distinctive fermented zip, around the time of the Halloween Party, high school students were limited to two glasses. Jerome McDuffie, a hefty, red-faced blond kid from South Carolina in his junior year, could not abide this limitation. Dever, who was in his dorm, said McDuffie drank some Wildroot Cream Oil hair tonic before the party on the theory that lining his stomach with the greasy stuff would prepare him for some heavy drinking. Dever said McDuffie sneaked into the kitchen late that night for more cider, then spent several hours barfing out his second-floor dorm window.

The calendar said winter began in the third week of December, but the season's dreariness was well established at Montour Falls weeks earlier. The colder it got, the more free time was spent playing basketball in the gym. There was the novelty of the first big snowfall and tobogganing on one of the hills on the seminary's grounds. We would fashion a run that climaxed in a launch over a concrete wall. I took the lead on one ride, my feet awkwardly crossed in front of me to accommodate three more students behind me. After clearing the wall the toboggan nosedived into the snow. In an instant my crossed legs buckled under me before the others piled onto my back, forcing my legs into a split. I lay writhing on the ground, the other students gathering around me helplessly.

"I don't think he'll ever have kids," I could hear Jimmy Smith, a third-year student, saying.

As the other students pulled me back to the building with me moaning and curled up on the toboggan, Father Owen rushed through the door asking what had happened. He directed that I be pulled to the garage, where he helped me into one of the cars and drove me to the Montour Falls hospital.

"They're going to hold you overnight for observation," he assured me after I was assigned to a room. "I think you're going to be fine."

It was the second time I felt deep concern from Father Owen, the faculty watchdog whose presence generally aroused anxiety, if not fear. The first time was weeks earlier when he came to my bed as I lay in a feverish stupor with other students during a flu outbreak. Before Father Owen reached me, I saw him, flashlight in one hand, moving from bed to bed with an alcohol compress, holding it to students' foreheads and gently rubbing their chests while muttering a prayer.

I remember his touch, tender like a mother's.

◆ ◆ ◆

Right on the heels of Thanksgiving came Advent, four weeks of spiritual anticipation of the observance of Christ's birth. Each Sunday during Advent one more of four candles set at the edges of an evergreen wreath was illuminated at Mass, a ritual that fired up even greater excitement throughout the seminary about the impending two-week Christmas recess and the trip home. While pulling my luggage from the attic the day before we left for the break, I was filled with anticipation I could hardly contain at the thought of reuniting with my father and two sisters—and seeing what this new family, formed in my absence, was like.

Early the next morning a charter bus pulled into the driveway. The driver switched on the interior lights, beckoning us from the frigid predawn, then stepped out to load up the underside luggage spaces. Holiday joy ratcheted up as the students broke out in Christmas carols while the bus rode south on Route 14 to Elmira. In an hour we were on the station platform as the Erie-Lackawanna's signature passenger train, the gray and purple *Phoebe Snow*, its engine bell clanging past us, slowed to a squealing stop. The conductor's "All aboooaaard!" was a welcoming signal to escape the cold, windy station. Everything continued Christmasy with more caroling and the train advancing on its five-hour journey through the bleak and wintry Pennsylvania Poconos to the terminal at Hoboken.

Scores of parents stood huddled alongside the track, then rushed to the doors as the train crept to a stop and let out a long hiss. My father's cousin, Aunt Dorothy to me, and her husband, Fred, were there to meet me and take me to their Bronx apartment where I would wait for my father to get off work.

On the one-hour drive north to Putnam Valley my father told of the hectic previous two weeks when the family moved into the new home. Everyone was excited about having me home for Christmas, he said. With some trepidation, I was, too, as he turned the car onto Canopus Hollow Road where, in the first quarter-mile, there was only one home before ours, a white, split-level house, surrounded by woods.

"Rich is home," my father announced as he set my suitcase in the foyer. Susan and Rosemary came running down the stairs from their bedroom. With the two of them hugging me, Eileen came from the kitchen drying her hands.

"Hi, Rich."

"Hi ,Mom."

We kissed.

"Why don't you show Richie the house and his room, girls?" she said.

"C'mon," said Rosemary, tugging at my hand. "See our bedroom first."

The three-bedroom home was bigger and more spacious than I'd ever seen, especially because the large, high-ceiling living room was devoid of furniture. Every available penny had been devoted to completing enough of the construction to move them from a drafty rented summer cottage at Lake Oscawana before winter's harshest offerings.

The girls showed me my first bedroom, furnished with a new bed and the walnut highboy that, until recently, had been my father's. I felt intensely happy and, for the moment, genuinely part of this family.

After dinner the family sat in the newly furnished den on the ground level watching television. The girls went to bed around 9:00 P.M. and, after watching the 10:00 news we went to the stairs leading to the bedrooms. As always, I kissed my father on the cheek and he said, "Good night, Rich. It's good to have you home."

"Don't you think he's a little old for kissing?" Eileen asked. Caught short, I felt embarrassed and hurt and carried those feelings to bed, where they morphed to anger. Much of it was directed at my father, who had appeared sheepish and weak and said nothing to dismiss her criticism.

In any case, we kissed no more.

The Christmas break went by quickly. My father was working extra hours much of the time and sleeping frequently at his mother's apartment in the city. This left a lot of time for my stepmother and me to spend together and my imagery of family coziness began to fade. Besides some forays into the woods, there was nowhere to go. The nearest store, a little convenience stop that was part of a gas station, was two miles away.

By the end of the recess, I was longing to return to St. John's.

John

As the holidays approached, we all started to become excited at the prospect of going home, getting presents, watching TV, eating sweets late at night, and sleeping in. My mother wrote and told me that my father wanted me to take the Long Island Railroad from Penn Station in New York City to our town, then to get a cab to the house. I said okay to that without a bit of hesitation. Before I went to the seminary, my father had often tried to entice me with promises of Rangers games or Yankee games to take a train to the city by myself. I had been too terrified by the idea, part of my global fear of everything. That, apparently, was gone.

I arrived home at dinner time on Thursday, December 20th. It was dark and cold. The meal was not memorable in any way. I watched TV, then went to bed. I awoke in the morning with a cold and asthma. I lay there wheezing and coughing for the first time in months.

My mother made me a soft-boiled egg, toast, and tea for breakfast; Campbell's chicken noodle soup, toast, and tea for lunch, my standard sick day fare when I was little. She made lots of tea, the Irish cure for everything. It was very comforting for a few days. She also offered to go to the store and buy me some comic books to read while I recuperated. I had read a lot of comic books before going to the seminary, especially when I was sick. I had not seen one since going to the seminary. I was very excited. When she returned with the comics, I immediately tore into them. To my amazement, I could not read them. They were such complete crap. I had been immersed in Melville, Stevenson, Dickens. These were like reading McGuffey's reader: See Spot jump.

I remained sick for most of the vacation, but my mother's tender care and the absence of conflict with my father made it generally pleasant.

When the time came to return to the seminary, I was anxious to do so. I then noticed that I had never unpacked my suitcase. As the years progressed, as each Christmas and summer vacation came and went, I never emptied my suitcase when I was home. I might exchange something too small for something bigger, or throw out something worn out, but the bag remained full, just waiting to go back where it and I belonged.

Mike

The first evening of my return to Lowell for Christmas break, the family gathered in the kitchen to eat and listen to my stories of seminary life. We were having roast beef, my father's favorite meal, and mine. The smell of beef heating in the oven, potatoes and bread baking, and corn on the cob boiling in a pot on the stove made me feel comfortable. I helped my brother set the table and asked my father, who was cooking, if there was anything I could do to help.

"No, just sit down and relax. Dinner will be ready soon," he said.

Relax? This was going to be my time to shine.

I jumped up and got myself a glass of water. Sat down at the table. Was up again, off to the bathroom to wash my hands and remember the stories I planned to tell and the order in which I planned to tell them. When the meal was finally ready and we were all sitting at the table, I launched right into my stories of seminary life. I talked about how different the priests at the seminary were from parish priests at St. Michael's, how interesting our classes were, how I was now an altar boy, how we went to Mass every morning, sports every afternoon, and study hall every night. They listened and looked impressed.

"How are your grades?" my father asked.

"I think I'm actually doing pretty good." I replied more confidently than I really was about my grades.

"That's good; we'll be looking forward to your first report card. We're paying a lot to send you to the seminary."

Even that didn't diminish my excitement. I rambled on, dominating the table talk until it was clear that everyone had had enough.

"It's time to clean up," Marie announced.

That night as I lay in bed, I remembered the looks on my father's and Marie's faces.

Surprise? Respect?

But in the days that followed I become aware of things that had made me uncomfortable in this place. The house appeared smaller and even more rundown. Pigeon shit lined the front stairs like sideline markers on a football field. The back stairs were so rickety you'd need health insurance to use them. The paint on the outside of the house was worn and wrinkled. It looked to me like the place was suffering from leprosy.

The signs of deterioration in the relationship between my father and Marie were obvious. They now slept in separate bedrooms. My father's drinking had gotten worse. Most evenings I was in bed before he arrived home, but I could hear him and Marie arguing and I'd put a pillow over my head to drown out the sound of his cursing. In the morning when he left for work, as part of our cleaning chores Paul or I would regularly remove up to six empty beer bottles and an empty pint of whiskey from his room.

Within three days I was desperate for the vacation to end and for my return to the solitude of the seminary.

Chapter Seven

Second-Semester Freshmen

Mike

One afternoon in January of 1957, John Tuohey and I found ourselves playing two-on-two basketball against Father Peter and Joe Silvia, another freshman. Father Peter was defending John, because he was by far a better scorer than I was. Silvia wasn't good, but we knew this would be a challenge because, when defending, Father Peter did a lot of pushing and holding to make up for his lack of speed.

"Foul!" John shouted as he fell to the floor, grabbing his knee.

"That wasn't a foul," Father Peter replied, "that's aggressive defense. You boys need to learn to be aggressive."

The game went on, and Father Peter kept muscling John whenever he tried to drive to the basket.

"Foul!" John yelled again.

"That wasn't a foul. You ran out of bounds," Father Peter responded. "Our ball."

"I didn't run out of bounds; you pushed me out, Father."

"You bumped into me and fell out of bounds. Our ball."

John's lower lip was quivering and he was glaring at Father Peter with razor-sharp eyes. We continued to play. John was becoming more and more frustrated over his repeated protests and the priest's denials. John's shoulders started to slump. The gym, empty except for the four of us, reverberated with the bouncing ball, continuing accusations of *foul*, and the denials. My play, always hesitant, became even more cautious as Father Peter muscled John and yelled to his own teammate, "Play aggressively; don't let these guys get to the basket."

John suddenly called time out. "I've got to go to the toilet," he said. I followed him into the locker room, where John was pounding his fist on a metal locker.

"Arrrrrh, he's mugging me," John shouted at the locker.

Let's start pushing him back," I suggested.

John drew a deep breath as he flopped down on a bench, a look of defeat on his face. I wanted to say something, but had no clue what. "I have an idea," John said, standing up. "Do you know how to set a pick?"

"What's that?"

"It's kinda like a block in football. I'll show you."

"Now," he said as we headed back to the court, "whoever Father Peter decides to guard will take the ball and the other guy will set a pick for him."

The game resumed. John began to dribble with Father Peter guarding him again. I ran over to Father Peter's blind side, as John had instructed me, and stood there making sure I didn't move. Father Peter barreled into me knocking me over. I heard an anguished grunt. He fell onto me, crushing me into the floor. I felt his weight but no pain, as I watched John dribble by and lay the ball into the basket. John's smile was as broad as a billboard as he gave me a hand up from the floor. We used the play again and again, Father Peter shouting in frustration to his teammate, "Joe, pick up the driver, pick up the driver," as John dribbled to the basket and scored. He began to push through me, but even when he knocked me to the floor, John had gotten well past him and scored.

Father Peter called timeout and took Joe to the sideline.

"He's going to start guarding you," John said. "He wants to be able to switch to me if you set a pick on Joe. When they do that, I'll start setting picks for you and you drive to the basket. Joe won't know what to do." When the game resumed, Father Peter switched to guarding me as John had predicted. John set the picks and I began scoring. After a few baskets by me, Father Peter began shouting.

"Moving pick."

John started taking extra pain to plant his feet and take the full brunt of the charging priest before Father Peter finally had had enough, declaring it was time to get back for dinner.

In the shower room John and I celebrated. "That was terrific!" John shouted. "Did you see how frustrated he was? I love it."

Ollie

When my father dropped me off in Hoboken after the Christmas break, my farewell was somewhat distracted. I was anxious to reunite with fellow seminarians. There also was a longing for St. John's, where my clothes and other belongings were like a staked claim to my existence in another realm. There was more to St. John's than friends or the countryside that took my breath away. There were clear and curiously comforting boundaries in the Rule, which were fair, logical, and evenly enforced. There were the admirable examples of older students who, by and large, responded to us freshmen charitably and with respect and tolerance. Everyone had responsibilities for their studies, for their clothing, and for neatness and order in their tiny living spaces, which were not much more than one's bed, the two feet around it, and one's closet. But individual order and cleanliness contributed to the stark and serene atmosphere of the common space, the dormitory.

St. John's functioned with the social precision of a beehive, including designated directions for traversing the sides of hallways and stairwells. I relished being part of this place, where everything was known and predictable. The teaching faculty did not have to do any prodding about assignments. Failure to keep up would hurt grades and students incapable of maintaining passing marks eventually were gone. The priests were generally evenhanded and levelheaded in classroom decorum. We held them in high esteem and respected their professionalism and intellects. Most of them inspired curiosity, academic excellence, and maturity. All it took for a priest to correct a student, encourage self-examination, or inspire a greater effort was a disapproving look or a gentle, sometimes sarcastic comment.

In the evening, Father Owen roamed the hallways reading from his breviary, a book containing the biblical Psalms, while enforcing general silence as students prepared for bed. In the half hour before lights out, there might be one or two students kneeling on the terrazzo floor in the second-floor rotunda doing penance for some infraction of the Rule. No one wanted Father Owen's attention. He would often stand in the first-floor rotunda waiting to nab an unsuspecting student for some Rule violation. Knowing that Father

Owen had him in his crosshairs, Bill Lewis, a sophomore, sneaked out of an emergency exit of the chapel one night and down a fire escape to avoid imminent discipline—however briefly.

But no one could dispute that Father Owen was fair and consistent, a benevolent father figure, clear and firm about guiding principles.

He summoned me one day with his foreboding index finger as we passed in the hallway between classes. *What did I do now?* I thought as I approached him anxiously.

He pointed to an article I had written in the school newspaper, the *Quill*, about a freshman-sophomore football game. "Olive, you have a gift for writing. It's something you should keep in mind."

That was it. Touched deeply by the compliment, I mumbled an expression of gratitude and tucked it into my heart for safekeeping.

John

Soon after Christmas break, an event occurred that gave me a painful look at myself and at a condition to which I had been exposed for as long as I could remember and that, by the age fourteen, was very much part of me: bigotry. Besides ingraining me with the lesson of keeping my dukes up and head down, my father also taught me to hate and watch out for everyone who was other-than-we. The familiar drumbeat was that every group had its demeaning title and its stereotypical, loathsome group characteristics. My father never referred to any group or individual by their proper names.

Jews were all cheap and clannish. They murdered Jesus and would burn in hell. It was not for nothing that Hitler had tried to rid the earth of them. Italians were greasy, ignorant, semiblacks. That the Pope was Italian and the seat of the Church was in Rome was irrelevant. Polish people were stupid, ate weird food, and spoke gibberish. British people were monsters who deserved to be blown to bits, a cause to which our family contributed funds. Oddly, my father had nothing bad to say about Germans. Perhaps he recognized in their recent past kindred spirits, political fellow travelers. We Irish were heavy drinkers and compulsive fighters, but, since that was us, those were admirable qualities.

Each group had its own vile epithets, names intended to carry contempt in most instances. Not surprisingly, given my father's worldview, his deepest hatred was reserved for Puerto Ricans and blacks. These he considered semihuman subspecies. They embodied all the worst characteristics of all other groups: filth, stupidity, laziness, bad smells, and ugly features. He believed that they should all "go back where they came from."

That the blacks did not come voluntarily, that they were here hundreds of years before my family's arrival around 1917, that their unpaid labor built the country to a large extent were of no interest to him. He would extend his arm, point at his skin, and declare that this demonstrated beyond doubt that we were superior and deserved everything we had. Their skin screamed that they deserved nothing.

We did not come in contact with any other ethnic groups, so they escaped comment. Once he did ask the nationality of a boy I knew. My answer, "Belgian," stumped him.

"Belgian? Well, what do you call him?"

"Belgian."

"Yeah. But what do you call him?"

I knew what he meant, but we had no name, no ready insult for a Belgian. I had no critical faculty to screen the endless hatred and baseless assumptions that spewed from his mouth. So I emulated him, becoming a small copy of this rude and ignorant man.

In the seminary, many of us made cracks about blacks and Puerto Ricans, using those terms we all now pretend we never said. We fervently took the side of the Arabs against the Jews, those killers of Christ. It was easy. There were none among us. We didn't say these things in the presence of priests. If I had been asked, I would have assumed that everyone shared the same opinions, used the same terms.

Then one seminarian did the most amazing thing. He gave a speech during an oratorical contest in which he said that Negroes were human beings; that God created them with human souls; that slavery had been an abomination; that this country had been built on their unpaid backs; that they were still treated like slaves; that it was ignorant and sinful to perpetuate bigotry.

Was he crazy? Did he actually mean any of that? This was Tom Gallagher, a well-respected junior who was also a very smart guy. How could he possibly say something so stupid? I found what he said so distressing that I sought him out.

"Gallagher, why did you say that stuff about *them*?" I used the standard epithet.

"Don't call them that. That's degrading. They are Negroes."

"What's wrong with it? That's what they are."

"It's insulting and you sound stupid."

What was he talking about? He was proposing that the sun comes up in the west, that it's hot in the winter.

"You don't really think they have souls, do you?"

"Of course they do. They're human."

"But they're really stupid."

"Tuohey, there are colored doctors, lawyers, judges, scientists, priests, and bishops."

Priests? Bishops? I had never even seen a colored Catholic. What strange universe was Gallagher talking about?

"Well, have you ever been around any of them? They all smell funny."

"Tuohey, everyone has an odor. Do you think that colored people don't think that we smell odd?" I had a sudden uncomfortable memory of Richard Basch giving me a map to the shower room, shower directions, and soap.

Gallagher gave me such a strange look. He wasn't angry; he was . . . what? Was it pity? Disappointment? I think both of those. I felt stupid and ridiculous.

Just as Bernard's telling me about sex had shattered me, so, too, did this talk. Could the endless litany of hate that I had heard and repeated all my life be completely wrong? This began to eat at me. In the seminary with me were Italians who were not greasy, Poles who were not stupid. So, those assumptions were wrong. How much more of the burden I lugged around was baseless, ignorant, hurtful, and sinful?

My process of undoing was now engaged.

◆ ◆ ◆

From the south and wafting between the hills on each side of the Catherine's Creek watershed, a soothing, determined breeze halted the Canadian cold and forced its retreat to Seneca Lake's northern reaches. Vague hints of green interrupted the drab gray that had dominated the hills for months. Robust daffodils had forced their way through the dirt around

St. Francis' statue near the gym and, with great determination, reached higher each day. Redwing blackbirds issued a symphony of trills with their feeding frenzy in the creek's cattails while dominant males, shiny black with shoulders flashing distinctive red, yellow, and white, guarded their stakes. The whole world, it seemed, was awakening.

John

Spring of our freshman year was memorable for Easter break and a concert in Elmira that almost ended my seminary career. Unlike Christmas recess when we went home, at Easter we remained at the seminary, but we had a week off school. That Easter week was beautiful, sunny, and warm, so warm that the side doors to the chapel were open, allowing sunlight to stream in and fill the chapel with smells of new life. The stained-glass windows were alive with color.

Just before midnight leading into Easter Sunday, most of the students were in their choir stalls in the dark, silent. Then a slow procession of acolytes in cassocks and surplices, one of them carrying the three-foot paschal candle, slowly preceded the rector into the chapel as organ music swelled. It was magical and great theater. From that moment, the Easter service was my favorite, the one I looked forward to all year.

During the week after Easter Sunday we had a lot of free time, beginning with a day trip on Monday for picnicking and hiking at Treman State Park in Ithaca, another of the many Finger Lake locations graced with magnificent waterfalls. The rest of the week was spent with some housecleaning chores, with much more time for softball and basketball, general relaxation, reading, and local hikes. It was wonderful.

Later in the spring we went by bus one evening to a concert in Elmira, arriving about twenty minutes early at the concert site. Jerry Waters invited me to join him and a few others for a walk around the block, to which Father Owen agreed. As soon as we were out of sight, Jerry took out a pack of cigarettes, lit one, and passed it around. Everyone unhesitatingly started smoking. I had no desire to smoke and certainly had no need to do so, but it was important for me to fit in, to emulate the cool guy, so I took a few drags. We circled the block, arriving in time to go inside. I remember Father Owen, looking at us in an intent way, as if he were mulling something over. He was.

Perhaps two days after that, long enough for my fourteen-year-old mind to have erased it, I walked into Father Owen's room to get a basketball. He sat behind his desk looking at me until I became uncomfortable. I knew I was in trouble, but was not sure why.

"Tuohey, what does the Rule say?"

I stared at him, running through the Rule, which actually said many things. As I scrolled the list in my head, I locked on the obvious one, the one that made me blush with recognition. Always a prodigious blusher, I was a bright beacon at that moment.

"Well?"

"Seminarians are not allowed to smoke, Father."

"So what do you have to say for yourself, Tuohey?"

"It was just a couple of puffs, Father. I didn't even enjoy it."

"That isn't the point, Tuohey. The Rule is to be followed. I am going to have to give a lot of thought into whether you can come back next year. You can go."

I was nearly out of my mind when I left there. This whole thing might come to an end over this stupid mistake? I might have to go home? I wanted to die.

It took me a long time to realize that Father Owen had not known we were smoking until I told him. He had picked the most likely candidate, baited the trap, and let me catch myself. It was pretty slick, but I was in no position to enjoy it. I told Jerry what happened and he chuckled. He did not seem worried or angry. He seemed to understand immediately how I had been caught.

Father Owen said no more to me about the incident and I avoided him as much as possible.

Sometimes events seem to conspire against us, however. This was one of those times. Near the end of the year, we had to deliver a speech in elocution class. I wrote my speech, folded it, and put it in my shirt pocket. I hung the shirt on the back of the chair by my bed and forgot to hang it in the closet. Later, the shirt was gone, and I realized that Father Owen had taken it—as my dorm senior had warned would happen if any clothes were left outside our closets. I considered going to ask for it, but not wanting him again thinking of me as a screwup, I decided not to.

A few days after that, I gave my speech, which I knew by heart. Afterward, Father Boniface Reidman, our elocution teacher, asked for my written copy. I had no idea he wanted the written copy. I told him, "Father Owen has my paper, Father."

"Okay," he said.

I thought nothing further about it until Father Owen grabbed me in the hall that evening. "Tuohey, aren't you in enough trouble with me? How dare you lie to Father Boniface and tell him that I have your paper?"

"You do have it, Father. It's in the pocket of the shirt you took from the dorm."

He looked at me as if I were contemptible. "I have real reservations about your being here, Tuohey," and off he went.

Now I was sure that I was finished.

Mike

We had a number of entertainers in our class and consisting, as it did, of fourteen-year-old boys, much of the comedy was anything but highbrow. There was, for example, farting, with Johnny Barbera heralded for deadly potency and Fred Delcimento for longest on record. John Zopf's talent was sticking grapes up his nostrils and blowing them across the classroom when a teacher was out of the room. One minute, total silence in study hall would be interrupted by a piglike snort, a soft spatter, and someone moaning. Everyone would turn to see Zopf grinning as he waved to his victim. In time, whenever we had grapes for lunch or dinner, everyone's study hall vigilance was heightened whenever a monitor left the room.

But it was Ollie, with a bizarre, over-the-top brand of humor, who could create the most inspired chaos. It was he who instituted a relentless assault on John Tuohey when the fidgety, high-strung Father Alphonsus was study hall monitor. Tuohey's desk was the last one in the only uneven row, which blocked the priest's path as he paced, nonstop, back and forth in the rear of the room throughout the study period. To provide for an unencumbered path, he'd direct Tuohey to move his desk to the front of the class. On the first few occasions when this occurred, nothing unusual happened. John would pick up both desk and chair and stagger awkwardly up the aisle with the bulky load, which included his books, while the rest of us went on studying.

One night there was a loud crash. John lay on the floor, the desk, chair, and books spilled ahead of him.

"Tuohey, what *are* you doing?" asked the annoyed and startled priest.

"I tripped on something, Father."

"Well, look where you are going. Pick up that desk and get to the front of the room."

"Yes, Father."

I saw Ollie smiling at Barbera and knew that somehow he was involved in the mishap. The next time Father Alphonsus monitored our study period, it happened again, and then again. Father Alphonsus was furious.

"How can you be so bloody clumsy, Tuohey?"

By now, Ollie had convinced others to stick out a leg as John staggered by with his load. Each time we had Father Alphonsus we waited for the inevitable and when it happened we exploded in laughter while Father Alphonsus went apoplectic. After a while Ollie seemed to tire of these episodes and they stopped. But we always anticipated something from him. And I was to become one of his targets.

Algebra was still stressful for me and tests were a particular source of anxiety because I had a tendency to become stuck on one problem and lose valuable time on others. I'd fidget and doodle and chew on my pencil eraser, puzzling over one problem, hoping that the answer would come in a surge of enlightenment. It seldom did. Often I failed to finish the test before the period ended and papers were collected. I needed a strategy to keep from loitering too long on any one problem, and I thought I'd found one. I didn't own a watch, but I had an alarm clock that I could stash in the well of my desk to keep track of time.

We were about halfway through a test when the whole class jumped to their feet at the fire alarm. Father Wilfrid hurried us from the classroom down the corridor to the stairway before he realized something was wrong. No one else was leaving their classes.

"Wait! Wait up class," he shouted as the leading boys began to gallop down the stairwell. "Wait up," he yelled again. He walked to a classroom where Father Alban was teaching, then returned looking embarrassed and amused. He ordered us back to our classroom where my alarm clock was still ringing.

"Mr. Connolly, boys, has brought his own alarm clock for fear he might fall asleep during one of my exams. Why don't you bring that up here for now, Michael, and you can reclaim it at the end of class." He seemed more amused than angry as he announced that due to the "untimely" interruption, he would reschedule the exam for later in the week. I could feel my face burning red as I walked to the front of the room and handed him the clock.

Later that afternoon when we headed out to play football, Ollie, who sat next to me in algebra, told me how he had set the alarm before class. "Did you see the look on Wilfrid's face?" he said proudly. I started laughing at the recollection of the episode while admiring Ollie's imagination and boldness.

Ollie

St. John's paid extraordinary attention to the *Triduum,* the Church's three-day observance before Easter of Christ's last supper with his apostles and his betrayal, death and burial.

It began on Holy Thursday with Mass in which Father Alban read from John 13:1-20. I closed my eyes, trying to picture the scene:

He rose from supper and took off his outer garments. He took a towel and tied it around his waist. Then he poured water into a basin and began to wash the disciples' feet and dry them with the towel around his waist. When he had washed their feet and put his garments back on and reclined at table again, he said to them, "Do you realize what I have done for you? You call me 'teacher' and 'master,' and rightly so, for indeed I am. If I, therefore, the master and teacher have washed your feet, you ought to wash one another's feet.'"

Then the rector, Father Wilfrid, removed his outer vestment, tied a towel around his waist and approached twelve students, two from each high school grade and two college levels, seated with bare feet. Kneeling before each one, he poured water over their feet into a large pan, then washed and dried each foot.

I had never seen this in a decade of regular, weekly Mass attendance and was mesmerized. A priest, the rector no less, kneeling before students. Washing their feet!

After Mass, the altar and all its flowers and finery were stripped and the lights were dimmed. Silently, somberly, we filed from the chapel to our dorms.

On Good Friday, despite blooming spring outside, we awoke very much aware of Jesus' impending trial and his resignation to death. There were no classes. Meals were sparse and the solemnity of the day was underscored by a six-hour silent retreat.

Holy Saturday was anticipation of prophetic resurrection, confirmed symbolically at midnight when the darkness was pierced as the chapel's 10-foot oaken doors opened to admit the Easter candle. Its single flickering flame was solemnly relayed among a hundred other candles held by us seminarians; the chapel's lights went up, revealing scores of Easter lilies around the sanctuary and priests in white vestments proceeding single file toward the altar. Simultaneously, the organ's full force reverberated, prompting the assembly into songful praise: *Hosanna in Excelsior Deo*.

◆ ◆ ◆

Every day of Easter week was a holiday with no classes, beginning on Monday with a trip to Treman State Park near Ithaca. The chartered bus pulled into the park and we watched in awe as a million gallons of rushing snow melt plunged over limestone cliffs into the pools below.

Piling from the bus into the snappy spring air and budding vegetation, we continued shedding winter doldrums with softball, hikes along the gorge's high ridges, and picnic fixings.

Back at St. John's later in the week some of us freshmen went nuts with the week's unprecedented freedom. After pulling out a boxful of tennis balls, someone beaned a student walking down the second-floor hallway. In no time tennis balls were flying all over, ricocheting off walls and pummeling students. The free-for-all mounted steadily with seminarians diving into dorms for cover and others being picked off like ducks in a shooting gallery. Raging adrenaline blotted out all consciousness of numerous Rules' violations that were taking place, including prohibitions against visits to other dorms and running or shouting anywhere in the building.

Finally, exhausted and sweaty, we quickly gathered the balls and returned them to the sports locker, relieved we were not caught, but uplifted by the rare opportunity to let loose.

◆ ◆ ◆

To guard against the formation of close relationships that was discouraged by seminary policy, dormitory assignments were shaken up every semester. It meant a new dorm senior and a whole new cast of roommates. The senior in charge of my dorm in our second semester was Barry Lonergan, who kept a hawk's eye on the charges assigned to him.

I was awakened from deep sleep one night by Kevin Kristoff, a classmate, kneeling beside my bed fondling me. It was my first experience of anyone but my mother thirteen years earlier or a physician touching me. Stunned and disgusted and feeling an overwhelming concern about being associated with such an act, I found myself restrained from making a sound lest it call anyone's attention to what was happening, I froze while Kristoff continued boldly touching me. Then I was alarmed to see Barry's silhouette against the window above his bed. He was sitting up reaching for his glasses.

"Get out of here," I hissed, and Kristof scurried back to his bed on hands and knees. Like a rat, I thought. It happened quickly and quietly. Barry's eyeglasses were virtual Coke bottles, so he could not have seen anything.

Neither Kristoff nor I ever acknowledged to each other what happened. I had never particularly liked him. Now I was repulsed by him. I felt violated and ashamed and would have enjoyed nothing better than to beat him up—and might have, were it not for the specter of immediate expulsion.

Kristoff seemed to have an affinity for two or three other freshmen and, following his approach to me, I came to suspect they were all queers, even though I wasn't sure what that meant. Outside of our shared classes, I made it a point to never associate with these guys. I treated them like they had something contagious.

Mike

Stimulated by our periodic pickup basketball games—especially our successful outing against Father Peter—John's good-natured ribbing about the Earl of Ham, and his general affability, I had warmed up to him and our friendship was taking root. We walked together around the building at night before study hall, and, before long, he confirmed what I had suspected. He wasn't at all threatened by my challenge on the stairwell on the first day we'd met. It was an irritation rather than a threat, "like a tack in my shoe," he said. I also learned that, despite his seeming confidence, he, like me, wanted to remain as invisible as possible at the seminary. We had something else in common: he despised his abusive father and wished he'd come from a different family. One night during one of our walks he said, "I'd like to change my name."

"Really? To what?" I asked.

"Deacon Flagg," he said

"Deacon Flagg?" I asked.

"Yeah, with two *g*'s."

"Why do you want to do that?" I was interested.

"When I came here I was pudgy, asthmatic, insecure, and intimidated by people; I'm not like that now. A new name would go with my new identity. How about you?"

"I wouldn't mind giving up Earlham, but what would I pick?" I stopped and thought for a moment, hoping something would come to me. I looked over at John who had stopped walking too. Next to him, all buffed up, I was a scrawny little kid. In fact, next to many of the guys at St. John's, I was a skinny runt. Scrappy, but scrawny.

"Hey, how about Rick Savage?"

John laughed. "Rick Savage. Yeah, that fits."

John

If for no other reason, I looked forward to summer vacation because it might relieve the pressure I felt every day, not knowing whether I would be allowed to return to St. John's for sophomore year. There were no friends I wanted to see back home. The only person I was anxious to see was my cousin Maureen, and that made me nervous.

I said to Denny Walsh, "When I go home I'm going to lock myself in my house."

"Why would you do that?"

"So I don't have to see any girls. They drive me nuts."

"Tuohey, half the world is women. If you become a priest, what are you going to do, just save male souls? You have to live among women. There is no way that you can lock yourself away from women in this world."

In the seminary we weren't avoiding the "occasion of sin" by dint of willpower. We were *good* because there was so little opportunity to be *bad*. There was little "occasion of sin," at least as I then understood it. The only females around St. John's were the elderly wife of the groundskeeper who lived in a cottage alongside the seminary grounds and a secretary who worked in an office isolated from the rest of the building. I was not afraid of "women in this world," as Denny seemed to conclude. I was afraid of just one, who was for me the embodiment of all women.

◆ ◆ ◆

As school ended in June and we scattered to our homes, I was about to bump my nose on a troubling truth. Although I had become a very different boy in my year at the seminary, I returned home to be the boy I had been, Johnny.

Again, I did not unpack my suitcase. I continued to go to Sunday Mass, but never went to daily Mass. I did not go out to play basketball or any other sports. I sought out no friends.

I rededicated myself to watching television. Endlessly I watched episodes of *Gunsmoke, Wyatt Earp, Sugarfoot, Maverick,* any show in which the good guy could exercise his option of killing guys who pissed him off. Thrown into the mix were shows like *Father Knows Best,* where a calm rational dad was sober, helpful, and nonviolent. On television that was a possibility.

I always watched Ed Sullivan. I suppose all Americans were duty bound to do so. Ed had had Elvis on twice, but we were away in the seminary and so had missed those crucially important cultural events. Perhaps I thought that it could happen again, and it did, although we were back in the seminary when it happened.

The one exception to my monasticism was my visit across the lawn to Maureen's house, where our activities were anything but conducive to one's preparation for the priesthood.

I had sunk into a sort of winter of the soul, waiting for the fall and my return to being John Tuohey. Of course, that was wishful thinking. I still had no idea if I would be accepted back at the seminary. I thought that I should prepare my father. Interestingly, it did not occur to me that I should prepare my mother. She might not be happy about my leaving, but she wouldn't give me a hard time about it. Whatever blowback I was going to receive would come from my father. I decided to broach the subject one night as we rode in the car.

"Daddy, I may not be going back to the seminary."

"What do you mean?"

"They may throw me out."

"What? Why would they throw you out?"

"Well, a few of us were caught smoking, and you can be thrown out for that." He looked startled, glanced inquiringly at me.

So are they gonna throw you out or not?"

"I don't know yet. They'll let me know."

"Oh." He did not say another word about it. I couldn't believe that there was no lecture. I convinced myself that he was both startled and pleased that I had done something rebellious, something that was somehow manlier in his eyes.

We were required to write a letter to Father Owen twice during the summer to let him know what we were doing, and in some instances, I suppose, to let him know if we planned to return. My July letter was sparse. I wrote about all the activity I was willing to discuss, like reading books and watching television.

In response to all the students, Father Owen wrote an update of the activities of each boy. In his letter he said that John Tuohey was immersing himself in reading, which should prepare him for sophomore English with Father DeSales.

I was in.

The relief was astonishing. My stars were aligned. My sleep was peaceful. I could breathe again.

I could then apply myself to one activity I had not mentioned to Father Owen, the one thing that got me out of the house every day, the one thing that burned like a fire in my heart, the thing I should not be doing: falling in love with my cousin, Maureen.

When Maureen and I saw each other at the beginning of the summer, it was as if there had been a tectonic shift. Suddenly I realized that, in addition to being beautiful, Maureen was the sweetest girl on earth; she was so easy to be with; she truly liked me. I was only fourteen, she, thirteen, but we were dealing with very adult feelings. We were like Terry Davis back in the Bronx with his blasting caps: playing with something that looked innocent enough, but

John became enamored with his cousin, Maureen, leading to a lot of necking during his first summer vacation. Eventually, she tired of his obsession, urging him to get a real girlfriend because "you don't seem to really want to be a priest."

was potentially explosive. We both knew that we should not have a romantic attachment. For one thing, kids that age are too young to be enmeshed in passionate love affairs. For another, we were first cousins, so this could never go anywhere. Our parents would be furious; my life could be at stake. I was going to be a priest, for God's sake. I was not supposed to go near any girl, certainly not my cousin. We knew all that. It didn't matter.

We latched on to each other like drowning people to a raft. Every day we went into her finished basement, put slow music on her record player, and slow danced for hours. In the process of dancing we kissed and kissed. Just kissing. Just lips, no tongues. No fondling. Always vertical. Whatever erotic fantasies I had concerned only kissing and involved finding some way that it would become okay for Maureen to marry me. I don't know how we managed to remain as chaste as we did. I don't know how we did not get caught. There must have been days when our lips looked as if we'd had silicone injections or a severe beating. Probably our parents could never dream that their innocent children (one headed for the priesthood, for Christ's sake) would be dancing on the edge of a carnal conflagration.

At times I tried to figure out how I might become a priest and also marry Maureen, which would have required some astonishing rearrangement of the known universe and the behavior of humans within it. When you start creating a dream world in which the Pope issues special dispensation for a Franciscan priest to marry his first cousin, and all their relatives glow with happiness at this cosmically ordained wedding of two people destined to produce genetically challenged children . . . well, you have strayed far down the wormhole.

Fortunately, Catholic guilt, Maureen's maturity, my timidity, and the arrival of September kept this picture more in the early Woody Allen genre, rather than mid-season Tennessee Williams.

Ollie

With one year behind us at the seminary, my parents drove to Montour Falls in June to take Johnny Barbera and me home for the summer. It was dark after the long ride when we left Johnny at the home of his sister in Highland Falls, twelve miles from Putnam Valley. I had no question about wanting to return to St. John's in September. Johnny's attitude was unstated. As the premier class clown, above average academically and involved, like me, on the junior varsity basketball team—however hapless it was—he had seemed happy with seminary life, but I thought his sneaking off with Moose Donovan now and then for a smoke was foolhardy.

In the middle of the summer Johnny and a kid we both had known in Parkchester hitchhiked to Putnam Valley. I was happy seeing my friend again, but the reunion was tempered for me by the presence of this other kid. There was a feeling that, perhaps, I had been replaced. Also, I was uncomfortable knowing Johnny's companion had been in trouble with the law.

They told me about how they had been having a blast while visiting Johnny's sister, including roving through backyards as Peeping Toms, where they had caught some girls and women in various stages of undress. I could not disguise my disapproval, and sadness welled up within. As intriguing as the thought of spying on naked females was, what they were doing was beyond me. Clearly, Johnny was straying far down a different path. Maybe, I thought, he wouldn't be returning to St. John's. No sooner had the thought crossed my mind than he confirmed it, almost casually.

Their visit was short, so short that I wondered whether he came just to deliver the message—or just to say goodbye. He would have known that I would be returning to St. John's. As they prepared to leave, presumably to hitchhike back to Highland Falls, I could see the end of our ten-year friendship, including six years as best friends. We had leaned on each other so often, through fun, mischief, and trouble. Now there was nothing left to say except, "So long; take care."

I never saw him again. I later heard that his father died of the brain cancer that had returned in our freshman year and that Johnny's mother died shortly thereafter, also from cancer. Ever cool, ever secretive, Johnny had never mentioned his parents' cancer.

This was my family's first summer in Putnam Valley. The change from city to country living was hardest for Eileen. A year earlier she was a twenty-six-year-old secretary at RCA in Rockefeller Center and in a whirlwind of New York City nightlife with my father. The romance lifted higher with a daylong wedding celebration at a posh country club, then a one-week honeymoon in Miami Beach.

When the newlyweds landed back in New York, the family moved to a remote, drafty lake cottage that would be a temporary residence while construction continued on the new house. Eileen found herself virtually stranded in the woods with two stepdaughters. My father's commute to the city and work consumed about sixty hours a week.

As a lifelong New York City resident, Eileen had never learned to drive—moot anyway because my father needed the car to get to the city. The nearest grocery store was six miles away. Except for dealing with his wife's morale, my father was in a lifelong dream come true. He had always wanted to live in the country, and he was willing to do whatever it took to sustain this new life.

I returned from the seminary with mixed feelings; happy that we lived in the country and for having my own room for the first time. But I was struggling with my reconfigured family. With no friends in Putnam Valley and with the house so isolated—the nearest neighbor was an aging recluse—I read incessantly, explored limitless miles of country roads and woods by bike and on foot, and navigated a strained relationship with Eileen.

My new close friend was Holden Caulfield. J. D. Salinger's classic was one of many books that summer, and Holden's deep alienation and unrest was odd comfort to me.

I spent countless hours reading in a massive oak tree, which eons earlier had pushed its way through a rock wall that was both a repository for fields of rock and a property line. A huge limb had fallen by some dint of nature—lightning strike, perhaps, or felled by its own sheer weight. One of its ends was on the ground and the limb led upward some ten feet, coming to rest wedged between another limb and a circular pocket in the trunk where I curled up with my book du jour, back and head against the trunk, one leg propped against another limb, the other dangling over the side.

Breaks from reading were just long enough for dreamily drawing in the leafy ceiling and the blue beyond, where ever-altering cloudscapes suggested horses, fish, elephants, dragons, and dispensed endless peace. All around nature's symphony harmonized with the wind through the leaves. Chattering squirrels and buzzing insects created a crescendo in July and August as marauding crows and jays vented mischief throughout the canopy.

"Rich, time for lunch," Eileen called from the back porch.

Most times she sat with me at the kitchen table, sometimes eating with me, other times just to chat, which was usually small talk and kind of annoying.

Out of the blue came a question that left me speechless and very uncomfortable.

"You don't like me, do you?"

I can think I don't like someone, even that I hate them. But I don't tell them, especially if the person is an adult. We were alone. No distractions. Nowhere to go. She waited quietly and patiently for my response. She had it together that way. Not mean or angry. Steady. So logical.

Why don't you leave me alone? I wanted to say.

All kinds of bad feelings erupted at the same time: anger, confusion, fear. I was angry for feeling confused. But still she waited for my response.

"No, I don't," I said, looking down at a half-eaten sandwich.

Her reply was quick: "Well, I like you."

I felt like a rat. Immediately. How could I tell someone who liked me that I didn't like her? I had never felt such turmoil within me. I told the truth, didn't I? No! It wasn't the truth. She had always been nice to me, so why was I so uncomfortable?

She waited at the table a few more minutes, quietly looking at me as if hoping for further discussion. I finished my sandwich in an awkward silence as my internal battle raged on.

Can't she do the dishes or something?

I drank my milk.

"Would you like some cookies?"

"No thanks."

I picked up my book and went back to the tree. But I couldn't read.

Mike

Summer break at the end of my first year at St. John's was disheartening. The street games that had once been a staple of our neighborhood were now rare. One morning I saw my next-door neighbor, Ned Reedy, walking down the street. I bolted out our front door.

"Hey, Ned, where are you going?"

"Hi, Mike. Going to football practice."

"You made the team?"

"Yeah."

"What position do you play?"

"End."

"Offense or defense?"

"Offense."

"Wow, that's great! Congratulations. When does everybody get together for street football?"

"We really don't do that anymore. A lot of us are on a team and the coaches don't want us to do anything where we might get hurt and can't play. Gotta go; I'm late."

"Oh . . . Well, good luck on the team this year."

He walked away without even looking back. I sat on the curb for a while throwing stones across the street at the sewer. Then I got up and went back into the house.

I spent most of the time by myself that summer reading books from Marie's library. *What else was there to do?* Father DeSales always encouraged us to write in our spare time. I didn't have much of that at St. John's. I did now. I wrote a poem. The poem was about my home life. It was a feeble attempt to imitate Edgar Allen Poe's *The Raven*.

Home

The house, a spot so bleak and dreary,
There I wander alone and teary,
Thinking thoughts of better days.
There I'm goaded, clearly lacking,
Lacking what my parents want.

Marie discovered it one day when I left it behind on the living room sofa.

"If you're so miserable here, why don't you just stay at the seminary?"

"We can't. We have to leave for vacations."

"Well, if you are going to stay in this house, you'd better show more respect for this family. Or find somewhere else to stay."

"Okay, I will," I replied, trying to sound apologetic without indicating which option I was agreeing to. I spent time wandering through the neighborhoods, reflecting upon my life and where it was headed. Father Peter's words tormented me: "It sounds like you're not just angry with your father, but with our Almighty Father as well." Several times I walked down to St. Michael's Church and sat there alone thinking about what life would be like if I'd stayed in Lowell. What I would be like. I began to feel comfort in the semi-dark solitude of the church. The cross above the main altar was like the one in our St. John's chapel. The two side altars with statues of St. Joseph and the Virgin Mary were similar too. It suddenly dawned on me: *You have a home. A real home. Not here in Lowell, but 400 miles away from here.*

My Aunt Sarah made my summers in Lowell tolerable. Since my mother's death, she had been my strongest supporter. I'd never forgotten the tender feeling of her arms going around me when she emerged from the bedroom after my mother's death. We were older now, but I could still feel those arms invisibly embracing me. I might be a failure in my father's and Marie's eyes, but to Aunt Sarah I was just a boy waiting for the right moment to reach his potential. She had paid for my piano lessons in grammar school. I gave up on them within six months. She encouraged me to become an altar boy, but I failed to master the Latin necessary for serving at Mass. She talked our church's choir director into inviting me to sing in the choir, but I had a singing voice that sounded like a rusty hinge. The choir director put me in the back row and told me to mouth the words to the hymns. This was proof enough for my father and Marie of my incompetence. None of this seemed to faze Aunt Sarah. It was a mystery to me, what she saw in me, but I trusted her.

Mike's Aunt Sarah, a gambler and horse racing aficionado, worked on her nephew's discouragement by pointing to long shots at the races that became winners through endurance and determination.

She played the ponies and every time she went to the racetrack, she'd bet on a long shot to win at least one race. It often did. "Betting isn't much fun if you can't take a chance on a long shot every now and then, Michael," she said. "When a long shot decides to run on a particular day, it doesn't run to place or show; it runs to win."

I found as many occasions as possible to be with Aunt Sarah, who lived on Beacon Street, just two streets from where we lived. On Saturday mornings I'd earn pocket money by doing housecleaning chores for her. On other days, I just went up there to be with her. Like me, she had lost someone she loved—her husband had died in his early thirties. Like me, she'd refused to replace the one she loved with someone else.

"How come you never married again?" I asked her, knowing that she was at least in her forties now.

"No one can replace my Richard," she said putting her arm around me and directing my attention to his picture on the parlor wall. "He was such a wonderful husband."

Aunt Sarah viewed life as an adventure to be embraced. I decided I needed to embrace it, too, with enthusiasm, like her.

I returned to St. John's for my sophomore year with a new sense of purpose. I'd passed all my subjects in freshman year, but I hadn't distinguished myself in any of them. I'd watched with envy classmates like Tom Dever, Richard Roulliard, and John Tuohey make the honor roll and gain reputations as excellent students. John and Ollie had made the school's JV basketball team and Ollie had begun writing for the school newspaper, the *Quill*. I'd done nothing beyond survive my first year. I was the long shot who hadn't even been able to place or show, never mind become a winner. As I waited for the train that would take me to New York City where I'd join other boys for the ride back to the seminary, I pulled a piece of paper from my notebook and wrote: "When a long shot decides to run on a particular day, it doesn't run to place or show; it runs to win."

I folded the paper and put it into my wallet, under the picture of my mother. It was time to run.

Chapter Eight

Sophomore Year, 1957

Mike

Returning to St. John's in September of 1957, I saw one of the ever-present realities of seminary life. Our freshman class had shrunk. Among those no longer present were John Zopf, Fred Delcimento, and Richie Olive's sidekick, Johnny Barbera. As Father Wilfrid had said, "Some of you will discover that the priesthood is not for you."

A smaller class brought us survivors closer together. I had maintained my friendship with John Tuohey, often playing with him in pickup basketball games and regularly walking with him around the building at night before study hall. A friendship with Ollie had begun to develop too. That seemed impossible when Barbera was with us—the two at times seeming inseparable. Now it was happening. John and Ollie played together on the basketball team and had gotten closer there. With Barbera gone, Ollie joined us during our nighttime walks. From the beginning, I'd admired him for his boldness and outrageous sense of humor. In freshman year he seemed too distant and too "cool" to ever consider a friendship with someone like me. The alarm clock incident had drawn us closer, but not made us friends. Now the genuine friendship I wanted was taking form.

John

I was sad to leave Maureen, but happy to return to life in the seminary. We were immediately back into the pattern of work, prayer, and study, having added French and geometry to our class schedule and losing algebra. Otherwise there were no surprises.

Our new Latin teacher was Father Alphonsus, the one priest who had gone out of his way to ride me in freshman year. When

I learned he would be our teacher, I feared that his personal and openly stated hostility to me would cause my grades to be unfairly skewed. I also feared that he would throw me out of class, as he had done in the past in study period. I worried in vain. He did not like me, but he was fair with me. That year he sometimes became exasperated with me, but he did the same with others. Exasperation was, I believe, a condition of his being. I learned to take it in stride.

French was wonderful. Father Alban spoke it the moment he walked through the door. He compelled us to answer in French, feeding us the answers. He always expected a lot from us, and we almost unanimously gave him what he wanted.

The strangest adjustment for me that year was in coming to terms with our losses. Gone were all the seniors from the previous year and several classmates from our first year. It brought home to me that this was a winnowing process:

For many are called, but few are chosen.

I was still here, a place where I had achieved a tremendous level of comfort after escaping the possibility of expulsion. I had become very confident of my place in the seminary. I would never smoke there again. In fact, I had done a personal novena, nine days of special prayers, the past spring. I had sworn to the Blessed Virgin that I would not smoke before I became eighteen, eight months after my expected graduation. I would not be thrown out for bad grades or rebelliousness. I was unlikely to lapse into heresy. I certainly was not going to discuss my cousin with any priests. So, as far as I could see, I had nothing to worry about.

Here in this world, I had grown healthy; I was safe from degradation and beatings; I received accolades; the rules were predictable and constant; punishment was fairly applied and rational. Despite all of that upside, a small voice asked me daily if I was supposed to be here.

Ollie

As much as I enjoyed the summer break, the woods, my perch in the tree, the long hours of solitude, I looked forward, once again, to returning to St. John's. We were required each summer to write to Father Owen, and he responded with a form letter to all students that, somehow, provided updates on everyone's activities. There was my name, with a reference to my hours of reading, which made me feel recognized—special.

It would be strange going back without Johnny Barbera, but I had accepted the fact of our different journeys.

There were scores of seminarians at the railroad station when my father drove me to Hoboken. It was clear who the freshmen were. They were the ones with parents. I spotted two of my classmates, Tom Dever and John Tuohey. As second-year students, we chuckled with a newfound sense of superiority about the anxious freshmen and speculated about how Father Owen would scare the crap out of them.

With St. John's students taking up much of one coach, the train ride was a celebratory reunion, sometimes raucous, with a lot of smoking. I tried two cigarettes and paid dearly for it with a couple of hours of nausea.

As we moved from the train to a chartered bus in Elmira, I lorded over a couple of freshmen with my year of experience as a seminarian—about what they could expect, the assignment to dorms, the nightly silence, etc.

That evening we stood silently in the refectory as the governing triumvirate made their dramatic entrance. However, Father Owen was in the lead, having succeeded Father Wilfrid as rector for the new school year. The new prefect, shuffling along with his long strides, was Father Alban, and Father Mark Traenkle, about eight inches shorter than Father Alban, brought up the rear. The new school year was underway.

After dinner, Father Owen told me he wanted to see me in his office. He always looked serious and, since I had just returned, I wasn't concerned about any major problem. What was unusual was being summoned to the office of the rector.

"Close the door," he said after I entered his office. "Olive . . ." There was a slight pause, a sure sign this was, after all, serious. "Were you and Kristoff engaged in improper conduct last spring in your dorm?"

I was stunned. Months had passed and I had buried the incident, way out of my consciousness. *How did he know? Of course, Lonergan. He saw. Oh my God! I'm going to be sent home.* In an excruciatingly long instant, my head swirled in confusion, shame, and inexplicable guilt, my eyes locked to the floor. I looked at the rector, who waited for a response.

"Yes, Father," I said, abandoning my penchant for lying. I began to shake, expecting the ax to drop. My imagination flashed to the next morning, me sitting in the back of the chapel with my suitcase; the satisfied sneer of that snitching creep, Lonergan; a long, lonely train ride back to the city; telling my father I was expelled . . . and the reason for my expulsion.

"Kristoff is no longer here," he said, which clearly sealed my fate. "Who initiated this?"

I told him what happened.

"Do you want to be a priest?"

I was on the verge of tears. "Yes, I do."

"Have you finished unpacking?"

Here it comes, I thought. "No, Father."

"Go and finish unpacking," he said.

◆ ◆ ◆

Kristoff wasn't the only one gone. So was about a third of our freshman class, including two others I suspected as being queer. Father Owen never said another word about the incident in the dorm. Somehow I felt he understood I was not a willing participant. And I began to feel I had somehow "made it," although I could not have said just what that meant outside of the sense I would not be one of the unfortunates sitting in the back of the chapel waiting for the bus to Elmira. I grew more attentive for a time to what some teachers offered, like Father DeSales in English, Father Edmond in history, and Father Alban, who introduced us to French in our second year. Once that year, and the only time, I placed on the honor roll's second tier with a grade average of eighty-eight percent.

I had grown nearly a foot in one year and maintained my enthusiasm for sports, scoring a career-high twelve points in one basketball game—noteworthy for a perennially horrible team that rarely finished with thirty total points. In touch football I relished the blocking contact and quarterbacking.

Being a sophomore helped my self-esteem. The higher grade carried no special privileges, but there was an unspoken expectation that, as upper classmen, we would be setting good examples of proper seminary decorum. With Johnny gone, my circle of friends expanded. There were some classmates for whom I had a special appreciation: John Tuohey for his wry, sharp wit; Tom Dever, par excellence for impersonating the friars who taught us; Mike Connolly, scrappy and tough enough to more than compensate for his small stature. We attacked each other relentlessly with good-natured putdowns we called "zips." When any of us went at each other about body odor, bad breath, or some personal characteristic, others would gleefully and dramatically declare "zip" whenever someone scored. These bouts generally avoided crossing the line between tasteful embarrassment and hurt feelings.

While my closest friends were among classmates, I enjoyed the company, particularly in sports, of some older guys, like Jerry Waters, an all-around athlete. However, the many hours we spent in class and study periods kept the different age groups generally segregated.

During recess and other free times students routinely walked around the building, either alone or with one or more others. Jimmy Hayes and I started hanging out on these strolls, but after a time I became uncomfortable about the frequent times he sought me out. He was two years older than I was and close friendships were unusual between students in different classes. Confused about my own discomfort, I started avoiding him, leading to an awkward, ongoing cat-and-mouse game. Hayes would look for me for a walk or inquire about my whereabouts while I dodged him in the halls or made sure my strolls were on opposite sides of the building. I heard from some that he was upset by my cold shoulder, which further heightened my anxiety. He cornered me one day and asked, "Did I do anything to hurt you?"

"No," I said nervously, hoping that would suffice. But he waited for more. Clueless about my own distress, I said, "I don't want to talk about it," although I had no idea what "it" was.

That pretty well did it. To my relief and, without another word, we steered clear of each other for the rest of the school year, going about our business as if the other didn't exist.

But my discomfort and confusion lingered.

Mike

For the most part, I'd been a spectator in the great variety of activities at St. John's. I'd done what was required spiritually, physically, and socially, but my obsession with study had kept me from really getting involved. The seminary experience was designed to be more than just religious exercises, study, and work. Dramatic performances were staged several times during the year; those interested in music could audition for the Schola choir; the *Quill*, the school newspaper, was always looking for writers, reporters, artists, silk screeners. Oratorical contests were a yearly event as was the Auxilium Latin contest.

Numerous clubs were available for those interested in photography, science, horticulture—whatever. Each year major Catholic mission events like the Catholic Students Mission Crusade, which took months of preparation, were held. Most of these were voluntary, but we were encouraged and expected to be involved in them. A future priest should, we were reminded, have a wide

Photo credit: the Quill

Class plays were periodic opportunities for aspiring thespians, including Mike who toiled over his one line in his one and only appearance.

berth of knowledge and experience. Or, as Father DeSales was fond of saying, should have the manners and depth of knowledge of an Elizabethan gentleman minus his lasciviousness. I'd not been involved in any extra activities in my freshman year and Father Peter and Father Owen had both noticed and mentioned it to me. It was time; I needed to get more involved.

My first adventure in extracurricular activity was in the production of *The Little World of Don Camillo*. Don Camillo was an Italian cleric and I was his altar boy. I appeared in one scene and had one line of dialogue. As Don Camillo entered the chapel where I was lighting the candles for Mass, I turned to him and said: "Good morning, Don Camillo." That was it, the extent of my role. I took this very seriously and practiced the line over and over—so often that I began to worry about forgetting the line at the big moment.

"*Good* morning, Don Camillo."

"Good *morning*, Don Camillo."

"Good morning, *Don Camillo*."

I managed to do my part, and when the performance ended, I had to endure days of John and Ollie performing their own versions of "Good morning, Don Camillo" for classmates.

John

Coming on the heels of Tom Gallagher's lesson concerning racial prejudice earlier in the year, there was a singular event in our second year. One of the new boys in our class was, as was said in those days, a Negro. I was shocked because I had not realized that Negroes could be Catholic, let alone priests.

Gallagher had been right.

Also, much to my surprise, I was worried about how he would be treated. I was not alone in my reflexive bigotry. But to my surprise, it seemed that everyone was trying to watch their mouths, but he must have heard that word more than once. I could feel his sense of isolation, and I wanted to be friendly. I tried. But it was as if there was some barrier. This boy and I seemed incapable of relaxing with one another. No real bond formed between us, and, sadly, none with anyone else. He did not return after Christmas and I recognized that we had failed him.

◆ ◆ ◆

Photo credit: Franciscan Friars of the Atonement, Graymoor Archives

Ollie (No. 6, far left) and John (No.14, far right) were on the school basketball team. Others shown (front row, left to right) are Ron Nickel, Coach Father Boniface, Denny Walsh and (back row, left to right) Joe Gagen, Brian Clendenin, George Nagel, Don Buonocore, Alan Hurley, Jerry Waters.

I had begun a friendship with Mike Connolly late in our first year, and now we began to forge one with Richie Olive, who had been set adrift by the loss of Barbera. Ollie, as we called him, was on his own and finding his way. He was more approachable now that he was alone, but always maintained an aura of distance; if not a wall, still a fence.

Ollie and I were on the basketball team and Mike joined us more and more for pickup games. The three of us were probably the most dedicated gym rats in our class. We seemed to like the same things, from books to girls. Once when we were standing in a classroom, waiting for class to begin, I was looking out at Route 14 and saw a nicely constructed young lady walking by.

"Look at that ass," I said.

Ollie looked at her and asked, "What can you do with an ass?"

I reflected on that for a second, then responded, "I don't know. But I'd really like to find out."

I would not have said that to many of our classmates.

Ollie

Except for the semester that I made second honor roll, I did nothing to distinguish myself academically. I resigned myself to life in the middle of the pack. Trying to match the class's two brains, John Tuohey and Tom Dever, was pointless. Tuohey achieved stratospheric grades effortlessly and with such a lackadaisical attitude that it bordered on lethargy. This drove Dever nuts because he had to study his ass off to stay close to Tuohey's near-perfect grades.

I contented myself with competing in sports, where I was a bit faster and stronger than many, though not quite the legend of my mind. Dever, endlessly energetic, was intense and competitive about everything. Relentlessly, he challenged me to wrestling matches he never won.

The year progressed with a sense of familiarity that made our activities more and more rote. Some of us talked and fantasized more and more about the outside world, which, the friars often reminded us, had many temptations that could divert us from the priesthood. The world, according to the consistent message in the seminary, was there, not here. Them, not us. If you opted for there, the door swung one way. It would hit you with full force when you left. A brief stream of light from the rotunda would slice into the chapel's darker space when you opened the ten-foot high chapel door to catch the bus. Some would turn to see who the person was. Later, there would be murmurings.

Did he want to leave? Were his grades poor? Did he get into trouble?

Whatever the reason, the collective conclusion was he did not belong here. Once gone, the departed were quickly forgotten.

Commitment to the religious life was years away, but the tension between the two worlds was real and now. Seminary life was secure and predictable, weekdays and weekends virtually identical. Boundaries were as definite as the seminary property lines that defined our physical limits. At the same time, the world, with all its temptations, represented unknown and broad horizons. There were people and places there I loved: my father and sisters, other family members, the tree in Putnam Valley. Also, there were some enticing forms of entertainment out there—television, new movies, and rock and roll. Our isolation from there was even more established by the censorship in the library, where provocative pictures of women or anything racy were redacted from newspapers and weekly magazines. The only times we had access to popular culture was Saturday night, when Father Alban would show a movie that was, at least, a few years old. Otherwise, we would have to wait for Christmas and summer breaks to sample current culture. It was increasingly evident that committing one's life to poverty, chastity, and obedience was not child's play.

On one of my parents' visits my father took me to the vacant Havana Glen State Park and let me drive around the dirt road circling the ball fields. With him alongside me in the passenger seat, I looked out over the hood ornament trying to imagine the open spaces and freedom beyond. It was like being handed the keys to adulthood.

Mike

"You ought to try out for the basketball team," John said to me one afternoon as we walked across the bridge over Catherine's Creek to the football field.

"You gotta be kidding. Someone my size will never make it."

"Size doesn't matter. You're getting better. You've made a lot of progress. You're a good athlete and you're scrappy. Try out."

I thought about it that afternoon and for days afterward. I liked basketball and was spending more time playing it during free times. My intramural team had made it to the finals the previous year. But seeing the size and the skills of the other boys who'd made the team in freshman year, I wasn't sure. Father Peter also encouraged me to try out. "You've gotten more aggressive, more confident. You ought to at least try out. Who knows what might happen!"

Try. I'd been hearing that over and over again in my life but hadn't *really* been hearing it. I had grown too used to failure even though some adults, Aunt Sarah in the lead, had been consistent in their effort to teach me one lesson: *try*.

I tried out for the team. I didn't make it. But on the day of final tryouts, the coach, Father Boniface, took me aside and said. "Try out again next year; you're improving. I think you may have a good chance to make the team next year." *Try.*

I tried other things that year. I tried writing some articles for the *Quill,* but I either threw them away unfinished or they never made it into the paper. I tried writing some religious poetry. When I showed it to Father DeSales, he tactfully suggested I might try another form of writing. "Prose, perhaps." What I tried the hardest at, what I most wanted, was to make the honor roll. I'd learned some of the discipline and some of the skills of study in freshman year, but I wasn't doing as well in tests as I needed to. Jealousy, we were taught, was a sin. But I was jealous. I watched classmates like Tom Dever and John Tuohey consistently make the honor roll. John's ability to do it was particularly frustrating. He did it with the ease of a master key fitting into a familiar lock. The nights before important exams, while I sat anxious and sweating in study hall, trying to force as much information as I could into my mulish memory, I'd glance over at John and see him reading—usually a war story or some novel. When tests were handed back, his grade was almost always the highest or one of the highest.

Dammit! Why couldn't I have been born with a brain like that? I came close a couple of times. But I failed to make the honor roll.

◆ ◆ ◆

Travelling home for summer break, I was overwhelmed with discontent. *Failed. You can't finish anything. The horse had finally decided to run but the result was the same—failure.*

I'd found some ways to limit my stays at home during vacations. At Christmas, I'd spent five days with Joe Silvia, in New Bedford, Massachusetts. I listened to his father's stories of the fishing industry and was happy with the Silvia family, a real family, and with life in New Bedford. I spent the first two weeks of summer break in Marblehead, Massachusetts, with Richard Roulliard, another classmate.

Thomas Wolfe, a favorite of mine, had written *You Can't Go Home Again,* but sometimes you have no choice, and home is where I spent the eight remaining weeks of summer. Life there was much the same: no street games, no one to hang around with, the family as chaotic and miserable as ever. I read more books from Marie's library, did my household chores, mowed neighbors' lawns to get money to go to a movie, and visited Aunt Sarah every Saturday. The week before I was to return to St. John's, she asked, "What's the matter, Michael; you seem so unhappy?"

I didn't want to tell her; I didn't want to tell anyone. I felt her arm around my shoulders. "Come over here and sit down," she said, steering me to a sofa. "What's wrong? You look more miserable than I've seen you in a long time."

There was a long silence, me remembering, *Connolly men don't cry*. Finally, the words burst out like a volcanic eruption: "I can't do it. I'm no good at anything. I screw up everything I try. I'm just a jerk."

"What are you talking about? You're not a jerk. What makes you think you're a jerk?"

Her hands felt warm, silky. And her voice; there was something about it that made me want to spill out all my misery the way I had years earlier to my mother when Mrs. Brown had taken all my marbles.

"I can't do it, Aunt Sarah. I'm just a failure. I'll always be a failure."

"What are you talking about?" she said, tightening her grip on my hand and pulling it closer. "What do you mean you're *just* a failure?"

"Remember how you told me last summer about the horse that finally decides to run? How it isn't going to run to place or show? How it's going to run to win? Well I tried last year; I tried to run to win, but I didn't win. I didn't win anything."

"Go on," she said.

"I tried to make the school basketball team, but I didn't make it. I tried to write for the school newspaper, but none of my articles were accepted. I tried to make honor roll, but I didn't."

She moved in closer to me and put her arm around my shoulder. I could smell her lilac perfume.

"Look at me." she said.

Reluctantly, I looked up. The lines that usually marked her face seemed to have smoothed out. Her eyes were on fire with excitement. She was smiling, almost laughing.

"Michael," she said in a voice as soft as a love song, "when I told you that when a horse that has never won decides to run to win, I didn't mean he always wins on that day. He has to learn how to run to win. He has to stay determined. If he does, one day he wins. You're not a loser just because you don't achieve the things you want to on your first try. Don't give up. One day you'll be a winner. I'm betting on you."

I thought about what she had said when I went down to St. Michael's the next day for Sunday Mass. Kneeling, I prayed silently. *Lord, don't let me be a failure. Help me be a winner.* After Mass, I went home and pulled out my wallet and found the paper on which I'd written: *When a long shot decides to run on a particular day, it doesn't run to place or show; it runs to win."* Under those words, I wrote: *"I'm betting on you, Michael"—Aunt Sarah*. And I underlined it.

John

Returning home for the summer filled me with ambivalence: anxious to see Maureen, sorry to be going home.

Once again, I did not unpack. For a time, I resumed my routine of sleeping late and getting lost in television. However, my isolation was watered down by my obsession with Maureen, the suffocating control and lunacy of my father—on full display in a disastrous, very brief visit from Jerry Waters—and a weeklong visit in upstate New York with Ollie and his family. Mr. Olive led us in saying grace before meals and we engaged in conversation at the dinner table. Everyone was relaxed with each other. It was a new experience.

"Come with me," my father said one morning, yanking me from isolation. "We're going to Charlie Chilion's house."

Charlie Chilion, my father's friend, was the father of an eighth-grade classmate, Lorraine Chilion.

"He's getting his basement finished. You're gonna help the workmen."

"What will I do? I don't know anything about construction."

"You don't have to know anything to carry boards or dig holes. And you're not gonna sit around the house all day."

For the next month, I spent every day in and around the basement of Charlie's house, carrying stuff in and out, holding stuff up, cleaning things up. An elderly plumber who came to build a septic system made the project memorable for me. He was short and rotund, with white hair and thick hands. He was a quiet, patient teacher and he took a shine to me. He had me dig the large hole for the septic tank and the sloping ditch from the house to the hole. We lined the hole with concrete blocks. He taught me how to cut pipe and showed me how thick felt was tamped down into the space between the fitting and lead was melted into the crack, cooling to a watertight seal. No one had ever taught me how to do something like that.

"John, when you get out of high school, you should go to plumbing school." he said one day. "I'd sponsor you. I'm not gonna be doin' this forever. Maybe one day you could take over the business."

I was flattered, but didn't he realize that my future lay in the translation of obscure Latin documents in some papal library in Rome?

"Thanks, but I'm going to be a priest."

While working at Charlie's, I got reacquainted with his daughter, Lorraine. She was now very pretty, with an amazing body and a deep, sexy voice. She was friendly in a flirtatious way. I found her scary. Sometime in July, my father announced that he had told Charlie that I could tutor Lorraine, who had failed Latin and geometry.

"I don't want to tutor Lorraine, Daddy."

"He's a friend, and she was your classmate. You're supposed to be such a hotshot. Help her pass the tests."

"Daddy, I don't know if I can help her."

"I told him you'll do it. Do it."

So Lorraine and I met in her family's finished basement three hours on Tuesdays and Thursdays; Latin one evening, geometry the other. Stretched out side by side on a rug with the program du jour, we established a changeless pattern. I would launch into the topic, ask questions, and have her write things. I used sample exams and fed her the answers with such redundancy that she would remember. Lorraine had a really short attention span. Within half an hour she wanted to watch TV or play cards or wrestle. Or something.

It was the something that had me worried. Lying horizontal beside me, she would start tickling me, mussing my hair, rubbing up against me. I wanted to rip her clothes off and do what people do, whatever that was. I just knew that I was very aroused and terribly scared. "Lorraine, put that magazine down. Pick up your book. Stop playing with my hair. Don't tickle me. Stop looking at me. Don't lie there like that. Yes, you do know what I mean. Stop stretching like that. I didn't say I didn't like it. We're here to do Latin (geometry)." And on and on, twice a week.

I wanted to give in so much. It just happened that I wanted not to give in a little more. If that was a test from God, it was a dandy.

Toward the end of the summer, all tutoring completed, my father said, "Lorraine's parents are throwing a sixteenth birthday party for her. You're invited."

"I don't want to go. Besides, she didn't invite me."

"Yes, she did. She put you on the list. Besides, I'm invited too. You're going."

The evening of the party was sultry. I had always been self-conscious about my prolific sweat production, and after walking the seven blocks to Lorraine's house I was wet. The Chilions' garage door was open and there were about twenty teenagers inside. The sound of rock and roll drifted out. My father headed toward the house with me close behind.

"Grown-ups in the house, kids in the garage," announced Lorraine's mother.

"I'd like to stay with my father." I was pathetic.

"Go join the kids; you'll have a lot more fun out there."

Really?

I walked to the opening of the garage and stopped. Some of the kids noticed me. Except for Lorraine, I knew none of them. My sweating went into overdrive, large beads rolling down my face and soaking my shirt. It was that sweat of terror that carried a sour funk totally unlike the sweat of vigorous sports and infinitely more offensive. Some kids looked at me, then turned and said something to others, who then glanced at me. In my effort to not be noticed, I had made myself the center of attention—which made me sweat more.

I stood there for more than an hour. Then I told myself to do something. So I walked to the backyard, took out my rosary, and prayed, as loud music and laughter echoed behind me. Feeling calmer after finishing the rosary, I decided to go in the garage. I walked a few feet beyond the bay door with the intention of leaning on the wall, in casual repose, engaged but removed. Sadly, I never noticed that where I put my hand was a sheet of unattached plywood leaning against the wall. When I leaned on it, the bottom of the sheet slid out and I crashed to the floor. The noise was startling and people were suddenly clustering around to check on the strange boy in the doorway.

After several *are you okays* they returned to the party and I resumed being mute. The party went on for another hour or two. I never conversed with anyone, never was asked my name, never asked for anyone else's name.

That was my first teenage party. I was never invited back.

Despite the summer's various activities, Maureen remained the center of my world. Like a cat bringing in dead mice, I brought all my needs and longings and loneliness and laid them at her feet. When Maureen pushed back about our dancing and making out—"Johnny, we should stop doing this"—I came close to saying, "Okay," but resisted. I wanted a fourteen-year-old girl to curtail her social life, be available every day, risk embarrassment, and violate her conscience. Essentially, I wanted her to take care of me.

◆ ◆ ◆

Jerry Waters, who also lived in Long Island, came to visit one day with two of his friends. The four of us were in the kitchen when my father came in with his new puppy trailing behind him. Very excited to see new humans, especially ones making a fuss over him, the puppy peed on the floor. My father, cursing, grabbed the dog and frantically snatched the metal leash hanging on the wall. Pressing the puppy's body against the floor with one hand, he beat the dog's head with the chain, saying over and over, "This'll teach you. This'll teach you." All the while the puppy screamed in pain and terror. I knew the feeling well.

Jerry and his friends watched in shock; I in utter shame.

Exhausted, my father let go of the pup, which ran screaming to hide somewhere.

"That's how you train them. Right from the get-go. He won't think about doin' that again. So, you boys want a sandwich?"

"No, that's okay. We just stopped by to say hello," Jerry said. The three boys muttered goodbyes and left.

I dreaded seeing Jerry back at St. John's, but at the same time I wanted some validation of my perception that my father was insane. But Jerry did not return. I never saw him again.

Ollie

Summer continued to mean freedom from classwork and chapel time, and such niggling minutiae as folding a towel over the bottom rung of my bed and washing my socks every day. I devoted endless hours to reading novels, watching television, listening to pop music, and hiking through the woods that surrounded our home.

My family and I remained secluded socially, except for periodic visits from family friends and relatives. I knew no one my age in this very rural area and was happy when two classmates from St. John's, Dever and Tuohey, came from Long Island for separate one-week visits.

Tuohey and I hitchhiked one day to Peekskill to go to a movie. Brigitte Bardot was featured at one theater in *And God Created Woman*. Glancing over her shoulder from the movie's billboard, the sultry, naked Bardot beckoned from a pool of water that barely covered her breathtaking hips. Feigning casual curiosity, we nevertheless gaped, entranced.

Half jokingly, I said, "Shall we?"

Tuohey nodded.

"Serious?"

"Let's go," he said.

I headed for the ticket booth while reaching into my pocket.

"Of course it would be a mortal sin," he said.

This, I thought, is not going to happen. Hoping that my disappointment was not obvious, I said, "Had you there for a minute, didn't I?" We chuckled at the notion of two aspiring priests going to a movie condemned by the National Legion of Decency, the Church's censorship arm that nixed certain films for lewd or morally objectionable content. *And God Created Women* qualified.

In the alternative, we wandered aimlessly around Peekskill before settling for a stop at a soda fountain.

Chapter Nine

Junior Year, 1958

Ollie

My grades began slipping in my third year. It didn't really hit me until report cards came out after the first quarter when I saw my average in the seventies. I thought I'd recoup, but grades on tests in most of my subjects in the second quarter showed no signs of recovery.

Slipping grades coincided with some risky adventures. At first there were a couple of postmidnight kitchen raids with Tom Dever, which yielded leftover desserts. While the Rule was silent about sneaking into the kitchen specifically, we knew instinctively there would be serious consequences if we were caught. With regard to another activity—leaving seminary grounds without permission—there was no question about what would befall us. This, the Rule emphasized, was "gravely serious and will ordinarily bring about expulsion." With that hovering over our heads, Dever and I met at 2:00 A.M. on the basement level and quietly opened and closed the door. We dashed down the driveway until slowing to a walk in the neighborhood adjacent to St. John's. Adrenaline flowed with the sense of adventure and we whispered excitedly as we walked the four blocks toward Montour Falls. At the Blue Ribbon Cafe on Route 14, which was open twenty-four hours, two truck drivers, their rigs humming on the highway shoulder, were the only customers. They sat at the counter, chatting with the waitress, the three of them smoking. She looked up as we entered and sat at a table near the door.

"Be right back," she said to the men, flicking, then resting her cigarette on an ashtray and picking up two menus. "You boys traveling?" she asked while looking out to the parking lot and handing us the menus. That stumped me. I was happy to hear Dever speak.

"No. We'll just have . . . two Cokes, please."

She gathered the menus. Her smirk suggested she figured we were from the seminary or, at least, up to no good. Before returning, she paused at the counter and took another drag from her cigarette. She said something quietly to the truck drivers, who turned to look at us, and the three chuckled as she returned with the Cokes.

"Okay, boys. Will there be anything else?"

I felt myself blushing, like we'd been caught.

"No, thanks," Dever said.

I took a couple of swigs thinking, *All this for a Coke?*

We stared at our drinks without speaking until Dever said, "You ready?"

"Yeah."

We walked to the cash register where we were joined by the waitress, still smirking. "That'll be twenty cents."

As we headed for the door she called, "You boys be careful now," and the truckers started chuckling again.

We walked back toward the seminary quietly for a couple of blocks before Dever said nervously, "I hope no one saw us leave."

Mike

When the new school year began, I recognized a particular positive change in me. At five-seven and 145 pounds, about the same size of many others in my class, I was no longer "little Mikie." I could drop the mask of Earlham, the runt who wanted to be a tough guy but wasn't. And I was now an upperclassman.

"Are you going to try out?" There it was again—*try*.

John, Ollie, and I were walking across the bridge after a football game, on our way to take a shower and prepare for supper. It had been a good afternoon for me; I'd caught a touchdown pass, thrown a few good blocks on run plays, and even run the ball for yards a few times myself.

"I don't know, maybe."

"Come on, try out," John said, shouldering me into the bridge railing.

Basketball season would be starting soon. Ollie and John had been on the team since freshman year and were guaranteed to be starters this year.

Photo credit: Gerry Whitfield

Regardless of athletic ability, participation in sports was mandatory for all students four hours weekly. Sports enthusiasts devoted many hours to games of choice on Wednesday, Saturday and Sunday afternoons.

"There're some open slots on the team and you oughta try out," Ollie said grabbing my T-shirt and shaking me as if I was a stuffed toy.

"I'll think about it," I said as we entered the building.

Heading to the gym for a pickup game about this time, Father Peter asked: "Are you planning to try out for the basketball team this year?"

"I'm thinking about it, Father. Maybe."

"You should; you're bigger now, taller, and you've filled out. You're tougher. Give it a try."

I had been thinking about it—a lot. A few times, I'd taken the paper from my wallet: *I'm betting on you, Michael.*

When we received the first quarter report card, I carried it to my desk and put it face down, not daring to look at it. *What if I . . . what if I didn't* . . . I sat staring at the back of the card, hands folded in front of my face, my breath a warm, wet tempest of emotion. *Lord, please remember my prayers; don't let me miss again.* I drew a breath, so deep I felt my chest would float off, a hot air balloon on a journey of its own, and flipped over the card. It didn't register right away. And then: *I did it; I made the honor roll!*

This was something to celebrate: I had begun to learn how to run to win.

"So," Ollie said, "now that you're on the honor roll, do you think you might honor us with your presence on the basketball team?"

"Yeah," said John. "Next week; tryouts."

Two weeks later, I made the team.

John

The end of summer break was to return to the only sane, safe place on earth. In our third year we were, once again, smaller in numbers. There was one addition, Ronnie Driver, from Massachusetts. He seemed to have come to us through a complete fluke. Few of us displayed a great deal of spirituality, but most of us had our moments. There were days when we turned inward, became meditative. There were moments when we contemplated the big picture. Ronnie had no "inward" that we could discern. If he had a spirit, it was the spirit of Puck, if Puck were a well-built, handsome Italian kid. To call Ronnie irreverent would make irreverence blush. His countless whimsical misdemeanors included prostrating himself when no faculty were around in the center of the chapel, accompanied by a collective gasp from all of us assembled there. Another was climbing the altar and turning himself into a statue, which we had to carry off—he maintaining his statue pose—before the priests arrived. Either of these things would almost certainly have resulted in immediate expulsion.

We had a science course instead of math, but everything else was the same, same Mass, same chapel, same basketball. There was great safety in sameness, in the almost complete predictability. I began to consider that I had escaped to this place because I was so fearful of that place outside. Outside was unpredictable, coarse, dangerous. It was also seductively attractive. Maureen was outside; other girls were outside. Outside there were television and cars, late nights and late mornings. What did I want, really? How much did I love God? What would I be willing to give up forever? I still had Mike and Ollie, and they shared my fears and puzzlement.

◆ ◆ ◆

I went to Confession one day with Father Peter. Even though he fouled me a lot when we played pickup basketball, I liked him.

"Father Peter, can I ask you a question?" I had never spoken the name of a priest in Confession or asked a question of one in my life.

"Sure, Tuohey, go ahead." In such a small school, living with the priests as we did, there was never the slightest chance that your confessor did not know you. That probably made it easier to behave well. We had no anonymity.

"Father, is it a sin to think about kissing girls?"

"Are you talking about just kissing them, nothing else?"

"Yes, Father, just kissing."

"On the lips?"

"Of course." What in the world did he mean by that? Where else would you kiss them? More correctly, where would you think about kissing them?

"Well, Tuohey, I believe that it's not a sin. But I want to suggest something to you. You're a man crossing a desert. It's not in your best interest to keep thinking about water."

I was very happy to hear that it wasn't a sin, but I had every intention to keep thinking about water.

Mike

Ollie was a terrible liar. Not because he lied often or was good at it, but because he was terrible at it. His lies were often so bad they left those he lied to slack-jawed. He was, we knew, also an expert at creating comical chaos, like the days of tripping John Tuohey or the alarm clock incident in algebra class. The combination of being a bad liar and a master of turmoil made Ollie the hero in many stories we told each other. One of the "liar, liar, pants on fire" stories was one in which Ollie, who loved war books, was secretly reading one during a class lecture by Father Edmund. Our desks had a shelf under the desktop where we kept the book and notebook we carried to class. Ollie had rested his book on the lip of the shelf and was pretending he was listening to Father Edmund while alternately glancing down to read the book. He'd been doing this for half the class. I sat next to him, admiring his cunning.

"Mr. Olive, what are you doing back there?" Father Edmund's voice startled me.

Ollie's head jerked to attention. There was a loud metallic clang at the back of his desk where he had tossed the book.

"Nothing, Father."

It took seconds before a burst of laughter from the class fractured the silence. Even Father Edmund couldn't stifle a smile.

Our French teacher, Father Alban, had a peculiar talent that we admired and wanted, somehow, to disrupt. Whenever he entered a classroom he would give the door a casual backhand push and it would close with a soft click. So precise and easy was the closing that it annoyed us. We were determined to find a way to make the door not close so correctly. Maybe have it close and bounce back open. Just once. One day Ollie conceived a plan from a game of trashcan basketball that some of us played between classes. He gathered three wads of paper, pulled the chair from behind the teacher's desk, and carefully balanced them on the upper rim of the door. "There," he said, chuckling. "Let's see what happens now."

We could hear the familiar *fa-lip fa-lop fallipty-flop* sound of Father Alban's sandals as he came down the hallway. Expectation began to build. I struggled to wipe the grin off my face and noticed others struggling to do it, too. I bit my lower lip and held my breath. The room was electrified with suppressed excitement as Father Alban appeared in the doorway. He gave the door his usual backhand swipe. We watched as one, then another, and finally the third paper wad dropped and bounced off the priest's head, one of them landing in his cowl, the hood around the back of his neck. He turned to us with his characteristic smile: "What's going on here?"

Silence threatened to stretch into eternity. Finally, Ollie said, "I'm sorry Father. A bunch of us were playing trash bucket basketball and the papers got caught up there." The lie was so ludicrous—the odds of three wads of paper somehow landing and balancing on the top of the door was so crazy—that there was a moment of silence. And then the whole class and Father Alban broke into laughter. Father Alban let us savor the moment for a while before he closed his eyes and began the prayer that signaled the beginning of each class.

Ollie

I was really getting into reading novels and war books, especially stuff about World War II. None of it had anything to do with class work. With the full seminary schedule, there was so little time for such reading. So I began smuggling pocket books to the chapel—not during Mass in the morning, but during the noon spiritual reading and the night prayer. I would hold them behind whatever we were supposed to be reading. In *Stuka Pilot* by Hans Ulrich Rudel (New York, Ballantine Books, 1958), I was completely absorbed in the ace pilot's dive-bombing exploits on Germany's Eastern Front while the rest of the student body was focused on more Godly agenda.

Study periods were an excellent opportunity for my reading. I could pull it off in some classes as well, but got caught one day in American history by Father Edmund.

One March day the prefect, Father Alban, called to me as I crossed the hall to another class. "Instead of going out for sports period this afternoon, you have an appointment at three with Father Normand, the spiritual director."

This was something different. I had never had an appointment with a spiritual director, and this priest, Father Normand Prevost, was a pretty mysterious guy. He didn't teach any classes on the high school level, but he would show up now and then to play tag football and kick ass when we tried to block him as he rushed for the quarterback. He was built like a bull. What was funny, though, once he broke through the line, never a problem for him, he couldn't find the quarterback because he was blind as a bat. Every once in a while we would see him leave his room, which was on the second-floor rotunda near the prefect's office. It seemed to be mostly around meal times, when he'd take the elevator upstairs, where the faculty had a dining room on the fourth floor. We didn't know what he did at the seminary.

I knocked on his door and, from within, his sonorous, somewhat spooky voice said, "Come in." The shade in the tiny antechamber was drawn and the room was strangely dark for 3:00 P.M. Quietly, I closed the door behind me.

"Is that you, Mr. Olive?"

Father Normand, arms in his sleeves across his chest, was sitting in an easy chair in front of the window. The only other furnishings were a light, which was off, and another easy chair, which faced him from a distance of about eight feet. Looking in my general direction, he said, "Be seated."

There was no small talk. I was still settling into the seat when he asked, "Do you think you have a vocation for the priesthood, Mr. Olive?"

The question rattled me. No one had ever asked me this and, until now, I had proceeded thoughtlessly hour to hour, day to day with such short-range goals as recess, a basketball game, Christmas and summer vacations.

I . . . uh . . . yes, Father."

He didn't move and said nothing. I waited until the silence seemed silly.

"Yes. I think so, Father."

"You should pray about this, Mr. Olive. Pray about this and come back and see me in three days at the same time."

Is that it? I waited to see if he had anything else to say and began wondering if he had fallen asleep. His eyes seemed to be directed toward the floor. Finally, he broke the silence. "Do you have any questions, Mr. Olive?"

"No, Father."

"That is all then."

◆ ◆ ◆

We were praying—or supposed to be praying—all the time. Seemed that way. But pray about whether I had a vocation? Come up with an answer in three days? How does this work? I went to the chapel once and looked up at the large cross. I didn't know what to say to it. But there were these thoughts: *If I was to be ordained, that would take forever. Another decade, anyway. If I did not have a vocation, I would be leaving. That felt so drastic, so sudden.*

I stumbled through classes, spiritual exercises, and sports over the next couple of days, straining to imagine life away from the seminary while, at the same time, lending ears to a siren song calling from the outside world.

"Come in," Father Normand said. It sounded like a recording from the first appointment. Entering, I noticed his single bed behind a partition, back in a space that clearly was small. I sat down even as Father Normand invited me to do so.

"Have you prayed, Mr. Olive?"

"Yes, Father. And I don't think I have a vocation."

The words were out of my mouth. I had punched my own ticket home.

"Very well; I have been praying for you as well. Now you should take this information to Father Alban."

"Thank you," I said, not realizing how our brief meetings—together no more than ten minutes—were changing my life.

He nodded.

I crossed the small alcove to Father Alban's room.

"Yes?" he called, responding to my knock.

"Father Alban, it's Richard Olive."

Coming from his living space to the antechamber and his desk, he motioned me toward an empty chair. I realized this was one more step out the door. I hesitated briefly.

"What is it, Mr. Olive?"

"Father, I've met with Father Normand. This has helped me . . . realize . . . that I do not have a vocation."

I found it difficult saying this for the second time, pushing myself closer to the door. Father Alban, my French teacher for nearly two years, now charged with keeping close tabs on every seminarian's life, remained expressionless. He sat for an unusually long moment in silence looking at me. Then his lips began moving, but I could not concentrate on his words. My mind was absorbing my radically altered world and the things I'd be facing immediately—calling home, packing my bag, being here when I just wanted to disappear, facing or avoiding friends. I heard him talking about my leaving, which would be in less than fifteen hours.

God, I thought, *am I having a dream?*

I was to call home and retrieve my luggage from the attic at 5:00 P.M., pack while everyone was in study period before supper at 6:15. He said something about best wishes for the future and fell into silence. The meeting was over. I needed something else from what was happening, but couldn't say what it was. Mixed, unidentified feelings surged within me, but I steeled myself.

"Thank you, Father," I said, not clear why I was thanking him. I stood and left his office, suddenly and irrevocably a former seminarian.

John

One day in mid-March 1959, Ollie announced that he was leaving. What?! Why now, so close to the end of the year? Why not finish high school, or at least the year? And the one burning question: how could he leave Mike and me? We didn't ask. There was probably not going to be an answer. Ollie was still a guarded guy, and I was certainly not going to tell him how much I would miss him.

The next morning in chapel, Ollie was the boy in the suit, suitcase beside him, seated in the back. Then he was gone, the parted water closed, and all trace disappeared, seemingly forever. Mike and I were stunned. We had had no intimation that Ollie was approaching that decision.

"What do you think happened?"

"I don't know. Did he tell you?"

"No. How about you?"

"No."

What did this mean for us? Would one of us walk into the chapel one morning and see the other there in a suit? If one of us could so easily blindside the rest, anything was possible. We had seen so many people leave or fail to return, but this was intensely personal. Unspoken, at least on my part, was the question of how he had been convinced to move on, how he had found the courage. I had to admit to myself that Ollie had always been bolder and more confident than I. I could see him coming to a decision and then boldly moving on with it. I doubted I could have the courage to leave.

Mike

Over time I would recognize that my father's warning "Connolly men don't cry" didn't refer just to crying or the emotion that prompted it. It meant Connolly men don't display emotion. With one exception—anger. When my father said "Connolly men" he meant "real men." Real men might feel sadness, disappointment, concern, affection, any number of emotions. But they kept those feelings behind an unemotional expression.

Anger was different. Anger was for self-protection. Broadcast it. It shielded you from danger and protected your private space, the space where other feelings hide. But displays of anger were discouraged in the seminary. I had to find another shield. I often found it in the sarcastic mantra "I care." If my parents didn't write, if I didn't make the honor roll, if I failed to make a team, wasn't selected for a role in a dramatic production, had an article turned down by the *Quill* staff, or heard that another boy thought I was a jerk, I'd duck behind "I care," spitting it out with a snarl or trumpeting it as if I was King of Cool. Sometimes I'd whisper "I care" to myself at night as I tried to let go of some disappointment and drop off to sleep.

But real men, and boys like me determined to act like them, do cry. Just not when others are around.

One day, Ollie pulled John and me and another classmate, Tom Dever, aside.

"I'm leaving tomorrow."

"Where are you going?" John asked.

"Home. I don't have a vocation."

What? What the hell are you talking about? Why now? You're leaving us?

Was I the only one whose mind these questions raced through before skidding to a stop? I stood there staring at Ollie, trying to absorb what he had just said.

"It's time," he said. "It's the right decision."

I was fighting to hold back tears.

There were no "I cares" on our three faces. We did care, but we were too shocked and too hurt to admit it. Besides, Ollie looked like he didn't want to talk about it any further. We parted for our dorms to prepare for supper. Ollie and Dever walking down one corridor, John and I down another.

"What do you think is going on?" John asked.

"I don't know. Did he say anything to you about this?"

"No," he replied. "You?"

"No, nothing."

"I thought everything was okay with him."

"Me too," I said, almost choking on my sorrow.

That night a Connolly man did cry. No one saw him. He made sure of that. The dorm lights were out and the other boys had drifted off to sleep.

◆ ◆ ◆

The next morning, I sat staring at the pews in the back of the chapel, waiting for the inevitable. The chapel door would open. Ollie would come in dressed in street clothes. He'd sit preoccupied and apart from us. Then at some point during the Mass he'd get up and leave. He'd be gone forever from our lives. I stifled the urge to cry again. *Save it,* the voice inside me demanded.

Ollie

As I walked to my dormitory from Father Alban's office, the others were returning from the sports period for showers before study hall. Some in my dorm seemed to take notice that, for the second time in a week during sports, I was still in class clothes. No one asked why I hadn't gone to the gym and I didn't say anything. I lingered around my bunk and closet as the others dressed and went downstairs.

Taking the elevator to the attic to retrieve my luggage, my whole body felt like a throbbing thumb after being pounded by a hammer. Solitude and loneliness swallowed me whole. Even though the words had been spoken and the process for leaving was underway, even though I had brought it to this point, a heavier impact was settling in. My friends were here and, at the same time, we were no longer together. Besides being known and accepted by more than 100 high school and college seminarians and faculty, I was stepping away from a coveted post as assistant editor of the school newspaper, the *Quill*, which, by tradition, had me positioned to become editor in senior year. And suddenly, the allure of the outside world did not have the same sheen.

But it was a done deal.

Returning to the dorm with the suitcase was eerie. I had walked the hallway on the second floor thousands of times over three years, but had never been in it alone. My mind struggled to catch up with the reality of the moment. I had almost completed packing when the bell rang for supper and I joined classmates going down to the refectory.

It seemed everyone was looking at me, but a quick check around the tables confirmed that my imagination was running amuck. For them there was nothing different about the moment. And when the rector's bell gave permission for talking, the familiar suppertime chatter followed—the latest homework, incidents in the classroom, gossip. I had nothing to say. I noticed Dever looking at me curiously a couple of times.

After supper I sought out Dever, Connolly, and Tuohey for a stroll around the building to tell them.

"You're kidding!" Connolly said.

I didn't respond and no one asked why. That had to come from me. I simply said it was my choice. No one asked when. They knew these departures were quick. The four of us had shared many times the attractions of the outside world, like girls, and fantasized about what life would be like "out there." But one of us in that tight-knit circle was now actually leaving?

"Why not wait till June?" Dever asked.

"It's too late," I said. And as I did, I realized that staying for another two and one-half months would be torture. I just wanted to get on with it. "I'm going to get a driver's license and save for a car," I said, not knowing what the point of that was. I was still numb and disoriented. Did I want to convince them, or myself, that I had a well-devised plan? That I had it all together? Was I saying, "Don't feel sorry for me," while, at the same time, tossing some bravado onto my exit? Was I trying to make them envious? Whatever, it only saddened me. The sudden gap between us was widening.

We lapsed into recalling good times, memories about Johnny Barbera, the silliness in freshmen year with classroom farting, the tennis ball battle. Recollecting trailed into silence for almost a full turn around the building before the bell gave its five-minute warning for study period.

"You going to study period . . . well, I guess not," Tuohey said.

"No. I have to finish packing."

"We'll see you, Ollie," Connolly said.

"See you guys," I said.

They went to study hall, I to my dorm. My packing was virtually completed, but there wasn't any place for me to go. Or to be. I was an outsider. When the bell ending study period rang I headed for night prayers in the chapel. With community prayers over, the whole student body, as always, filed out in silence; I, for the last time, feeling extremely strange.

The packed suitcase next to my bed spoke volumes to my dorm mates.

◆ ◆ ◆

The next morning, I waited until everyone left the dorm before carrying my suitcase downstairs and placing it in the rotunda outside the chapel. With the service underway, several boys stole glances toward where I sat in the dimly lit back. It was a very long fifteen minutes before I gathered my coat and stepped to the chapel door. As I crossed the rotunda, passing the life-size statue of St. Francis, praises echoed from the chapel as seminarians joined the angels with hosannas:

Sanctus, Sanctus, Sanctus. Dominus Deus Sabaoth . . .

I recited along with them as I stepped through the main entrance into morning darkness.

An alien in familiar terrain, I walked down the center of the wide driveway under the canopy of denuded elms, stepped off the shoulder of Route 14, and crossed to wait for the southbound bus. The seminary's tall facade loomed across the way, the barest hints of eastern gray sky behind it. The bus hissed to a stop.

"Destination?"

"Elmira railroad station."

I paid the fare and lugged the suitcase to the rear seat. From there I watched the seminary for about a minute until it disappeared behind the hills as the bus rounded a curve alongside Catherine's Creek.

◆ ◆ ◆

Height of irony, the March 1959 monthly magazine of the Franciscan Friars of the Atonement had an article entitled "First Steps to the Priesthood," aimed at boys thinking about a future in the religious life. There, across two pages complete with photos, was me. There was no indication that this "model" seminarian was, in fact, gone. Because I lived relatively close to the friars' monastery in Garrison, New York, one of the friars had arranged for a photo shoot during the 1958 Christmas recess. Four pictures in the article showed me in a series of poses: prayer, kneeling, and reading my missal; study, in white shirt and tie at a desk complete with crucifix, the New Testament, and five other books; play, appearing almost ecstatic while looking skyward in the act of shooting a basketball;

and work, drying a dish. "Look at Richard, for example," the article read. "When he *studies,* he *studies.*"

"What to Do," read a final subhead before continuing, "This year study like Richard—real hard."

Meanwhile, I was entering the world, completely unfamiliar with how to be someone a month shy of seventeen out there. The sudden absence of years-long routine, with virtually every minute monitored and accounted for, was discombobulating, as were the freedom, extensive downtime, and wide-ranging choices. The thought of attending nearby Peekskill High School, public and coed, was overwhelming. At my request, my parents enrolled me in Catholic Archbishop Stepinac High in White Plains. I had no clue about the challenges. Thirty-five miles from home, Stepinac was an all-boys school with more than 2,000 students. As a third-year student entering weeks before summer vacation, I was a nonentity.

The basketball season had just ended and I told the coach about my three years playing at St. John's. He invited me to scheduled tryouts, which I interpreted as a step away from being given a uniform. Anxious to show my stuff, I found myself among scores of boys in the gym taking shots—all hoping to crack the twelve-man varsity team or even the junior varsity, both of which were all-metropolitan caliber in a league that included the best Catholic high teams in New York City. Several assistant coaches organized simultaneous scrimmages on six courts to eyeball prospects. After airballing one shot and quickly losing a ball to a steal, I was among the first told to return to class.

Carpooling daily, I arrived just before first period and left immediately after the last period, which left no time for extracurricular activities. It seemed, too, that every junior and senior had a car, many of them recent vintages or brand new. I was in the wrong league.

One day in history class I answered a question with some witticism that cracked up the class. The recognition encouraged me to assume the niche of class clown, earning for me the appreciation of some classmates and the disapproval of the institution. At the same time, my relatively respectable academic record from St. John's was tanking.

My first stab at dating, a movie followed by a stop for ice cream, was disastrous. I didn't have a driver's license and Pat was surprised as I escorted her to the car, where she discovered we were double dating with my parents. In the back seat on the way home she let me hold her hand, but it was sweaty. I tried calling her afterward, but could never catch her when she was home.

Mike

During our third year at St. John's, John decided I needed a girlfriend. Around and around the school building we went, and I listened as John told stories of his encounters with girls in Central Islip. The girls he described were sweet and beautiful, and they found John attractive. I was silent.

"What's the matter?" John asked.

Silence.

"What's the matter?" he said prodding me in the ribs with his elbow.

"Nothing."

Finally, I relented. "Remember that girl Phyllis I told you about. The girl I was attracted to in the eighth grade?"

He nodded, "Yeah?"

"Remember how I told you she was so popular I didn't even dare talk to her?"

"Yeah."

"Well, during summer break I decided to ask her out."

"You did?"

I told him how on the train from Hoboken to Boston and then on the bus from Boston to Lowell, I had rehearsed different ways I would ask her out.

"Two weeks after I got home, I decided to do it. I called her several times, but hung up before her phone started ringing. Then one day I called again and let it ring. Her mother answered, and I asked if I could talk to Phyllis. She asked who I was, and I told her Phyllis and I had been classmates at St. Michael's. When Phyllis picked up the phone, it was obvious she didn't remember me.

"'I'm the one who decided to go to the seminary after eighth grade,' I said.

"'Oh,' she said, 'I think I remember you now.'

"She invited me to come to her house the following day, and she took me into her parlor and invited me to sit down on the sofa.

She sat down next to me. 'It's good to see you again,' she said. She asked about the seminary and how I liked it and what we did there. I answered without giving a lot of details; I was anxious to get on with what I had come for. When I finally summoned the courage to ask her out, there was a long silence. I watched her pulling on some strands of hair behind her neck. Finally, she said, 'I'd like a glass of lemonade, would you like one?'

"When she returned with the lemonade, she handed me a glass and then sat in a chair opposite me.

"'I'm going steady with someone,' she said. 'And when we graduate from high school, we plan to get married.'

"'Oh, I'm sorry, I didn't know.' I was sweating profusely. All I wanted to do was get up and leave.

"'But since you are in the seminary and are going to be a priest, maybe I can call my boyfriend and ask him if I can go to a movie with you this one time.'

"For the rest of that week, I didn't spend much time at home. I didn't want to take her call. When she did call, I told her I couldn't go on the day she could go and that in a few weeks I would be going to visit a seminary friend, and after that, I'd be returning to the seminary.

"'Maybe we could do it next summer,' I told her."

John laughed, then apologized, seeing he had hurt my feelings.

A few weeks later, John invited me to visit him in Central Islip. We'd have some fun during summer break and I could meet his cousin, Maureen, and some of the other girls I'd heard him talk about. We were months away from summer break, plenty of time for me to worry about being a seminarian who was planning to get involved with girls. Maureen's letters to John mentioned how excited she was about meeting one of his seminary friends. She talked about things we could do together. Nothing too provocative, but exciting enough to make me want to visit. I passed spring nights thinking more and more about Maureen and hoping she was everything John had said she was, and that in real life she was as beautiful as she was in the one picture he had of her.

I'd always left St. John's during Christmas and summer breaks reluctantly, knowing I would miss the rhythms and routines of seminary life, where expectations were clear. Where there were friends and support from teachers. Being in Montour Falls soothed my spirit, pacified my anger. But this summer would be different. There was the promise of adventure and . . . I wasn't sure what the *and* might be, but I was both nervous and looking forward to it.

John

Life stabilized after the loss of Ollie. Mike Hunter and I became good friends. That came about in a very circuitous way.

There was a boy named Richard Ebert who was a year behind us, although he and I were the same age. We had always gotten along well until one night in our dorm. We were horsing around, kind of meaningless bumping and pushing. Suddenly I was on the floor, and he had me pinned. All the others looked on in some surprise because I was considered by many to be a tough guy. I was terribly embarrassed by losing to someone in a lower grade and Ebert was encouraged to become a thorn in my side. He would walk up and fake punches at me, tell me how much he'd like to beat me up, just to be a general pain in the ass. I finally had enough.

"Why don't you and I go out to the football field tomorrow afternoon and settle this thing," I said.

"Yeah. I want to beat the crap out of you."

The next day, Saturday, after our general chores, Ebert and I crossed the bridge over Catherine's Creek, walked to the middle of the field, and engaged in a wrestling match. We wound up entangled on the ground. Neither could gain any real advantage. We wound up agreeing to stop when we were both exhausted.

My feeling was that it had not been satisfying, but we had worked it out. Ebert's feeling was that he should continue to bust my balls. I wanted to kill him, but I clearly lacked the talent to put him away. One day I talked of my frustration with Hunter, who at that point was the toughest or next-to-toughest guy in the place.

"Why don't you beat the shit out of him? You're way stronger than he is."

"I'm stronger, but I really don't know how to fight."

That was true. I had avoided fights throughout grammar school. In the seminary there was very little fighting, and my early growth spurt and strength had made me an unappealing target. I had a reputation for toughness that was completely undeserved.

Photo credit: Brian White

A busy schedule notwithstanding, students found time for horsing around in the dorms, even though aware that "loud laughter, shouting … are forbidden."

"I can teach you to fight if you want to learn," Hunter offered.

"You can teach me?"

"There's an ex-Marine who lives in my neighborhood. He's been teaching me combat judo for years. When we go home in the summer, he works out with me most days. I can teach you to fight like I do. You'll be able to take Ebert apart."

The prospect of beating Ebert up was dizzying, so I signed on. Little did I know that I had signed a pact with the devil. Hunter was now Cato to my Clouseau. From the middle of the year until the end, Hunter taught me. We began on mats in the gym, where he threw me and choked me and made my joints go in funny directions. He took this very seriously and expected me to do the same. As I progressed, he decided to add variety and surprise to the mix. I would enter a room and Hunter was on my back. He jumped me on the stairs, walking around the building, on the fields, in the gym. I was achieving a state of perpetual readiness. I was also starting to get better at it and much more comfortable with mixing it up.

At the same time, there was a freshman named Gerry Whitfield who brought boxing gloves to the seminary. He had boxed in

Catholic Youth Organization and was pretty good. He began teaching Mike Connolly and me to box. It was crazy. Here I was in a seminary learning boxing and combat judo so that I could beat the crap out of a fellow student. It was not very priestly, but it was a lot of fun. For the time being I was content to avoid Ebert's provocations, knowing that he had a surprise coming his way in the fall.

◆ ◆ ◆

We began playing softball in late May. There was a very sweet, totally unathletic boy, Paul Galka, on the team I captained. At bat one day, Paul was a nervous wreck due to a complete absence of confidence.

"Don't worry about it, Paul. Just keep your eye on the ball," I told him as I retreated down the third base line.

He stood there with the bat on his shoulder as a soft strike floated by him.

"Paul, you have to swing if it looks good. Just take a swing and try to hit it."

He watched another strike float by. I called time and walked up to him.

"Paul, on this pitch I want you to swing the bat. Even if the ball rolls up to you, try to hit it. Can you do that for me, Paul?"

"Okay, John. I'll try." He still looked worried. I moved down the third base line.

The pitch came in and Paul swung as hard as he could and let go of the bat. I saw it come at me in slow motion, make one full rotation, then explode into my face. I was knocked back as if, well, as if I had just been hit in the face with a baseball bat. My hands had automatically gone to my face and were soaked with blood. I was standing, but dizzy. I had trouble breathing due to all the blood. My shirt was soaked with it. Concerned students made me lie on my back, which made it impossible to breathe. Blood was running like a faucet down my throat. I was choking and swallowing it as fast as I could.

"Let me up. I can't breathe," which came out in a froth of bloody bubbles and sounded like God knows what. As I periodically vomited blood I had swallowed, a couple of boys walked the half mile with me back to the seminary, where I was put to bed in the infirmary and had ice applied to my nose. I did not wake up for two days, other than to urinate. When I came to, they took me to our doctor for my last such visit, the first in over two years. An X-ray showed that my nose was broken.

The next time I saw Paul, we were passing in the hallway. He shrank against the wall, terrified.

"Paul, it was an accident. I'm not angry. We're still friends. Just let it go."

I could not stand to have another see me in the same light as I saw my father.

◆ ◆ ◆

The summer after my junior year was filled with epiphany and shame. I thought I would pick up where I left off with Maureen. She, however, had turned that page.

"Johnny, we can't do this anymore, and I mean it. You need to find a girlfriend."

"I can't get a girlfriend. I'm a seminarian. And I don't want a girlfriend."

"Come on, Johnny. I am not your girlfriend. I can't be your girlfriend. And you don't seem to really want to be a priest."

I pouted for a few days. Then Maureen continued to take care of me by reconnecting me with Donald Donovan and Joe Ruiz, two boys with whom I had been friendly in eighth grade. They lived two blocks away, but I had neither seen nor spoken to them in three years. Suddenly my life accelerated. Joe and Donald caddied at a country club about twenty miles away. They were up by 5:00 A.M. and hitchhiked there. They invited me, and we three did that all summer.

Sometimes, after caddying, we went for long runs or skinny-dipped in the Great South Bay. The first time we went swimming was uncomfortable for me. Joe and Don went to schools where the boys took communal showers after athletics. I had been in a place where we never took our clothes off without being shielded from all others' eyes. But I quickly learned that the pure joy of stripping down after a run and diving into the bay far outweighed my discomfort.

I was a terrible caddy. I had trouble gauging where the ball landed and I had no idea what clubs should be used for what shot.

Being around wealthy people, many of whom never acknowledged my existence, was also discomfiting. I felt for the first time what it is to be a servant. Once, after I had been searching for a ball that a lady had hit into a marsh, I came out onto the fairway covered with mosquitoes. I was slapping my T-shirt and khakis and leaving bloody splotches all over myself.

"Oh my God, Elaine, look at all those mosquitoes. Let me get the bug spray," said one of the two women I was caddying.

She unzipped a pouch on her golf bag and retrieved a can of spray. She sprayed her partner, head to toe, back and front. She gave the can to her partner, who did the same for her. She took the can back, put it in her bag and zipped it up. Off they went.

"Don't worry about me, ladies. I'll be okay," I said, too softly to be heard. I wasn't comfortable returning to being nothing.

It quickly became clear that Donald and Maureen were interested in one another. Donald had just ended a relationship with a pretty blonde, Cathy Anderson, who was still in the social mix, which made the two of us the unattached particles in the electron ring. In short order, she and I were together a lot. I kissed her one day. "Finally!" was her comment. Once I realized that she was not offended, I spent every available moment kissing her, just kissing, just the lips. I had a girlfriend! I thought I was a stud. One night, as we all walked the neighborhood, which we did every evening until almost 11:00 P.M., I was doing my best to never come up for air.

"Johnny, why don't you give it a rest? You shouldn't be kissing her all the time." Maureen was lecturing me.

"Why don't you shut up and mind your own business," I cleverly retorted. I wanted very much to add, "This was your idea," but I did not.

I had an epiphany one Sunday at Mass that marked the beginning of the end of my pursuit of the priesthood. I heard a baby fussing, not yet wailing, but amping up. My gaze drifted toward a nicely dressed young couple, probably in their twenties. She was quite pretty and had an infant in her arms, gently bouncing and rocking the infant, the baby softly cooing. The man beside her looked down at them, a soft smile on his face. The three made a beatific tableau.

I will never have this. I will never have a beautiful wife who loves me and has my baby. I will never have someone to grow old with. One day I will die alone and lonely, surrounded by strangers who don't care about me. This thought came unbidden in an electric thunderclap that made me want to sit down. I felt as if I had been hollowed out. The emptiness of the life before me took my breath away. How could I turn away from that beckoning image of love and connection? Why would I do that? Would I do it? I left the church that day, if not changed, then open to the idea of change and with an enhanced hunger for it.

In the living of life as it is, not as we wish it to be, our experience of wonder can be invaded by horror. It was then time for horror. In my life horror was my father's domain, and so it was this time.

Uncle Ray, Maureen's father, was painting his chimney white. Earlier he had painted the house light green. One day he left the white paint can and brush by the chimney and my three-year-old brother, Michael, discovered it and began painting the house white. Not imagining the repercussions, my uncle said something to my father, who raced out our kitchen door, ran the thirty feet to where Michael stood at the chimney, grabbed his arm, and punched him in the head. Michael's body went flying into the air, swinging like a pendulum. Each time he swung back toward my father, another punch or kick sent him flying away again. Blows and kicks propelled him toward our house, accompanied by the beast's litany of "teach you a lesson, you little shit." He dragged Michael up the steps, opened the door, and threw the poor, wee thing across the kitchen, where my mother collected him and put him in bed. My father stood outside, continuing his rant about teaching lessons and not putting up with any shit.

I stood there the whole time, doing nothing, saying nothing. I was too terrified of him. I failed that little innocent, and I would never be able to wipe that shame from my mind. Later I spoke to my mother about it.

"I should have tried to stop him."

"What are you talking about?" She seemed genuinely puzzled.

"I should have tried to stop Daddy from beating Michael."

"Are you crazy? Your father has always wanted to kill you. If you tried to stop him, he would have had the excuse he always wanted."

Holy shit, my mother had just confirmed what I had always sensed, always believed. She was telling me that my father had always wanted to kill me. In addition, she was telling me that she had always known that . . . and done nothing.

Ollie

After several months at home, I was yet to find a mutual comfort zone with my stepmother. The art of walking on eggs around each other failed us in a battle of wills involving a stray German shepherd mix that I declared mine. Great dog, the first I ever had. He followed me everywhere, sensing I was his only real friend. A neighbor claimed the dog was chasing his sheep. My stepmother, who didn't like dogs to begin with, which bugged me, started talking about getting rid of him.

"Don't worry," I said. "The dog will be okay."

But complaints from the neighbor continued.

"Richard, I've been called again about the dog. This isn't working."

The dog sat between us, his eyes and head shifting with the dialogue.

"I'll keep him in my room when I'm not around, okay?" I snapped.

That night I heard her talking to my father in their bedroom. "I'll be damned if I'm going to let some seventeen-year-old kid run this house." My father rolled over without a whimper and the dog was gone the next day. I didn't talk to her for two weeks. My father came into my bedroom one night and, pulling up a chair, sat down with the backrest facing me.

"Here's the deal. You are one of five people in this household and I'm not going to let you upset it. I don't like your attitude and the way you're treating your mother. If you can't follow some simple rules and be civil in this family, you're going to have to make other arrangements."

I glared at him, furious about my own sense of powerlessness. I wanted to say, "She is *not* my mother," but I checked myself.

"Do you understand?"

I continued to glare, thinking he never stands up to her. He even slows down when she tells him he's driving too fast.

"Do you understand?"

"Yes," I muttered.

"Good," he said. And he swung a leg over the backrest, pushed the chair against the wall and walked out.

Mike

Maureen was the first person I noticed when the Long Island Railroad arrived in Central Islip. She was standing between John's parents waving excitedly at me and John, her long auburn hair blowing tenderly in the summer breeze. She was smiling, a smile that lit up the dreary train station. *Who was that smile for? John? Me? Both of us?*

First to greet us as we stepped onto the platform, she wrapped her arms around John and gave him a sisterly kiss. She hugged me too and gave me a look that I wanted to mean, "You are as cute as I hoped you would be." On the drive to John's house John and Maureen talked about things that had been happening to them since they last saw each other. Occasionally she looked at me and smiled. I was too self-conscious to say anything. I sat admiring John's gift of gab and Maureen's beauty and charm. Whenever the car turned a corner and her leg brushed against mine, I felt a rush of excitement.

When we arrived at the Tuohey house, I was taken to the room I would have to myself. As I unpacked, I was thinking of how clumsy I was around girls. I was shaky enough to consider telling John and his parents I was sick and needed to spend some time alone in my room, but I sucked it up and came out for supper. After supper, John announced we would be going to Maureen's to listen to some music with Maureen and her friend, Lorraine Chilion. Once there, I sat mute and moody while John charmed both of them, filling in for his incompetent companion.

When Pete Seeger sang "Little Boxes," he must have been thinking about Central Islip. Every house was exactly the same: a small seven-room ranch with a fifty-foot-wide front yard running to the street; a backyard big enough for a clothesline, a sandbox, and a small garden; a strip of land between adjacent houses that you could cover in four steps. The only thing that set houses apart was the color they were painted and what people chose to do with the inside of them. Maureen's house was much more upscale and stylish inside than John's. Her living room was decorated predominantly in white and gold. The sofa and chairs were immaculate. Maureen's parents had charm and grace and good looks. They were a well dressed and distinguished couple, the Ozzie and Harriet parents I wished I had. Downstairs, where we went with Maureen and Lorraine, the room had been built for ease and comfort. Walnut paneling, plaid sofa and recliners, cabinets for games and records, soft lighting, and the hi-fi we had come to listen to.

When John put on the first record and Paul Anka began to sing *Put Your Head on My Shoulder*, Maureen jumped up and pulled me onto the floor to dance. While we danced, she did put her head on my shoulder. We danced without talking through that song and the next. I kept thinking of the dance book I'd purchased the previous summer. How I'd studied the silhouetted dance steps in that book. How I'd practiced them on our kitchen floor with a broom until my awkwardness was replaced by a measure of comfort. When Maureen and I sat, she began asking questions about me, my life at St. John's and in Lowell. Her voice was as soft as a satin pillow. I found that my tongue loosened up and I could talk to a girl who reminded me of Rita Hayworth. As Lorraine and John jitterbugged the night away, Maureen and I talked, stopping only occasionally to dance the slow dances. Before the night ended, we all agreed to meet at Lorraine's the next day. That night in bed I kept thinking of Maureen and of how desperately I had worked to keep her from knowing my penis was rising every time I danced with her—and of what I would do the next time it happened.

The next day John asked me to go next door and tell Maureen we'd leave from the Tuohey's to go to Lorraine's. He was busy slapping on Old Spice and putting the final touches on his pompadour and duck's ass. I rang the doorbell at Maureen's house. "Come in," I heard a female voice call from somewhere in the house.

"Hello?"

"In here," the voice replied.

Maureen was sitting at a dressing table in her bedroom combing her luxurious hair. She invited me to sit on a pink and white canopy bed that smacked of royalty. I sat while she chatted away like a chickadee celebrating a spring morning. My heart was going nuts and my palms and armpits were drenched. Maureen was wearing a white sweater, cut just low enough around the neck and shoulders for glimpses of cleavage. I sat mesmerized by the sight of her whenever she turned to address me. It was difficult to breathe. The smell of Ambush perfume, hair spray, and lavender body powder filled the room. I wanted to believe they were causing my short, strangled gasps, but a rising hard-on suggested otherwise.

"Is something wrong?"

"No," I said wiping my hands on my pant legs, "everything's fine."

"Are you uncomfortable with me?"

I was in a panic. I didn't know how to respond.

"Why are you uncomfortable with me?"

"I'm not uncomfortable with you," I heard myself saying in a voice I didn't recognize. "I'm uncomfortable with me not knowing what to say or do when I'm around you. I like being with you."

She got up and came over to where I was sitting. "I like being with you, too. Why don't you just relax and be yourself?" She bent over and started tickling me. I jumped up and started tickling her back. We were both laughing wildly when she fell forward into me and I lost my balance falling back onto the bed with her on top of me. I saw her eyes, warm with excitement. She bent down and kissed me.

Later, when we joined John, he asked, "Hey, what kept you two?" Maureen made a comment about having to spend as much time with her hair as he did with his. Then we were off to Lorraine's. We walked the three blocks together, John and Maureen making plans for the day while I was thinking of my first kiss and the words to a Johnny Mathis song:

You ask how long I'll love you; I'll tell you true,
Until the twelfth of never, I'll still be loving you.

I had experienced none of the awkwardness I expected from a first kiss. Our lips had met and they had transported me to a world I'd begun to dream about in the seminary, but never visited. I'd closed my eyes, felt the warm pressure of her body against mine, tasted delicious lips, surrendered to sweet smells, and wished to stay there forever. Approaching Lorraine's door, I could feel sweat running down my sides. *Oh God, did I put on deodorant?*

My chest felt like someone had parked a bus on it. This was the big leagues, I thought. My only experience with kissing was practicing on myself, mugging my forearm when nobody was around, trying to get the positioning of my lips right, trying to get the right amount of pressure into a kiss. When John Wayne kissed Maureen O'Hara in *The Quiet Man,* she turned to putty in his arms even though she had at first tried to resist him. That's what I was thinking when Maureen took my hand and led me away from the pool table in Lorraine's basement and whispered, "Why don't we let John and Lorraine play and you and I can be alone for a while in the other room." The moment of truth had arrived and I felt more like Jerry Lewis or Lou Costello than John Wayne.

"Let's dance," Maureen said, pulling me close. From the other room we could hear Connie Francis singing "My Happiness." "I'm so happy to be with you," Maureen sighed.

It was at this point that I worried about farting . . . or Lorraine's parents coming into the room. Instead, Maureen lifted her head from my shoulder, put her hand under my chin, and looked straight into my eyes. We stood still for a moment. In the background, I could hear Connie Francis:

Every day I reminisce
Dreaming of your tender kiss
Always thinking how I miss
My happiness

Then I kissed her, long and lingering, with no disasters. And, at that moment, I came as close as ever to feeling like John Wayne.

Chapter Ten

Senior Year, 1959

Mike

I returned to St. John's as optimistic as I had ever been. I'd made the varsity basketball team, I was writing regularly for the *Quill*, I'd made honor roll the previous two semesters, and I felt like I was developing spiritually, even if a bit slowly. I had a girlfriend. I was confident. This was going to be a great year. Two years of college would soon be part of my future. The horse that'd been used to losing had finally learned how to be a winner. This was where I wanted to be. This was home.

As seniors, we were required to return a week earlier than the underclassmen to help get the building and grounds ready for the school year. I was okay with that. When the day's work details were finished, I'd have time to play basketball and go on hikes. Most important of all, I could pump John for information about Maureen and how much, I hoped, she missed me.

Soon after we arrived, my optimism about senior year soured.

"I don't like him," I told John as we shot baskets in the gym.

"Why not?"

"He's arrogant. Didn't you get that feeling?"

"Kinda, but it's too soon to tell."

We were discussing first impressions of the new rector, Father Theophane Murphy. This was one of the many changes that were about to alter the course of our futures. Father Owen was gone. Father Theophane was in charge.

"I didn't like the way he swaggered into our rec room to introduce himself to us. And the way he talked to us. Like the master sergeant, talking to a bunch of 4-F inductees. He doesn't like us, John. Can't you see that?"

"You might be right. Let's wait and see."

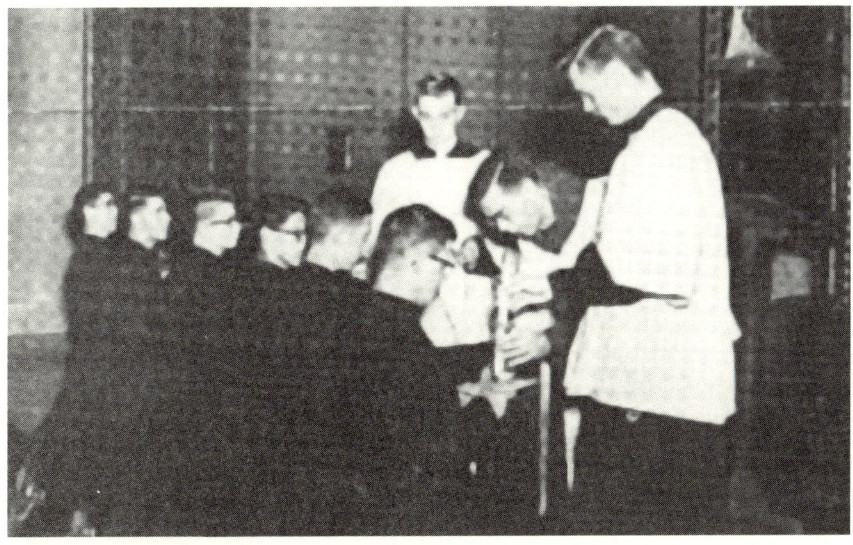

Photo credit: the Quill

Mike Connolly (left) and Richard Roulliard, help Father DeSales initiate new novices into the Third Order of St. Francis.

It didn't take long.

Days later we were caught by Father Theophane on Main Street in Montour Falls during a Saturday afternoon hike. He had given John, Richie Roulliard, Ronnie Driver, and me permission to take a hike to the falls at the west end of town. We knew that permission did not give us license to go into town, but we did anyway. Roulliard and Driver enjoyed flirting with the girls at the drugstore soda fountain and John and I were interested in getting a soda. When Father Theophane came walking down Main Street with a group of our other classmates, he had no trouble identifying us, especially when Driver, dressed in a pair of bright aquamarine pants and blazing cobalt paisley print shirt, stopped in the middle of the street and waved before making a run for it with the rest of us down a nearby side street.

Each of us was summoned individually to Father Theophane's office later that afternoon. There he hammered us with verbal abuse about how we were a bunch of conceited, overindulged seniors who were not good role models for other boys. "You're an arrogant, self-centered bunch who think you're special. Well, you're not."

"He planned that," I told John later on. "He knew we'd go into town. He came with those other guys to catch us. He hates us."

A few days later, I was called into Father Theophane's office again.

"Michael, I've noticed you spend an inordinate amount of time with John Tuohey."

"We're friends, Father."

"That may be, but let me remind you of our seminary Rules." He paused and glared at me like a prosecuting attorney. He picked up a copy of the seminary rule book. "Do you have a copy of this?" he asked, wagging the book at me, his eyes cutting through me.

"Yes, Father." I tried to look over his shoulder at the picture on the wall of Father Paul Wattson, the founder of the Franciscan Friars of the Atonement.

"Look at me when you speak to me," he demanded. "Do you have a copy of the seminary rule book and have you read it?"

"Yes." My stomach was churning, a cement mixer blending bitterness with fear.

"Yes, what?!?" he shouted.

"Yes, Father."

"You have it? Or you have it and you've read it?" His stare locked on me.

"I have it and I've read it, Father."

He read from the book: "High school and college students are to keep to their own group, but within each group every student shall be friendly, cheerful, and neighborly to all."—pausing, he shifted into emphasis mode, delivering each word like a carpenter hammering nails—"without . . . picking . . . anyone . . . as a . . . constant . . . companion . . . to the . . . exclusion . . . of others."

"I am friendly, cheerful, and . . ."

"Don't interrupt me; I'm not finished," he said rising from his desk and coming around in front of me. He held the rule book in front of me. "Read those last words," he said poking his finger at the words.

"Without picking anyone as a constant companion to the exclusion of others."

He slammed the rule book on his desk. "That's it!" he said. "If you want to remain here, I don't want to see you with just John Tuohey."

Later John told me Father Theophane had given him the same ultimatum. "Well, the Rule doesn't say we can't hang out together;

it says we just can't do it to the exclusion of others. So when we're together, we need to make sure other guys are with us," I said.

Having this guy as rector was going to be a problem. But I was determined to deal with it. I wanted to finish two years of college at St. John's and then decide what to do next with my life.

John

On arriving at St. John's for our senior year, we discovered a complete change in the administration. Three friars we had never seen were now in charge, led by Father Theophane Murphy, the new rector. Fathers Alban and Mark, though still on the teaching faculty, had been replaced as prefects by Fathers Kieran and William. Father Theophane was middle aged, short, and stout. Fathers Kieran and William were young and looked to be in good shape. All three seemed friendly enough.

We seniors arrived a week earlier than the lower classmen for general housecleaning. It was easy, mindless work and we had time to play basketball and go for hikes. One hike sent us into conflict with Father Theophane, suggesting that we were dealing with a very different breed of priest. It occurred when Mike Connolly, Ronnie Driver, Richard Rouillard, and I were granted permission to hike around Montour Falls. Our permission was limited to hiking to Shequaga Falls on the outskirts of town. I had not consciously breached any rules since the cigarette episode three years earlier, but this was an unusual week and, while I knew stopping at a soda fountain was a stretch, it seemed a relatively minor issue.

I was called into his office later and was shocked by what came down. Besides saying, "You seniors are spoiled, stuck-up, and conceited," he said our ways "are going to have to change. I'll see to that."

When Father Owen had gotten on me, he had cited precisely how I had strayed from the Rule and what I had to do to make amends. He had never called me names or attacked my character. He told me I was an introvert, but did it to help me and made sure I understood. This guy, however, who had known me a few days, had concluded that I was conceited and stuck-up, that I thought I was better than everyone else. There was a wide range of faults for which I routinely flagellated myself. Conceit and superiority were not among them. No priest had ever accused me of any of those things. In fact, aside from Father DeSales trying to get me to edit my work and Father Peter trying to get me to rebound better, no priest had ever criticized me.

Father Theophane reminded me of my father, a first in that place. I never trusted him again.

Life moved on. I forgot about the incident. Theophane did not.

Mike

Father Theophane waited until the underclassmen arrived before delivering a crushing blast to us "conceited overindulged seniors." With the entire student body in the refectory awaiting his general introduction, he swaggered in with his new prefects, Fathers Kieran and William. He mounted the dais and, after a brief welcome, in a voice as harsh as the bite of a whip on a bare back, he effectively ended the seminary career I had foreseen. "I want to remind all of you that there has been a Rule change that will affect all of you gathered here today and will be of particular significance for you seniors." He paused, glancing at me and then at John and Ronnie Driver. "The governing body of the Friars of the Atonement has decided that, beginning with *this* senior class, students who wish to continue their seminary training will go to novitiate for a year before continuing on with their educations. I will be calling on each of you seniors before Easter break and asking if you intend to go on to novitiate and continue your training for the priesthood."

I felt like a passenger in a car spinning out of control. Going to novitiate would mean taking a year off from classes and dedicating most of that time to prayer and silent meditation. I looked at John and Driver. John looked like he'd been punched in the stomach, his face red and contorted, as if he was gasping for air. Driver seemed unfazed. For weeks after that we talked about this radical shift before returning attention to the demands of daily life. We had actually been told back in November of the previous year that this decision was being considered, but with only a year of high school still ahead of us we had filed it away as of no importance right now. But here was Father Theophane reminding us that "right now" was about to arrive.

John and I were cocaptains of the basketball team, I was still writing for the *Quill*, and I was determined to keep making honor roll. And then there were those other tests to prepare for, the Regents Exams and Catholic University Exams. If we passed them, we would be granted a diploma not only from St. John's, but also from Catholic University in Washington, D.C., and from the State of New York. That would be an achievement that would far surpass anything I might have done at Keith Academy. That would make me college material.

John

Our basketball team was awful. We only had time to practice three hours a week and we played the occasional team whose shortest guy was taller than our tallest. All we had going for us was that no one smoked, no one drank, no one dated, and no one went to bed later than 9:30. We kept games close solely on our virtue. As is so often true in life, virtue does not always triumph. In our case, it triumphed once all season. Mike Hunter should have been on the team and would have made a difference. He was a talented player and, at six-three and 220, he was a force. Sadly, Mike's grades were marginal at first quarter, so he was not allowed to go out for basketball.

Hunter and I continued the routine of attacks we had started as juniors. All in all, I believe I was his closest friend. Perhaps I was his only friend. Nevertheless, he freely gave me his time; he was truly proud of me when I occasionally got the best of him; he treated me with a deference and respect that would have gone so far for him if he had shown it to others.

So it was with complete surprise that I found out that he was leaving. He never spoke of leaving or of any concerns or reservations. Sure, he seemed like odd priest material, but that was true of most of us.

"Tuohey, Tuohey," a voice said, and I felt a great weight press my mattress down. It was pitch black, well before 5:40 A.M.

"It's me, Mike. I'm leaving."

Suddenly awake, I realized Hunter was sitting on my bed.

"What are you talking about? You're not leaving. We're seniors, for God's sake. Just stick it out a few more months and we'll graduate together."

"No. It's time for me to go. I just couldn't leave without telling you goodbye."

"When are you planning to go?"

"Right now. After mass. My bag is packed. I have my suit on."

It finally sank in. He was actually leaving us, leaving me. I was crushed. I felt like hugging him, but that was only acceptable when we were trying to break each other's neck.

So another chapter closed. From the original freshman class of thirty, six of us were left. Another boy had had courage or the insight or whatever it took to say "enough" and take the bus. My doubts and fears, my overall confusion about the rightness of my being in the seminary were accelerating at a worrying speed.

Hunter's departure punctured my innocence. One evening when Ronnie Driver, Mike Connolly, and I were walking around the building, the subject of Hunter's leaving came up. I expressed my shock and wondered aloud what had made him do it.

"He was told to leave because he was coming on sexually with some other guys," Ronnie said.

"What the hell are you talking about?" I said. I had stopped dead and was peering at Ronnie in the dark.

"Mike was reported for making sexual advances to other boys." Ronnie said.

"That's complete bullshit. Whoever said that is a liar. Mike would never do something like that." I was shaken, furious. How could anyone say such a horrible thing about my friend, and a guy who was bigger and tougher than anyone? From the little I had ever heard on the topic, people who engaged in homosexual activity were little pansies.

"I'm the one who reported him," Ronnie said.

I looked at Ronnie in silence, mouth agape. I realized instantly that it was true. Ronnie was not the kind of guy to report people. He had no malice toward anyone. If he said he did it, then it was true.

Finally, "What happened? What did he do?"

"He started talking to me about sex and showed me some sexual passages in books. After a while he tried to get me to show him mine and he would show me his. There were others involved, too. They would get together and jerk each other off, shit like that."

Ronnie then named several other boys, boys who had suddenly been in chapel, dressed in suits, bags packed, gone on the bus, vapor fading in the morning sun. It all hit me like my fated baseball bat. For years I had seen inexplicable departures. Now I knew the explanation in many of the cases was sex, and sex of a variety I had never imagined. This was as if blinders had just been taken from my eyes, and what I saw was ugly and perverse. I was Adam after biting into the fruit from the tree of the knowledge of good and evil. I wanted to go back to not knowing. Was the whole world a place of dark desires, littered with the snares of the devil? Even here, even in my one safe place, the ground was treacherous. What was real? What could I believe?

Ollie

Less than six months removed from the seminary, I was friendless and adrift in a world that for three years I had only visited briefly, a fifth wheel in a family that had defined a way of living fitting for a couple with two girls, seven and twelve. It was like we didn't quite know what to do with each other. Some relief from my general discontent came with a job at Food Fair in Peekskill, which provided thirty dollars toward a drivable 1950 Chevy that I waxed all summer. There was some dating with a couple of girls—one from the store—with slightly detectable facial hair whom my father, to my considerable discomfort, called "Hairy Mary." But I didn't have a driver's license yet, so, outside of hitchhiking the ten miles to Peekskill for work and the occasional movie date, I was pretty much stranded.

All summer I dreaded going back to Stepinac, where I still hardly knew anyone. Things brightened somewhat about the time school started when I finally got my driver's license. While the Chevy was not the kind of car other boys would gather around, it was enough to help me upgrade girlfriends and maintain part-time hours at the store.

Getting off work one Friday night at 9:00 P.M. I wished there was something to do—some place to go—other than home. Deep inside something stirred, a signal similar, perhaps, to that experienced by migrating birds in changing seasons. This was the first September in three years I was not returning to St. John's. I'd just gotten paid. With gas at nineteen cents a gallon, why not go? If I was there the following day, which would be a free afternoon, I might see some of the guys. I gave no consideration to the fact I'd already been up for fourteen hours or the seven hours of driving time it would take. No thought of telling my parents. I turned out of the Food Fair parking lot and headed toward the Bear Mountain Bridge and Route 17.

Hour upon hour, revved by the spontaneous adventure, I blasted rock and roll on the radio, singing along with my favorite songs. I hated coffee but forced myself to drink a few cups along the way to stave off drowsiness. I felt so much a part of the road, my car, radio, and me, cruising along with overnight truckers, quick flicking my brights to let them know I was passing, switching my directionals back and forth to say "hi" and "thanks," and delighting in their on-again, off-again brights, which said "okay partner."

I was going back to my favorite place in the world.

I stopped at a truck stop on the other side of Hancock and wolfed down a large stack of pancakes and more coffee. Driving through the town moments earlier I had tried to locate the restaurant where the Barberas and I had stopped for lunch three years earlier, but everything along the main drag was closed. By the time I reached Binghamton at about 3:00 A.M., there was no sense in pushing on to St. John's because that would get me there before dawn. I had been struggling to keep my eyes open, anyway, so I pulled into a rest stop, curled up in the back seat, and quickly fell asleep.

The sound of truck traffic on Route 17 awakened me at dawn to the general terrain where I had come to feel so much at home, in this case high green hills on both sides of the Chemung River Valley that stretches from west of Elmira through Binghamton into northern Pennsylvania. Exhilarated and excited, I drove another fifty-five miles to Elmira and stopped for more pancakes. At the restaurant, I phoned home.

"Hi, it's Rich . . ."

"Where are you?" my stepmother asked.

"I'm going to Montour Falls. I'm in Elmira now."

After a pause, she said, "Your father has been very worried. He checked with the police to see if there'd been an accident."

"Is Dad there?"

"No, he had to go to work."

"Well . . ."

"I suggest you come home. I'm sure your father will be calling, but I think you should get home as soon as you can."

"Yes. Okay . . . but I've got to go now. Someone is waiting to use this phone," I lied.

I left the restaurant and began the final leg on winding Route 14 to Montour Falls. In twenty-five minutes the seminary appeared. My heart accelerated. I slowed to a crawl and, riddled with nostalgia, gazed at the building and grounds. In a moment, feeling oddly like a voyeur, I stepped on the gas and turned onto West Main Street in Montour Falls. My plan was to return after lunch in the hope of seeing some friends during their free time. It was a warm morning with the rising sun shining onto the froth of Shequaga Falls tumbling over the cliffs at the end of Main Street. I parked and lay down on a bench close to the falls and absorbed sounds of the crashing waters, inhaling their cooling blast. I squinted at the changing autumn leaves above me and the puffy, white clouds in a brilliant blue sky and, feeling at peace, dozed off.

◆ ◆ ◆

Awakening, there was still time left before lunch was over at St. John's. I drove to the Blue Ribbon Cafe, where Dever and I made our early morning escape the previous spring and ordered a hamburger and strawberry malted. Then I drove to the seminary grounds. There, on the knoll north of the building, were some students, among them, Connolly, Tuohey, and Dever. Father Peter, as always, was out playing touch football with the guys and coming from the building were several other students and Father Normand. Connolly looked curiously at my car as I parked, then he recognized me when I stepped onto the grass.

"Will you count me in?" I called.

My three friends trotted toward me, making the trip worth every mile and minute.

"What the hell . . ." Dever said.

Acting the traveling man with places to go and glorying in the attention, I said I was "driving through" and stopped by to see if anyone was around. No one, fortunately, asked me where I was going.

"I'll take Ollie," Connolly said.

It was like I'd never left. As always, we double-teamed Father Normand futilely as he bowled his way through the line and stumbled around looking for a ball carrier. I went out for a long pass—Connolly to Olive—and picked up a good forty yards. Heaven. With no clock or scoreboard, we played up and down the field to our hearts' content until, finally, the two priests said it was time for them to go in. We played some more, but it was getting late and I felt that some of the guys were playing longer than usual to accommodate me.

"Hey, guys, I gotta hit the road."

"Yeah, I have to get in," a student I didn't know said.

Tuohey, Connolly, and Dever walked to the car with me, the questions flowing:

"Where're you going to school?"

"Have a job?"

"Do you have a girlfriend, Ollie?" Connolly asked.

"Yeah," I said without mentioning I didn't really like her.

"What's it like?" Connolly asked.

I suspected he wanted to know what it was like to feel up a girl—or more—but I had no experience in those areas.

"It's okay," I said, with all the cool I could muster.

The small talk got smaller. We were done. I was feeling deep sadness and dreading the loneliness of the long drive.

"Well, gotta go."

"Good seeing you, Ollie."

I stepped into the car and they turned toward the building. Turning south on College Avenue, I slowed to watch my old friends enter the seminary through the side door. It slammed shut and I stopped the car, looking once again at the building for a couple of minutes. Then I put the car in gear and moved onto Route 14 for the long drive back to Putnam Valley.

John

One evening, after a retreat day light on food and drink in which we maintained silence, prayed, and meditated, we had a singularly extraordinary experience. A friar from another order came and delivered a chilling homily to us. We had never seen him before, would never see him again. He was not introduced to us; there was no explanation for his presence. We merely filed into chapel and he appeared on the altar where he launched into his unforgettable talk about vocation. To paraphrase him: when God calls on a young man to be a priest, it is not only a great privilege; it is an absolute imperative to obey.

The privilege derives from being an instrument of God in the salvation of souls. Only a priest can administer the sacraments, including hearing sins and conveying forgiveness. It is the priest, in the administration of last rites, who assures the eternal salvation of wayward souls. The power and authority are immense. Balancing this immense power is a fearsome responsibility. God does not call a young man lightly. God does not make mistakes. If God has put this path before a young man, then that young man must follow. If, for reasons of doubts, weakness, carnal desires, that man turns from the path before him, then he will face a two-pronged destruction.

First and foremost, he will lose his soul, go to hell. God has no tolerance for those who turn their backs on the holy path that He has chosen for them. For these people, even the likelihood of last rites is dim at best.

The reason for that outcome emerges from the second prong of the skewer. In his willful disregard for God's desires, the straying seminarian not only will lose his soul for choosing a worldly life, he will also find no peace or comfort or joy or satisfactions in that life, which is all illusion and sinfulness. Its rewards are meaningless, yielding only unhappiness and despair. God, in His infinite love and mercy, has laid the path to salvation at your feet. If you choose another path, you will be lost forever, in this world and the next.

In case his message had been too subtle, he then told us a case study to clarify his point. There was a young seminarian who was clearly called by God to be a priest. This young man gave in to the temptations of the devil. He was weak, wanting to be with women, live a worldly life. So this young man left the seminary and went out into the world. Ultimately, he married, had children, had a career. Sadly, however, and yet inevitably, he was never happy. Not one day of joy or fulfillment lay ahead of him, for he had chosen a path other than God's path. Finally, in the ultimate act of despair, he went into his garage and hanged himself.

Wow. Talk about a bedtime story. Perhaps other tired, food-deprived boys let it all wash over their heads, but not me. I was the boy with the image of that young couple and their baby seared into his memory. It was I who hungered to have what they had. I wanted the physical and spiritual intimacy of a woman who loved me. Now, however, I was faced with the prospect that that temptation was a "whited sepulcher," beauty covering decay and despair. I could see myself swinging at the end of a rope. My only consolation was that my family had no garage.

Mike

Father Theophane's reminder about the alteration of seminary training drastically accelerated my thoughts about the future. I had hoped to delay any decision about whether to remain with the friars until after two years of college at St. John's. Such a deferment was now impossible. Going to novitiate would include taking vows of poverty, chastity, and obedience in return for the brown habit of a Franciscan Friar of the Atonement. My feelings for Maureen would have made any decision to go to novitiate complicated. But even before that relationship I had decided that I did not have a vocation to the priesthood. I was getting better at mastering the demands of obedience in seminary life.

But poverty? And chastity?

I had counted on those two years of college education. I had not anticipated having to surrender so soon the stability and feeling of family I found here at St. John's.

Damn you Father Theophane!

John

One day I sought out Father Normand for spiritual guidance. He had a deep voice, slow and resonant. It seemed to me that he exuded spirituality. Who knows? Perhaps he was just quiet.

"Father, I'm having a tough time with my vocation. I've come to realize that I obey the rules because I don't want to get caught. I don't want to get in trouble. I know that I should obey because I love God and sacrifice with a glad heart to please Him. But, I do what I want if I think I won't get caught. That doesn't seem like acting for love of God."

"You don't love God."

What? Had I heard him right? Did a priest just tell me that I don't love God? All my life I'd been told that I love God and God loves me. The world was being turned upside down.

"How could you love God? You don't know God. You are a child. You have been nowhere. You have seen nothing, done nothing. How could you love God, let alone know Him?"

Could he have fully understood the enormity of what he had said? From age five and the Baltimore Catechism: *Who made you? God made me. Why did God make you? He made me to know, love, and serve Him in this world and be happy with Him in the next.*

I had repeated and repeated an endless litany of my love and God's love. I had been told, and I came to believe, that saying this over and over constituted belief. This priest had just completely undermined all of that. He had not shaken the pillar, but obliterated the temple. Did I believe anything, or had I just repeated it so often that I had installed an empty automaticity that meant no more than saying "God bless" to a sneeze? Moreover, he had suggested—no he had stated unequivocally—that I did not, could not love God. And yet, the world continued to turn.

Some days later, I arose before everyone else at the sound of my alarm clock at 4:45 A.M. to prepare serving Mass at the St. Joseph altar at 5:30. Due to some sort of brain cramp, I forgot that day was Sunday, when there were no Masses on the side altars. I went into the dark, quiet sacristy dressed in my black cassock and white surplice. I lit candles, readied wine and water, laid out the vestments for a priest who would not be coming. Then I waited and I waited.

Suddenly I remembered it was Sunday. I thought that I could go back to bed and get another forty-five minutes of sleep. As I considered my options, I had an abrupt thought about why I was there, alone, at that hour. Perhaps God had made me get up and come here. If so, what was the message? What was I supposed to do? I came to the conclusion that God wanted me to do the stations of the cross. Furthermore, I was to do them in the dark, on my hands and knees. Symbols of the stations, depicting Christ's trial and pivotal points of His torture and crucifixion, were on the walls around the chapel's periphery. The journey on the cold terrazzo floor would be a tribulation, but nothing compared to that of Jesus.

I walked to the altar and knelt in front of the first station, where I briefly prayed, then crawled on my way. I prayed at each station, waiting for God's message to suffuse me. I tried to tell myself that God was pleased with me. After the fourteenth station, I sat in the back pews, where all the departing boys had sat. I looked at the sacristy light on the altar. The first soft light of dawn lit the stained-glass windows, allowing the statues, the altar, and the cross to gently emerge from the darkness. I looked at this as the departed boys had looked at it for the last time. I looked inside myself, seeking some kernel of ecstatic revelation, some clarity. I had abased myself in service to God's will so that He would reveal something to me.

And He had.

He had revealed a silly seventeen-year-old kid who mistook forgetting what day it was for a message from God; a boy who thought that crawling around on his hands and knees in the dark would please a God in whom, as it happened, he had only a tenuous belief. He had revealed to me that I, like the others who had sat in this vantage point, was already gone. What remained were mere details. And in the details, as we all come to know, lies the devil. I had no intention of leaving St. John's before finishing two years of college because I truly liked most things about the seminary. I just did not want to be a priest. I believed that I could continue to play the game for two years to get what I wanted, but that I could not, would not, take vows that meant nothing to me.

But that was taken out of my hands when we were told there would be no more college years at Montour Falls, that the next stop in our training would be the novitiate. It would serve neither my ends nor the Order's for me to go to novitiate. The die was cast.

◆ ◆ ◆

About a month before Easter, each senior had an appointment with Father Theophane to tell him whether we planned to continue to the novitiate or leave after graduation. The interview proved to be far more complex than a simple *yes* or *no.*

"Well, John, how are you?"

"I'm fine, thanks, Father."

"Well, have you given any thought to whether you are going to continue to the novitiate?"

"Yes, Father, I have. I've decided to leave after graduation."

"Oh. And why have you decided that?"

"Well, Father, I love it here. This is the best place I've ever been. It's safe and orderly, and I fit in very well. But over the years I've come to see that I'm terrified of the world outside. It scares me a lot. I don't understand it and I don't think I fit into it. And I've begun to think . . . in fact, I've kinda thought for a long time that my main motive in being here is how scared I am of that world. Then I think that I'm cheating God because I'm not here to serve Him but to protect myself from what I'm scared of. And then I think that I'll never forgive myself if I don't face up to the world and prove to myself that I'm not scared of it. You know what I mean?"

Father Theophane mulled that over a bit, and then said to me something so unexpectedly insightful, so genuine and personal, that it amazed me.

"John, have you ever wondered if, perhaps, places like this exist for people like us?" *People like us?* Were he and I alike? Were some or all of the seemingly confident priests around me as eaten up by the anxiety engendered by the world and the guilt of not facing up to it? Was it all devotion and love of God, or was it self-preservation? For a moment I felt that I had misread Theophane. Perhaps we could have been close.

"Father, I never thought of that. What an amazing idea that is. But doesn't it make it even worse if I stayed? Acting out of fear, not love of God?"

He sat up straight and any intimacy we may have touched upon disappeared behind his familiar stern mode.

"Well, it really doesn't matter. We weren't going to allow you to continue. You're not the sort of boy we want."

What? Was he kidding? I was no trouble. I was the best student in the place. I'd won a lot of academic awards. I was captain of our very bad basketball team. How could they not want me? They had been planning to dump me? What the hell was going on?

He swiveled in his chair, removed a folder from a file cabinet and looked inside it. "You've grown smug and conceited here. You think you're really something. Well, it's easy to appear smart in such a small group. But I have your IQ here in front of me, and you're not very intelligent at all. When you go out into the world you'll constantly come in contact with people much brighter than you are and you'll be put in your place. Thanks for coming in. Send in the next boy."

Stunned, out I went. I walked around the halls obsessing about all this. Smug? I was so insecure it drove me crazy. Unintelligent? Had I really fooled all these teachers all these years? Was I about to enter a battle for which I had no skills? When Mike Connolly came out after his interview, I reached out to him for a breath of sanity.

"What did you tell him, Mike?"

"I told him I'm leaving."

"What'd he say?"

"He said that they were planning to drop me anyway. Then he told me that I'm not very smart and that I'll never be accepted in any college. I have no future in any academic field. What did you tell him?"

"I'm leaving."

"What did he say?"

I told Mike what he said, then we stood there looking at each other in disbelief. Then Ronnie Driver came out.

"Ronnie, what'd you say?"

"I told him I'm going to the novitiate."

"What'd he say?"

"He said that he was pleased, that they wanted me to go on. He said I'm the kind of boy they want."

"But you don't plan to go on. Why did you say that?" Mike was incredulous.

"Why should I make things uncomfortable for myself? Maybe I'll change my mind." Ronnie smiled his devilish smile. He was a lot smarter than I'd given him credit for.

Mike and I looked at each other, mouths open. They did not want Mike or me, but they wanted Ronnie. We loved him, but he was a marginal student, utterly irreverent, and we knew that, actually, he had no intention to go on. Then we began laughing. It was all bullshit, just bullshit.

Yet, that night in bed I pondered how fragile was the confidence I had built over almost four years. How much of it depended on staying right where I was, where I was no longer wanted. We were entering the endgame. Events continued to accelerate. I was rushing toward the world, and the world was about to come rushing toward me. Thank God that I still had a home to go to.

Mike

By the time Easter vacation approached, I had decided against going to the novitiate and, like the rest of my classmates, I prepared—with trepidation—to meet with Father Theophane. He wasn't like Fathers Peter, Owen, DeSales, Alban, and others who seemed secure with themselves. It seemed to me that Father Theophane needed to build himself up by putting others down.

"You seniors aren't as smart as you think you are. You boys have an inflated sense of yourself. You are misguided in your opinion of yourselves," was the sermon he was constantly preaching to us.

I paced back and forth in the corridor outside his office. John was in there going through the ordeal I would soon experience. My chest felt as if someone was standing on it, my heartbeats accelerating in rhythm with my footsteps. I was thinking about how I would respond to his question of my intentions. I knew the answer, of course, but I kept going over and over how I should word it. John and I had rehearsed the responses we would give. But a rehearsal was not the actual performance. I wanted to see the look on John's face when he came out, so I could gauge what to be prepared for. I even considered putting my ear up against the door. Finally, the sound of a chair being pushed back. The door snapped open and John appeared, his shoulders hunched, a look of shock on his face.

"Connolly," Father Theophane called.

John saw on my face the question I wanted to ask.

"I'll tell you later," he muttered as he walked by.

"Michael," Father Theophane said as I waited in the doorway, "come in and sit down." He motioned to a chair that seemed like a toddler's compared to the one he sat on behind his commanding mahogany desk. His expression was solemn, even a bit angry. I glanced at his desk, not wanting to meet his eyes. Scattered about it like toys in a child's playroom were files and loose paperwork. *He's a slob.* The room was stuffy with the smell of cigarette ash. It reminded me of my father's bedroom.

"So Michael, how are you doing?"

"Fine, Father."

"How has your senior year been going?"

"Fine, Father. I really like my classes and my teachers and I think I'm doing very well."

He was smiling now, ready to get down to business. "Michael, some time ago I asked all of you seniors to pray and ask God's guidance in determining whether you wanted to continue in your preparation for the priesthood by going on to novitiate next year." He was still smiling. There was a long pause. I took a deep breath and exhaled. Not too visibly, I hoped.

"I love it here at St. John's and I really appreciate what you and all my teachers have done for me here, Father. I've grown so much and learned so much and made so many friends and I'm so grateful for . . ."

"Michael, let's dispense with all of the tributes and get to the question at hand. Do you or do you not plan to continue with us in your preparation for the priesthood?"

"Well, Father, after much prayer and reflection, I've come to the conclusion that I don't have a vocation and I don't believe I should continue."

His face hardened, his eyes darkened. I could hear his breathing now, raspy and labored. The smell of tobacco got stronger. He gathered himself. "That's a good decision on your part, Michael. The faculty and I had decided that we were not going to recommend you continue on to novitiate." His smile had faded into a smirk. "You're not the kind of boy we think should go on."

It was my turn to gather myself.

He waved a finger at me. "You know, son, you've grown used to being a big fish in a small pond here, but where you are returning to you are going to find that you're a minnow in an ocean of sharks." His eyes were now as shiny as new dimes. "I don't know how you will survive out there, but I wish you well. Please send in the next boy."

I sat struggling to contain myself. I wanted to . . . I wasn't sure what I wanted to do. But, whatever it was, I knew I couldn't do it. Not after four years and all the good that I'd experienced here. I gripped my pant legs with my fists. *He has chosen to shoot me down in words only one rung above my father's "you're just a stupid little asshole."*

"What are you waiting for, Michael? Send in the next boy."

I didn't get up. *I'll show you. Someday I'll come back here and show you what a big fish in a small pond can do. Someday I'll come back and show you I'm better than you ever thought I would be.*

Finally, I got up and left without looking at him.

The next boy was Ronnie Driver, who had told John and me he was not going to go to novitiate, but he intended to say he planned to go. "No reason he needs to know that now. Lots of guys change their minds over the summer," he had said with a smile. Ronnie gave me a sly grin now as he brushed by me into the rector's office.

John was pacing up and down the rotunda.

"Did you tell him, John?"

"Yeah, I told him," his voice sounded like someone had been kicking him in the throat.

"Are you all right?" I asked, calmer now.

"He told me I wasn't the kind of boy they want here. That I wasn't going to be allowed to continue. He told me I was smug and conceited and that I wasn't very intelligent."

"Are you kidding? You don't believe that bullshit, do you? You've just won a full-paid scholarship to any university in New York State. What does that son of a bitch know anyway? He told me the same thing. He told me I'd been a big fish in a small pond and that when I left here I'd be eaten alive by bigger fish. And, oh yeah, he said he and the faculty had not planned to have me back anyway."

We walked back and forth in the rotunda, talking.

"John, you're not taking what Theophane said too seriously, are you? He's nothing like our other teachers. He's vindictive. He doesn't want to acknowledge that you're bright or smarter than he is."

"Yeah," John replied. But he didn't sound convinced.

For the first time in our four years at St. John's we were sent home for the Easter break. I had dreaded telling my father and Marie that I wasn't going to return to the seminary after my senior year, but was surprised and relieved by their reaction. There were no comments about my never finishing anything. There were no accusations about me being a "stupid little asshole." There was only the question of what I planned to do next. "I want to go to college," I said. "I'm an honor roll student now and at the end of this year I'll have three graduation diplomas. I think I'll be able to get into a good college."

"Where?" my father said. His tone put me instantly on the alert.

"Merrimack College; it's a Catholic College and I'm sure they will want me when they see my Catholic University diploma."

"And how do you intend to pay for it?"

"I was hoping you'd be willing to help me." I was working to control the shiver in my voice.

"We've already paid for your education. Four years of it. It's your brother's turn. We'll pay for your brother's college education and then your sister's. You've had your chance."

I looked over to Marie, hoping for some support. She sat across from me, a stoic expression on her face. It was hopeless, I decided; I was never going to college.

"You need to start thinking now of where you're going to get a job when you get home; you're not going to be just sitting around here living off of us. You're going to start paying your way here," my father said pushing his chair back. "End of conversation."

◆ ◆ ◆

"You don't have to give up your dream of a college education," Aunt Sarah said, trying to snap me out of my self-pity. "You may just have to get to it a different way." We were sitting in her parlor and I had been rehashing my discussion with my father and Marie.

"What do you mean? You mean I have to get a scholarship? My grades aren't that good, especially my freshman and sophomore grades."

"No," she said, looking up at the picture of her husband, Richard. "You can go to work and then pay for the rest of your education, like he did, and I did."

"Do you know how much it costs to go to Merrimack College? Five thousand dollars just for one year. And that's before paying for any books. By the time I earn that kind of money, I'll be too old." I was watching the sun descend on my dream of college education again.

"Why does it have to be Merrimack College? You know, Michael, sometimes we have to be willing to take a different route to where we want to go. Lowell Tech and Lowell State cost a whole lot less money than Merrimack and you don't need a car to get to either of them." She saw me frown.

"Why that look? You know sometimes the way we want to go to get somewhere may not be the best way for us to go." She got up from the corduroy upholstered chair and sat beside me on the sofa. "Look," she said, "sometimes the way we want to go is blocked or closed, and we have to be willing to go a different way. I didn't get to go to the nursing school I really wanted to go to, but I went to one here in Lowell and I got my nursing degree."

I opened my mouth. She was ready for my "yeah but . . ." She took my hand to stop me.

"You remember the horses?" I nodded. "Well, sometimes to get to the front of the pack a thoroughbred can't just barrel right on ahead. Sometimes there's an obstacle, another horse, in front of him and he has to be willing to take a different route to get around him. He goes either to the outside or to the inside. You understand?"

I nodded and got up to leave.

"And by the way," she said, "did you know that your mother went to Lowell State?"

"She did?" I said, a look of doubt on my face.

"It was called Lowell Normal School back then and it was only a two-year college. But it's where she got her teaching degree." She wrapped her arms around me and gave me a determined squeeze. "See you Saturday."

John

Prior to Easter, we seniors had taken the competitive exams for New York Regents College scholarships. These were four-year scholarships to any participating college or university in the state of New York; in essence it included almost all schools. I did well and won a scholarship. So it was that I went home at Easter with the burden of telling my parents I was not going to be a priest. I would be easing that message with the news that I had a four-year scholarship to college. I figured that those two things would balance out. True, I would be coming home to live, but my college would be largely taken care of.

I had no intention of discussing with them my terror of making the wrong choice, my fear of failing in the world and burning forever in the flames of hell. Neither would I reveal how I dreaded and feared not living in the seminary, how I dreaded losing that safety, the quiet, the order. I had never been asked to discuss my inner life with my parents and had no confidence that it would be welcomed by them. We had never had a conversation about such things before. Why would we start now?

As soon as I arrived home, I told my news to my mother. My father was working evenings, so was not home. When he did get home, my mother and I sat at the kitchen table with him as he had something to eat. In what ensued, my mother said nothing.

"Daddy, I'm leaving the seminary. I'm not going to be a priest."

"Yeah. Well, what are you gonna do?"

"Well, I won a Regents' four-year scholarship to college. I'll go to college."

"You're not going to college. You had your chance with the seminary and you fucked it up. I'm not paying any more money for you to go to school."

"But, Daddy, I have a scholarship. That will pay for school."

"Oh yeah? How much does it pay? Does it pay it all? Cause I'm not paying a penny."

"If it doesn't pay it all, I'll get a part time job and pay the difference."

"You can't work and go to college. You don't know shit about it."

"Daddy, my teachers say I'm brilliant and I should go to college." Not the thing to say to him.

"Who the fuck do you think you are? You're no better than the rest of us. If you go to college, find a place to live, because you sure as hell are not living in this house."

"Please, Daddy, I have no place to go. I need to come home."

"Tough shit. If you go to college, you're on your own. Here's what you're going to do. You're going to go to nursing school."

"Nursing school? Girls are nurses."

"Yeah, well plenty of men are nurses. Besides you're not a real man. You'll never be a real man, never be able to do the work of a real man. Nursing'll be fine for you."

This first foray into a family discussion continued for a while. The endpoint was this: choose right now, nursing school and a home, or college and live on the street. Before we rose from the table, I had capitulated, as I always had. I had not considered not having a home to go to. No seminary and no home was overwhelming. I absolutely had to have a place to go. I had not yet begun to implement my plan to join the world, and my life had already begun to crumble. I thought of that friar and the man hanging in the garage. What had I done?

◆ ◆ ◆

Once back at the seminary, I began getting letters of invitation from colleges. Each letter was a laceration in my soul. Students who knew I was leaving asked what college I would attend, and I told them, "Central Islip State Hospital School of Nursing. I'm going to be a registered nurse." They would look at me, shocked.

My father had not killed me, but he'd cut off my balls, and I had held them steady for him. At that moment, it seemed that everything I had crafted over four years of work and discipline had been wiped away. It was as if it had never happened. I was no longer somebody, I was nobody. And I hadn't even gotten started yet.

The remaining shred of dignity left to me was the anticipation of my graduation. In prior years there had been a pattern for graduation that would suit me well. Each year only a few students graduated. Our class would graduate nine students. It was not time-consuming. Each graduate would be called up for his school diploma. If he passed all of the Regents' exams, he would be called for that, too. The same applied to passing all four years of Catholic University exams.

Then Father Theophane told us just before graduation that to save time each graduate would come up one time and get whichever diplomas he had won. What kind of savings were we talking about? In my narcissism, I felt that Theophane was deliberately changing things to punish us, to punish me. In retrospect there might have been some other reason. Of course, I could still console myself with being called up for the award for "outstanding student."

The tension and excitement of finals and the impending graduation were leavened by our almost fanatic interest in the Floyd Patterson versus Ingemar Johansson heavyweight championship fight. In the months after the first fight, we had devoured every article we could find about Floyd. He was an American, Catholic, happily married, and a model of humility.

Johansson, on the other hand, was a brash, flashy, foreign, non-Catholic. He also openly traveled around the world with a tall, statuesque Swedish blonde who was not his wife. As delicately as they could in those days, the papers alluded to the fact that they slept in the same room.

We had no access to television and were forbidden to have radios. There was a radio, however, in the infirmary. It was a perk of being ill to listen to radio. After lights out on June 20, 1960, groups of boys silently found their way to Radio Free St. John's in the infirmary. We clustered around static-ridden radio and listened with barely restrained joy to the defeat of evil at the hands of Floyd. For that night, at least, "Ingo" and his paramour would probably sleep chastely, which pleased me greatly.

My father did not come to my graduation. My mother, my grandmother, and my four-year-old brother came. Father Theophane called my name and handed me three diplomas. I wanted to turn to the assembled parents, tell them that I had passed all those tests, gotten three diplomas. Tell them that, for a little while, I had really been somebody.

Father Theophane then announced that he was giving the award for the outstanding student: "This young man has maintained consistently high grades; he has excelled at athletics; he plays the organ and edits the school newspaper . . . Thomas Dever."

Just like that, it was over. I felt as if I were awakening from a beautiful dream to find myself lying naked and cold on the side of a strange road. *Where am I and what direction do I follow?*

We filed out, said our goodbyes, and got into the cars with our families. My mother began driving down the driveway. Father Theophane had promised me that he would bring me down a peg, and he had kept his word.

My mother broke the silence.

"That Father Theophane called Big Mom and me into his office to talk about you. He said that he thinks you are mentally ill and will wind up in a psychiatric hospital."

I thought that Father Theophane, perhaps, had treated me worse than anyone ever had. I thought that only briefly.

As we drove down the driveway I looked at the seminary through the rear window. So many priests had been good to me. I had been encouraged to become so much more than I was when I arrived. I was probably alive because they had taken me in. I would not allow the anomaly of Father Theophane to contaminate the overwhelmingly beneficial effect of so many priests.

Mike

The return to St. John's after Easter break was something I didn't look forward to. It was like traveling backward. My life was over here—that's how it felt. The rule change sending my class to novitiate after graduation had shattered my dream of a quality college education at St. John's. Going back was really about preparing to leave, getting my diplomas, saying goodbye to classmates, walking around with John, remembering the good times, and making plans with him for the future. I went to classes and did my work, but without the passion I'd once had. Being there felt like being at another funeral, saying goodbye to something you had once loved and had loved you, but now was gone.

One afternoon during free time, I sat in chapel thinking about what the last four years had been all about. The oily smell of freshly polished pews was comforting. Sunlight coming through the stained-glass window bathed the pews in an array of vibrant colors that seemed almost supernatural. Staring up at the cross, I asked and then demanded, "What has this all been about? Why did you bring me here only to force me to leave?" No voice came from the heavens. Eventually I gave up expecting some kind of answer. I started thinking back to my life in Pinehurst and to my mother's death. My eyes hadn't left the cross since I'd knelt in prayer and then sat back to try to make sense of it all. It was a battle now between my anger and my tears.

Maybe you don't appreciate it, Michael, but Mrs. Brown is trying to teach you and your friends a lesson.

What lesson?

She's trying to show you that you have to learn how to lose. You have to learn how to accept losses. We all do.

All that was left was the graduation ceremony, which had always been an extended celebration of the successes of the senior class. This, Father Theophane decided, was a waste of time. Rather than honor graduates for several separate achievements, each of the seniors was called up once and handed his three diplomas. Other awards seniors had earned in speech, Latin, and other academic activities were handled the same way. The ceremony was brief. Not so much a celebration as a send-off. A funeral.

I care? I really didn't. As our Chevy pulled onto Route 14, I didn't look back. Instead I was thinking about Father Theophane's Easter message to me, "You've been a big fish, Michael, in a small pond. Now you're going to be a minnow in an ocean of sharks. I don't know how you'll survive."

The Chevy accelerated toward that ocean where Theophane didn't believe I'd survive.

We'll see, Father Theophane! We'll see!

Epilogue

Life Begins Again

On the last day of our reunion, we relaxed on the wrap-around porch of our three day-lodging, a century-old farmhouse along Route 309 in the hills above Watkins Glen. Leaves on the front yard's massive maple hung motionless in late afternoon heat. In the farmstead across the highway, a horse grazed lazily in shoulder-high grass. All agreed it would be good to surprise Father Owen with a call and let him know where we were. His voice mailbox was full, so Ollie called the receptionist at his retirement home for help in making contact.

"I'm sorry," she said, stammering, "but Father Owen passed away this morning."

Clearly stunned and looking to the others waiting anxiously, Ollie said, "He just died."

The prolonged grind of a cicada high in the maple seemed to fade instantly, allowing for total silence. Very suddenly, an eerie westerly blast shattered the lull. It ripped leaves from the maple and other trees, sent loose papers on the porch flying and clapped loose boards on the barn nearby. The horse across the road snorted and bolted.

And with equal suddenness, after about fifteen seconds, the wind ceased, restoring stillness and silence.

Mike's eyes brimmed with tears. "He's been with us the whole time," he said.

The following morning at breakfast before separating and heading home, John and Mike recalled a conversation they taped with Father Owen when they visited him in 2004.

"You must have known back in those days as prefect of St John's that many of the boys who came to the seminary would not become priests," John asked. "What were your hopes for boys like us who came and left?"

The authors (left to right: Mike, Ollie, and John) on the steps to the main entrance of the old seminary, now the New York State Academy of Fire Science, during their reunion in 2012.

Father Owen paused and looked into the distance as if his eyes were time-traveling back to those days. Finally he replied: "Yes, I actually looked at the numbers once and recognized that we were losing a much larger number of boys than we were sending on to the priesthood. I pointed that out to our rector Father Wilfrid and I said, 'We're investing a great deal of time and money taking boys into preparatory seminary at age thirteen and very few of them will

Photo credit: By permission of Franciscan Order of the Atonement, Graymoor Archives

Father Wilfrid Brennan, St. John's Atonement Seminary rector during the authors' first year, noted in his welcoming remarks, "Some of you will leave us in time with the knowledge that the priesthood was not your calling."

end up becoming priests.' He replied, 'That's true, but we will be having a great influence on these boys' lives. They will be learning the truths of the Catholic faith and we will be providing them with a good Catholic education.'"

Father Owen paused again: "He was correct and I was satisfied with that."

The three of us were not among the few who were chosen to be priests, but we are among the many whose lives have been profoundly affected by years spent under the guidance of the dedicated priests at John's Atonement Seminary. Their influence and the teaching of the Catholic faith changed the lives of the three of us and many others who didn't complete the path to the priesthood.

Albert Schweitzer wrote: "I don't know what your destiny will be, but one thing I do know, the ones among you who will be really happy are those who have sought and found how to serve." That was a lesson we learned in the seminary, at a time when we believed happiness had eluded us.

PostScript

Mike Connolly followed his Aunt Sarah's advice and in 1965 graduated from Lowell State College. Inspired by the example of Father DeSales, he became a high school English teacher. In 1968 Mike served as a chaplain's assistant in Cu Chi, Vietnam.

After the war he returned to the United States and became a school principal. He worked for forty-two years in middle and high schools in the United States and in international schools in Thailand, Costa Rica, the Netherlands, and Vietnam. He currently serves as a Eucharistic Minister, distributing Communion at All Saints Catholic Church in Hampstead, North Carolina and at a local nursing home.

Mike is married and has four children. He is the author of three books: *What They Never Told Me in Principal's School; Teaching Kids to Love Learning, Not Just Endure It;* and most recently, *Young Enough to Change the World: Stories of Kids and Teens Who Turned Their Dreams into Action* (coauthored with his wife, Brie Goolbis).

Mike and John Tuohey have remained friends and stayed in contact with one another since they left the seminary. In 2004, they travelled to Graymoor, home of the Franciscan Friars of the Atonement in Garrison, New York, to visit Father Owen. He informed them that their St. John's classmate, Richard Olive, had also visited him over the years, and lived in San Rafael, California. They located Ollie through social media, leading to the reunion of the three in 2012.

Richard (Ollie) Olive was clueless after high school about his future until he wandered into a Navy recruiting station. Recalling Father Owen's encouragement about pursuing writing, he applied for and was accepted in journalism school at the Naval Training Center, Great Lakes then served for forty months as a journalist aboard an aircraft carrier.

He parlayed his Navy journalism experience into a twelve-year career with daily newspapers, The Associated Press, and United

Press International. The rest of his working life was divided among service as a business agent for The Newspaper Guild, a labor union; public relations; and fund-raising. He retired in 2014 and is devoted to writing, family, and a nondenominational ministry on San Quentin's Death Row. He and his wife, Ana, have seven children and six grandchildren between them. Besides family, friends, and faith, he is grateful to be playing racquetball and for his recovery from alcoholism, which began in 1986.

John Tuohey became a registered nurse in 1964, graduating from Nassau Community College. He joined the Army in 1966. In 1968, after active duty, he remained in the Active Reserve until 1998, retiring as a lieutenant colonel. In 1970 he received a BA in psychology from the University of Wisconsin-Oshkosh. In 1977 he became a family nurse practitioner through the University of Southern Maine, and received his Masters of Education degree in counseling from Rivier College. He obtained a Master of Science in Nursing in critical care from the Massachusetts General Hospital Institute of Health Sciences in 1994. Throughout his career he worked primarily in emergency rooms, cardiology, and urology clinics before retiring in 2011. At retirement he also had been nationally certified as a family nurse practitioner, psychiatric nurse practitioner, and urology nurse practitioner.

He is currently a volunteer English teacher for new Americans, a participant in a French conversation group, and a member of a writing group. He has completed riding his bike in forty-nine states, with Alaska scheduled in 2018. He is a practitioner of Sayoc Kali, a Filipino martial art.

Throughout his hospital career, John has never forgotten Father Owen tending the sick during the flu epidemic and has tried to model that priest's care and concern for his patients.

He has three daughters from a first marriage and two stepsons from his marriage to Pam, who has made his life a delight in every way. All the children still speak to him, which he considers his major accomplishment.

Index